CROSS-CURRICULAR TEACHING AND LEARNING IN THE SECONDARY SCHOOL

What is the role of the individual school 'subject' and 'subject teacher' within school? Is it to teach a set of core subject knowledge, skills and understanding in a way that remains faithful to long-standing subject cultures and pedagogies? Or is there another way to consider how the curriculum, and the notion of individual subjects and teachers' pedagogy, could be constructed?

Working from the key principle that there is no curriculum development without teacher development, *Cross-Curricular Teaching and Learning in the Secondary School* argues for a new, skilful pedagogy that embeds an authentic, cross-curricular approach to teaching and learning in the work of the individual teacher. This approach respects and builds on individual subject cultures, embracing and exploring links between subject knowledge and subject pedagogies in an enriching way.

Drawing on examples and case studies taken from innovative practices in different schools and subject areas, as well as summarising lessons from key pieces of research evidence, this book includes:

- clear theoretical frameworks for cross-curricular processes of teaching and learning
- a lively account of key issues blended with engaging stories of current practice
- an analysis of the use of language, ICT and assessment as key components of a skilful pedagogical practice that affects how teaching is delivered and how pupils learn in cross-curricular contexts
- practical tasks and questions for reflective practice.

This timely textbook is essential reading for all students on Initial Teacher Training courses and PGCE courses as well as practising teachers looking to holistically introduce cross-curricular themes and practices in their own subjects.

Jonathan Savage is a Reader in Education at the Institute of Education, Manchester Metropolitan University, and Managing Director of uCan.tv. His research interests include implementing new technologies in education, cross-curricular approaches to teaching and learning, supporting gifted and talented students, creativity and assessment.

Cross-Curricular Teaching and Learning in . . .
Series Editor: Jonathan Savage (Manchester Metropolitan University, UK)

The *Cross-Curricular* series, published by Routledge, argues for a cross-curricular approach to teaching and learning in secondary schools. It provides a justification for cross-curricularity across the Key Stages, exploring a range of theoretical and practical issues through case studies drawn from innovative practices across a range of schools. The books demonstrate the powerful nature of change that can result when teachers allow a cross-curricular 'disposition' to inspire their pedagogy. Working from a premise that there is no curriculum development without teacher development, the series argues for a serious re-engagement with cross-curricularity within the work of the individual subject teacher, before moving on to consider collaborative approaches for curriculum design and implementation through external curriculum links.

Cross-curricular approaches to teaching and learning can result in a powerful, new model of subject-based teaching and learning in the high school. This series places the teacher and their pedagogy at the centre of this innovation. The responses that schools, departments or teachers make to government initiatives in this area may be sustainable only over the short term. For longer-term change to occur, models of cross-curricular teaching and learning need to become embedded within the pedagogies of individual teachers and, from there, to inform and perhaps redefine the subject cultures within which they work. These books explore how this type of change can be initiated and sustained by teachers willing to raise their heads above their 'subject' parapet and develop a broader perspective and vision for education in the twenty-first century.

Forthcoming titles in the series:

Cross-Curricular Teaching and Learning in the Secondary School . . . The Arts
Martin Fautley and Jonathan Savage

Cross-Curricular Teaching and Learning in the Secondary School . . . English
David Stevens

Cross-Curricular Teaching and Learning in the Secondary School . . . Foreign Languages
Gee Macrory, Cathy Brady and Sheila Anthony

Cross-Curricular Teaching and Learning in the Secondary School . . . Humanities
Richard Harris and Simon Harrison

Cross-Curricular Teaching and Learning in the Secondary School . . . Using ICT
Maurice Nyangon

Cross-Curricular Teaching and Learning in the Secondary School . . . Mathematics
Robert Ward-Penny

CROSS-CURRICULAR TEACHING AND LEARNING IN THE SECONDARY SCHOOL

Jonathan Savage

Series edited by Jonathan Savage

Routledge
Taylor & Francis Group

LONDON AND NEW YORK

This first edition published 2011
by Routledge
2 Park Square, Milton Park, Abingdon, Oxon OX14 4RN

Simultaneously published in the USA and Canada
by Routledge
270 Madison Avenue, New York, NY 10016

Routledge is an imprint of the Taylor & Francis Group, an informa business

© 2011 Jonathan Savage

Typeset in Bembo and Helvetica Neue by Prepress Projects Ltd, Perth, UK
Printed and bound in Great Britain by CPI Antony Rowe, Chippenham, Wiltshire

British Library Cataloguing in Publication Data
A catalogue record for this book is available from the British Library

Library of Congress Cataloging-in-Publication Data
Savage, Jonathan.
Cross-curricular teaching and learning in the secondary school / by Jonathan Savage. –
1st ed.
p. cm.
Includes bibliographical references.
1. Education, Secondary. 2. Multicultural education. 3. Interdisciplinary approach in
education. I. Title.
LC1099.S29 2011
373.1102–dc22
2010009496

ISBN10: 0-415-54858-6 (hbk)
ISBN10: 0-415-54859-4 (pbk)
ISBN10: 0-203-84420-3 (ebk)

ISBN13: 978-0-415-54858-8 (hbk)
ISBN13: 978-0-415-54859-5 (pbk)
ISBN13: 978-0-203-84420-5 (ebk)

Contents

Illustrations

1

The Context for Cross-Curricular Teaching and Learning

Key objectives

By the end of this chapter, you will have:

- explored key principles for teaching which will shape your thinking about cross-curricular teaching and learning;

- considered the broader historical framework within which an approach to cross-curricular teaching and learning can be developed;

- examined the current educational climate and the associated curriculum frameworks and reflected on the possibilities for generating new approaches to cross-curricular teaching and learning;

- engaged in a range of reflective and practical tasks that will help you apply key ideas in this chapter to your own teaching practice.

Case Study 1: An opening: One teacher's journey

Writing this book has been a challenge, personally and professionally. Like most of the readers of this book, I started my teaching career as a subject specialist (in my case, a music teacher) working in a couple of high schools in East Anglia. I taught music to the various classes throughout each school and really enjoyed the associated challenges of creating what I considered to be an interesting music curriculum that related to, and drew inspiration from, the National Curriculum. Music can be an isolated subject within schools. Most music teachers work in a small department, often on their own or with a small team of visiting instrumental teachers. The music room is often geographically isolated (it can be noisy!) and, in terms of the educational processes and knowledge that underpin the subject, it can be something that appears distinct and separate from the work of other teachers. Music is often referred to as a 'Cinderella' subject; a 'shop window' for the school; something that can be wheeled out for special occasions (e.g. concerts, assemblies or open evenings) but otherwise is left alone to do its own thing. For all these reasons, teaching music can be a lonely experience and one that is not conducive to collaborative approaches to teaching.

As a music teacher I often wondered if my thoughts about my own subject, and its perceived isolation, were shared by other teachers as they considered their subjects. As head of department in my second school, and quite by chance, I discovered that one of my colleagues, a mathematics teacher, was also an active and very competent composer. We chatted about our teaching roles and shared musical interests (I was not quite so good at the mathematics side of things) and soon struck up a close friendship. This changed my perceptions about teaching music. Why? On reflection, it seems that two fundamental reasons have emerged. First, as a teacher I realised that I had ignored the fact that the majority of musicians work, and travel, across the boundaries of music and other areas of knowledge regularly. Sometimes their journeys are down well-travelled paths, for example film composers regularly work with images and draw their artistic inspiration from them; on occasions these journeys are more exploratory, for example investigating areas such as cognitive psychology or genetics for compositional ideas. Second, as my discussions with my mathematics colleague continued, I began to appreciate that the educational processes that underpin mathematics education were not so different from those that I was seeking to develop within my music classes.

So, for musical and educational reasons, the collaborative work with my colleague continued over two years. It resulted in a number of cross-curricular projects that will be discussed at points within this book but can be read about in full elsewhere (Savage and Challis 2001, 2002). The projects enriched my teaching in ways that I could not have predicted. They also transformed my thinking about how I should teach my subject. This was the start of my interest in cross-curricular ways of teaching and learning, which has stayed with me and developed over recent years.

Introduction

This book has begun with an extended personal narrative for an important reason. During the course of this chapter I will argue that teachers are at the heart of the process of teaching and learning. Their beliefs, aspirations and values are all important, informing elements of the design and delivery of a curriculum. The creation of an enriching pedagogy for cross-curricular teaching and learning (an important and often misunderstood term) can be achieved if teachers can reclaim some authority in curriculum development and delivery. Recent developments in the National Curriculum at Key Stage 3 present some exciting opportunities for this to happen.

However, we are getting ahead of ourselves. Before we begin to consider what an approach to cross-curricular teaching and learning might look like, three important principles that underpin this book will be introduced. Two of the principles draw on the key phrases and ideas from educationalists who, sadly, are no longer with us. The third springs from these. In choosing to start the book with these principles, it is hoped that the reader will recognise that, in several key respects, developing an approach to cross-curricular teaching and learning is embedded within good teaching per se. Obviously our concerns throughout the majority of this book will be to consider the book's title and associated themes in some detail. But, first, a platform about the curriculum, teachers and pedagogy needs to be built. It is time to examine three foundational principles of this book.

Principle 1: No curriculum development without teacher development

Fifty years ago, the Crowther Report stated that 'everything in education depends ultimately on the teacher' (Central Advisory Council for Education 1959). It is a sentiment that one of the greatest educational thinkers of recent decades, Lawrence Stenhouse, would have undoubtedly agreed with. Stenhouse was a firm advocate for the teacher. It was fitting that the teachers with whom he worked across East Anglia contributed a plaque in his memory. On it, they inscribed Stenhouse's own words: 'It is the teachers who in the end will change the world of the school by understanding it' (Stenhouse 1975, p. 208).

Stenhouse was well known for his belief that teachers could enhance their professional understanding by engaging in processes of educational research. His notion of the 'teacher as researcher' has done much to shape current thinking about professional development, reflective practice and action research. He was an outspoken critic of what he saw as the deprofessionalisation of the teacher through 'objective' based curriculum models. These, he said:

> Rest on an acceptance of the teacher as a kind of intellectual navvy. An objectives based curriculum is like a site-plan, simplified so that people know exactly where to dig their trenches without having to know why.
>
> (Stenhouse 1980a, p. 85)

For Stenhouse, such curriculum models were a symbol of distrust of the teacher. He worked hard to challenge such approaches. More than that, he developed alternative ideas that reasserted the teachers' role in curriculum planning and development. If, as he wrote, 'it seems odd to minimise the use of the most expensive resource in the school' (Stenhouse 1975, p. 24), it would be better to 'reinvest in the teacher and to construct the curriculum in ways that would enhance teachers' understanding and capability' (Ruddock 1995, p. 5).

It is this background that led Stenhouse to make one of his most famous statements: 'No curriculum development without teacher development' (Stenhouse 1975, p. 142). As Silbeck comments:

His theory of education is essentially a theory of teacher professionalism, autonomy and development. . . . It is the teacher, purposive and free, informed by knowledge and understanding, with clearly articulated values, and a repertoire of practical skills, that he [Stenhouse] saw as the central agent in the educational enterprise.

(Silbeck 1983, p. 12)

These are powerful arguments that have much resonance with current thinking about curriculum design and development. As we will go on to see, recent pieces of curriculum reform have placed a greater degree of ownership and responsibility on schools. The greatest asset of every school is its teaching staff. The 'localisation' of the National Curriculum presents an opportunity for teachers to respond to the challenge of developing themselves and the curriculum they offer to their pupils in tandem.

Practical Task 1

Think through a recent piece of curriculum planning that you have undertaken. This might be a single lesson plan or a scheme of work. Consider the following questions:

- To what extent was this an opportunity for your professional development as well as a piece of curriculum development?

- In regard to the content of the piece of planning, how did you recycle existing subject knowledge that you might have had?

- In respect of how you chose to organise the teaching and learning opportunities, how did you consider new teaching strategies – perhaps even those drawn from outside your particular subject area?

- Finally, given the opportunity to undertake another piece of curriculum planning, how could you extend your original approach to develop it more closely with Stenhouse's mantra of no curriculum development without teacher development?

Principle 2: Subjectivity is like a garment that cannot be removed

Alan Peshkin's work on subjectivity is important for anyone engaged in research activities (Peshkin 1988). As the second key principle for this book, the above phrase is drawn from the following paragraph of his seminal paper on the topic of subjectivity and its influence on the research process:

Subjectivity is not a badge of honor, something earned like a merit badge and paraded around on special occasions for all to see. Whatever the substance of one's persuasions at a given point, one's subjectivity is like a garment that cannot be removed. It is insistently present in both the research and nonresearch aspects of our life. . . . By remaining conventional wisdom, our subjectivity lies inert, unexamined when it counts, that is, beyond our control while actively engaged in the research process.

(Peshkin 1988, p. 17)

For our discussion, subjectivity can have a double meaning. In the sense that Peshkin is talking about, it refers to our personal qualities that affect the results of our work. It could include aspects related to our values, knowledge and understanding about a whole range of issues (both educational or, probably, more generally). These, Peshkin argues, cannot be removed. They are like a garment through which our gaze is mediated. They influence the way we feel, think and act. Our subjectivities need to be examined and understood in order for us to engage meaningfully with each other, with formal frameworks that implicate our professional practice, with our pupils – in fact, with every aspect of our lives.

However, there is another meaning that can be drawn. This relates to our 'subjects'' values, knowledge and understanding and how these have shaped our individual and collective consciousness about how they should be presented in classrooms, taught and learnt about. Either way, Peshkin's key point is that this subjectivity cannot be removed. It shapes or mediates our thinking and action in a whole range of ways. Therefore, it needs to be understood through a systematic process of reflection and self-interrogation. Chapter 2 will argue that this process is most helpful in helping us define our key principles for cross-curricular teaching and learning. These will stem from our understanding about the centrality of teachers as the key informant to curriculum development, but also, importantly, from teachers' own conceptions of themselves and, what might be called, their 'subjects' sensitivities'. These will affect how they seek to extend the opportunities for teaching and learning across traditional subject boundaries and engage in meaningful collaborations with teachers (i.e. representatives of other subject areas).

It will be important that teachers assert control over this process. To paraphrase and apply Peshkin's (1988) comments about research, 'subjectivity is insistently present in both the *teaching* and *non-teaching* aspects of our life'; by leaving it unexamined, it remains 'beyond our control while actively engaged in the *teaching* process'. This is an undesirable state of affairs and one that would not be conducive to meaningful and constructive curricula collaborations.

Reflective Task 1

What are the 'subjectivities' within your specialist curriculum subject? These are the key elements that make your subject unique, that are valued or treasured by the subject community at large. Try and make a short list of them now.

Compare your list with your subject's National Curriculum Programme of Study for Key Stage 3. Do the Importance Statement, Key Concepts or Key Processes listed there have anything in common with your list?

> Finally, how does your understanding and appreciation of these subjectivities affect the way that you might approach teaching your subject? What would be their impact on your chosen pedagogy?

Principle 3: Skilful teachers embody a skilful pedagogy

How do you define pedagogy? The *Oxford English Dictionary* defines it as 'the profession, science, or theory of teaching'. Other definitions of pedagogy extend this to cover the practice and process that underpin the activity of teaching. For example, Popkewitz develops a broad-based definition of pedagogy:

> Pedagogy is a practice of the social administration of the social individual. Since at least the 19th century pedagogical discourses about teaching, children, and learning in schools connected the scope and aspirations of public powers with the personal and subjective capabilities of individuals. This administration of the child embodies certain norms about their capabilities from which the child can become self-governing and self-reliant.
>
> (Popkewitz 1998, p. 536)

Bernstein picks up on this notion of pedagogy as process, defining it as:

> A sustained process whereby somebody(s) acquires new forms or develops existing forms of conduct, knowledge, practice and criteria, from somebody(s) or something deemed to be an appropriate provider and evaluator. Appropriate either from the point of view of the acquirer or by some other body(s) or both.
>
> (Bernstein 1999, p. 259)

The key principle that can be drawn from these definitions is that pedagogy is both a 'practice' and a 'process' through which certain things can be acquired or through which certain capabilities can be developed. In both definitions, references are made to something 'outside' the obvious context of an educational exchange (i.e. between a teacher and a pupil). In Popkewitz's definition, this is seen in the phrase 'scope and aspirations of public powers'; in Bernstein's by 'an appropriate provider and evaluator'.

This leads us to a second question. Where would one find 'pedagogy'? Is it something that one would find within a curriculum framework or associated guidelines? Or is it something that teachers, or pupils, possess? This is not a simple question to answer. It is something that will be considered frequently through this book. But, by way of a partial answer and as a way of leading to our third key principle, consider the following quotation from another great educational thinker, Jerome Bruner:

> In theorizing about the practice of education in the classroom (or any other setting, for that matter), you had better take into account the folk theories that those engaged in teaching and learning already have. For any innovations that you may

wish to introduce will have to compete with, replace, or otherwise modify the folk theories that already guide both teachers and pupils. . . . So your introduction of an innovation in teaching will necessarily involve changing the folk psychological and folk pedagogical theories of teachers – and, to a surprising extent, of pupils as well.

(Bruner 1996, p. 46)

Bruner's argument about the importance of 'folk pedagogies' implies that pedagogy relates to a set of beliefs or values about teaching that individuals (including pupils) have and which can be challenged, change and develop over time. They can also collide together and conflict with each other within a teaching context if there is a lack of sensitivity on the part of the teacher or pupil.

The third key principle of this book is that skilful teachers embody a skilful pedagogy. It places the onus of responsibility clearly within the teacher's role. They are responsible for its development and application. As part of this, to be sure, a consideration of the 'folk pedagogies' or alternative learning styles or contexts that pupils exhibit will need to be considered, maybe approved or perhaps rejected. But this is part of the overall skilful pedagogical approach that an effective teacher will bring to the classroom. This skilful pedagogy will need to have been developed at some point. In what follows, the ideas and practices of developing a pedagogical approach to cross-curricular teaching and learning may well, in Bruner's terms, 'compete with, replace, or otherwise modify' your current pedagogical thinking and practice. But it is more than that. As Bruner points out, the pedagogies that we adopt as teachers will impact on our pupils as well. As the arguments within this book unfold, you will notice how vital this particular strand of thought will become.

Practical Task 2

Choose a particular topic from within your subject area. Jot down a few ideas about how you might teach about it in a typical Key Stage 3 lesson within your classroom. What would you be doing? What would your pupils be doing? What resources would you need and how would you organise them? All these questions get you thinking about your pedagogy for this particular teaching context.

Now take yourself out of this context. In this new scenario, the pupils are at home but are going to explore the same topic. How would they do this? What would they need? Would it even be possible? What would be their learning strategy within this context and how would it differ from their role in the more formal context of your classroom?

How do these two alternative contexts and approaches to learning compare? How easy did you find it to associate with the pupils' alternative learning context?

In summary, the three key principles of this book are:

1. there is no curriculum development without teacher development;
2. subjectivity is like a garment that cannot be removed;
3. skilful teachers embody a skilful pedagogy.

Perhaps you consider this to be a strange way to start a book on cross-curricular teaching and learning? I hope not. But if you do, please be reassured that these general principles set an important overall context for the specific challenges associated with creating and maintaining a meaningful, cross-curricular approach to teaching and learning.

Reflective Task 2

This chapter has begun with the teacher. It has challenged the view that curriculum development can take place in isolation. It has posited the notion that the individual teacher and their 'subjectivities', whether related to them as an individual or to their subject, are vital considerations for curriculum development. It has argued that the creation of a skilful pedagogy is key to implementing change. Spend a few moments reflecting on the following questions:

1. What is meant by 'curriculum development' and could it be linked to my own professional development as a teacher?

2. Why is it important to develop a sense of my own 'subjectivity' and how would this relate to curriculum development and the construction of a skilful pedagogy underpinned by reflective practice?

3. How explicitly are learning and teaching linked together? What are the commonalities or differences between 'formal' and 'informal' approaches to teaching and learning in different contexts? How would these affect the pedagogy I choose to develop?

Defining cross-curricular teaching and learning

Defining the key principles of cross-curricular teaching and learning will be the main preoccupation of Chapter 2. However, at this point, I want to state clearly and simply what the working definition for cross-curricular teaching and learning will be throughout this book. This definition draws on a range of historical sources, some of which will be described and analysed below, but all of which will be considered more fully in Chapter 2. As a starting point for this book:

A cross-curricular approach to teaching is characterised by sensitivity towards, and a synthesis of, knowledge, skills and understandings from various subject areas. These inform an enriched pedagogy that promotes an approach to learning which embraces and explores this wider sensitivity through various methods.

This definition draws on the obvious semantic meaning of 'cross-curricular'. It also emphasises that subjects contain more than knowledge and skills. They contain 'understandings', which I would seek to equate to 'subjectivities' as discussed above. Finally, the emphasis on pedagogy in the second sentence places a key focus on the work of the teacher but, as we will see as the book unfolds, this pedagogical element can also be shared with, and to a point owned by, the pupil.

However, as with any educational philosophy or method, cross-curricular approaches to teaching and learning have been frequently discussed and utilised by educators. In the following part of this chapter we will take a brief look at historical developments in this area and consider what can be learnt from the development of cross-curricular approaches in the primary curriculum, before considering the main context that secondary teachers are facing today, namely the opportunities presented by a new National Curriculum at Key Stage 3 and a developing set of qualifications at Key Stage 4.

A historical oversight

Recent educational policies and initiatives and resulting curriculum frameworks all have a history. It is interesting to take the longer view and consider how these current initiatives have emerged from, or perhaps are distinct from, previous ways of thinking or working. In this section we will briefly consider a range of issues drawn from literature surrounding the implementation of the National Curriculum in the early 1990s. As we will see, some of the questions and issues that were raised then have an interesting parallel to issues being considered today.

The implementation of the first National Curriculum in 1992 was encompassed by extensive discussion amongst educators and politicians about a range of issues. Amidst this discussion, the inclusion within the National Curriculum of what were referred to at the time as 'cross-curricular dimensions, skills and themes' was hotly contested. Some of the arguments will be familiar. Dufour, writing in 1990, stated that:

> 'Education' and 'curriculum' have not been defined in any previous Education Act, although the Education Reform Act, 1988, which is about both, does depart from this tradition by providing a definition of the curriculum along with a prescriptive list of subjects that must, subsequently, be taught.
>
> (Dufour 1990, p. 1)

One can sense the tumultuous political arguments that are raging beneath his prose. Within, and beyond, this 'prescriptive' list of subjects there were winners and losers, for example music was included, drama was not; physical education (PE) was there in its own right, dance was not, etc. The sense of politicians 'meddling' in the construction of a curriculum was very real at this time. One could cite numerous examples of how individual subject content was changed in response to government 'interference', even at the level of individual government ministers (Verma and Pumfrey 1993, p. 21). Dufour goes on to say that:

> While the status and context of different forms of knowledge will continue to be influenced by political and ideological considerations, political partiality should not be allowed to influence the final choice and status of particular subjects and cross-curricular themes for the school curriculum. The only question that should be asked is an educational one – how can all the subjects and themes fit together into the curriculum?
>
> (Dufour 1990, p. 11)

Unfortunately this was not, and perhaps has never been, the case. Politics and education have a long and troubled history. But as one can see from the second part of this statement, alongside the inclusion of certain subjects, cross-curricular themes were also included within the curriculum framework. The National Curriculum Council defined these themes as:

> elements that enrich the educational experience of pupils. They are more structured and pervasive than any other cross-curricular provision and include a strong component of knowledge and understanding in addition to skills. Most can be taught through other subjects as well as through themes and topics.
>
> (NCC 1989, p. 6)

These cross-curricular themes included topics such as economic and industrial understanding, health education, environmental education and citizenship. But in addition to themes, the inclusion of cross-curricular skills such as communication, numeracy, problem solving, information technology and study skills was implemented. Writing in 1993, a year after the introduction of the National Curriculum, the prescribed subjects and these various cross-curricular components, Pumfrey commented that:

> The sheer rate of change that is taking place in education is unprecedented. The volume of paper reaching schools and requiring responses is daunting, even to the most committed professional. The core and other foundation subjects are currently centre-stage. Unless teachers and schools are vigilant, the benefits of cross-curricular themes could be adversely affected.
>
> At present, the National Curriculum is far from fully in place in schools. The way in which various subjects and cross-curricular themes have been introduced into the secondary school syllabus has not been of the highest order. Too little preparation and consultation have led to controversial changes.
>
> (Pumfrey 1993, p. 21)

As we will go on to see, in respect of implementing cross-curricular elements within a wider curriculum framework, little has changed in twenty years! The position facing teachers today is that the inclusion of cross-curricular dimensions within the new secondary curriculum is non-statutory. Given the raft of other new initiatives, this sends a strong message to teachers about where their priorities might lie. Crawford (2000) considers the role of policy makers and their relationship to practitioners in a fascinating study. At the level of the individual teacher who, in the early 1990s, as we have seen, was struggling to make sense of these monumental changes in curriculum policy and design and had to sideline cross-curricular themes in favour of core subjects, he quotes Ball, who stated that 'teachers were reduced to agents of policies which were decided elsewhere' (Ball 1990, p. 171). Perhaps there is nothing new there either. But more generally, whilst Crawford's belief is that the then Department for Education and Science was not against the principle of whole curriculum initiatives (i.e. an approach that blended together subjects with cross-curricular themes), his concluding thought is that 'the debate over the whole curriculum is representative of a conflict over the strategy of curriculum implementation' (Crawford 2000, p. 628).

In summary, this tumultuous period demonstrated many things. First, the marriage of subjects and cross-curricular themes within the curriculum is not an easy one. Second, the imposition of large changes in curriculum design often means that teachers will focus on what they know, that is, their subject, and not make the wider links that might have been envisaged by a 'whole' curriculum. Finally, although the benefits of a cross-curricular set of themes and skills were recognised by politicians and educators, the practical implementation of the curriculum itself meant that opportunities were missed and creative links were not established between subjects or between subjects and cross-curricular themes.

Reflective Task 3

Looking back can be very constructive. It can help us to avoid making the same mistakes again. Consider your education at primary and secondary school. Which lessons do you remember? Why? Were your lessons constructed around individual subjects, cross-curricular themes or a mixture of the two? Which were most effective in your opinion (as a pupil)?

Lessons from the primary curriculum

From the perspective of secondary education, the primary school can often be seen through rose-tinted spectacles. If classes are taught mainly by one class teacher, surely the opportunities for cross-curricular links between subjects and other curriculum elements will be easier to manage? Many primary teachers are trained as 'generalists' rather than specialists. If cross-curricular approaches to teaching and learning are going to succeed anywhere, surely they could within the primary school?

If this is your view, perhaps it will come as a surprise that the range of debates about this issue have raged within primary education in an equally vociferous way to the historical discussion outlined above. In fact, many of the points are precisely the same. The first version of the National Curriculum was criticised for its rigidly subject-structured model (White 2004), and Brehony (2005) asserts that 'the National

Curriculum adopted, in opposition to the primary schools' use of projects, the time-hallowed conception of the organisation of school knowledge into subjects' (p. 31).

Since then, of course, there have been a large number of changes to the primary curriculum. There has been a revision of the National Curriculum in 2000 and the implementation of National Strategies for Literacy and Numeracy. Boyle and Bragg (2008) have conducted an analysis of longitudinal curriculum data from across the ten-year period from 1997, which encompassed both of these developments. Their findings conclude that:

> The introduction of the National Literacy and National Numeracy Strategies, and the high level of external auditing and accountability of the implementation of those strategies, resulted in a pronounced reduction in cross-subject planning, linkage and teaching alongside an increased concentration of teaching time on English and mathematics which reduced time allocated to the foundation subjects. The introduction of the revised curriculum 2000 did not initially redress the balance. The survey data for 2001 provided evidence that the emphasis on single separate subject teaching was as strong as it had been prior to the revised curriculum.
>
> (Boyle and Bragg 2008, p. 17)

However, they are more optimistic about recent developments. In closing, their analysis quotes from a presentation made by the Director of the Qualifications and Curriculum Authority (QCA):

> The National Curriculum subjects are only part of the curriculum. . . . The real curriculum is the entire planned learning experience. This is about looking at how the curriculum can meet the needs of children now and in the future.
>
> (Waters 2006)

On this note of optimism, we will turn our attention to consider the recent curriculum changes at Key Stages 3 and 4 and the impact that these may have on allowing cross-curricular approaches to teaching and learning to develop.

The current curriculum context: Key Stage 3

The situation facing teachers today is one of considerable change. The new National Curriculum at Key Stage 3 has, in one sense, learnt a lesson from history and is being implemented over a three-year period. Key documents from the QCA have outlined the key changes in terms of function and design (QCA 2008a,b). Each subject has a new programme of study containing elements such as Key Concepts, Key Processes, Range of Study and Curriculum Opportunities. More generally, the 'big picture' of the curriculum (Qualifications and Curriculum Development Agency; QCDA 2009a) illustrates the vast number of curriculum elements that need to be considered. Individual subjects are just one small part of this.

Of particular importance for our consideration is the inclusion of what have been called 'cross-curricular dimensions'. In what has a striking resonance with the historical overview presented above, these (at the time of writing) 'non-statutory' elements of the curriculum cover the following areas:

- identity and cultural diversity;
- healthy lifestyles;
- community participation;
- enterprise;
- global dimensions and sustainable development;
- technology and the media;
- creativity and critical thinking.

Accompanying guidance from the QCDA (2009b) outlines the purpose of these cross-curricular dimensions. They have been chosen because they reflect some of the major ideas and challenges that face us and will help make learning 'real and relevant' (p. 1). Additionally, the dimensions:

- are unifying areas of learning that span the curriculum and help young people make sense of the world;
- are not subjects, but are *crucial* aspects of learning that should permeate the curriculum and the life of a school [my italics];
- add a richness and relevance to the curriculum experience of young people;
- provide a focus for work within and between subjects;
- are interdependent and mutually supportive.

(QCDA 2009b, p. 1)

For all these reasons, one might have thought that these dimensions should have been made statutory. Perhaps the QCDA is wary of some of the developments that recent history has taught it about overloading teachers with too much bureaucracy. However, time may have shown that some teachers would have sought to prioritise their work elsewhere were it not for a second, important development in the individual subject programmes of study.

A closer look at individual subject programmes of study reveals important new emphases on collaborative, cross-subject working. In every subject's Wider Opportunities statements you will find references such as:

- work on problems that arise in other subjects and in contexts beyond the school (Mathematics 4d);
- develop speaking and listening skills through work that makes cross-curricular links with other subjects (English 4f);
- make links between science and other subjects and areas of the curriculum (Science 4k);
- make links between geography and other subjects, including citizenship and

ICT, and areas of the curriculum including sustainability and global dimension (Geography 4i).

DCSF and QCDA (2007)

These subject references to cross-curricular opportunities are particularly helpful and represent a significant shift in the curriculum orders. They are, of course, statutory and a plethora of advice about how to implement these (and other) changes has been produced for teachers (QCDA 2009c). As an example, one of the QCDA guides on sustainable development (QCDA 2009d) includes very detailed planning materials about the learning objectives, typical teaching activities, advice on how individual subjects can contribute to the teaching of the dimension and more. It exemplifies many of these through numerous case studies drawn from primary and secondary schools.

Alongside the cross-curricular dimensions and the individual subject programmes of study there are other statutory elements of the curriculum at Key Stage 3 that all teachers have to embed within their teaching. These include Functional Skills in English, mathematics and information and communication technologies (ICT) and the Personal, Learning and Thinking Skills (PLTS). Both these sets of skills and competencies will require teachers to make imaginative links between their subject's knowledge, skills and understanding and other areas of knowledge. This has many similarities to what we might consider a more traditional cross-curricular set of teaching and learning approaches.

So, every teacher in every subject at Key Stage 3 is charged with developing a cross-curricular approach to teaching and learning. It is the law.

The current curriculum context: Key Stage 4

At Key Stage 4, the situation is a little more complex. The revision of the National Curriculum here includes only the core subjects but, as in Key Stage 3, each contains references to cross-curricular ways of working. For example:

English:
- Analyse and evaluate the impact of combining words, images and sounds in media, moving-image and multimodal texts (2.2i);
- Develop speaking and listening/reading/writing skills through work that makes cross-curricular links with other subjects (4.1f, 4.2f and 4.3f).

Mathematics:
- Work on problems that arise in other subjects and in contexts beyond the school (4d).

Science (in the Explanatory Notes):
- All pupils develop their ability to relate their understanding of science to their own and others' decisions about lifestyles, and to scientific and technological developments in society.

- Most pupils also develop their understanding and skills in ways that provide the basis for further studies in science and related areas.

(DCSF and QCDA 2007, p. 221)

Additionally, there are references to cross-curricular working with Citizenship (4j), ICT (4h) and PE (4f) as well as the non-statutory Economic Wellbeing and Financial Capability (4k) and Religious Education (RE) (4i).

Alongside these references within the programmes of study, additional components of the curriculum such as Functional Skills and PLTS (all of which extend the learning covered by pupils in Key Stage 3) present opportunities for cross-curricular practice.

However, perhaps the biggest innovation at Key Stage 4 has been the introduction of the diploma qualifications. These have resulted in a significant shift in the ways in which teachers from different subject specialisms are required to work together. As an example, the Creative and Media diploma contains elements from subjects such as music, visual arts, textiles, fashion, drama, dance, film and more; Travel and Tourism will involve subjects such as geography, history, economics, ICT, etc. In addition, each diploma has Functional Skills and PLTS built into the assessment framework. Teachers working on these new diplomas have had to collaborate extensively on the design and delivery of new schemes of work that relate to the specific principal, specialist and additional learning strands. This is further complicated by the need to include elements of work-based learning and the need to support an independent student project with appropriate subject specialist input. Teachers need to become more flexible in their approach to their subject and how it relates to these emerging qualifications. It is interesting to note that 'collaborative working' is one of the key areas that the Training and Development Agency, together with Lifelong Learning UK, have identified as needing further professional development for teachers working within these new qualification frameworks (TDA and Lifelong Learning UK 2008, p. 11).

Given these new components in the Key Stage 3 and 4 curricula, all teachers will need to consider their approach to teaching in a cross-curricular manner. But, as this book will demonstrate, to do this effectively one needs to go beyond the subject content itself and look more broadly. To reiterate, our working definition for a cross-curricular approach to teaching is characterised by a sensitivity towards, and a synthesis of, knowledge, skills and understandings from various subject areas that inform an enriched pedagogy that promotes an approach to learning which embraces and explores this wider sensitivity through various methods. The teacher has a vital and essential role to play in this. There is no curriculum development without teacher development. But what is the wider view on this? Is it really just down to the hard-pressed, individual subject teacher? In the final part of this opening chapter we will turn our attention to this issue. Whose responsibility is it for developing approaches to cross-curricular teaching and learning?

Practical Task 3

Consider the range of teaching that you are involved in at the moment. This may span across several Key Stages, subject areas or qualification specifications. Make a visual map of the various cross-curricular opportunities that are presented in your work. Make sure you include opportunities to collaborate with other subjects, cross-curricular dimensions, Functional Skills and PLTS.

Situating cross-curricular teaching and learning

Who is responsible for developing approaches to cross-curricular teaching and learning? Is it the responsibility of the whole school through the implementation of a whole school policy or strategy? Or is it the responsibility of individual subject teachers and their relationships with other teachers or wider local networks that encompass other professionals?

The short answer is that all of the above can play a part in developing approaches to cross-curricular teaching and learning. There is a shortage of data about how the recent curriculum changes in England have affected teachers' perceptions on this issue, but one survey by Ofsted (2008) presents some interesting findings related to how schools can successfully manage innovation in the curriculum.

Ofsted's survey of 30 schools indicated that at the whole school level there were four main categories of curriculum innovation. These included organising the curriculum around themes that were developed through different subjects. For some of these secondary schools, the thematic organisation was not subject orientated, but rather focused on a particular cross-curricular dimension or learning competence:

> Themes based on cross-subject or inter-disciplinary approaches incorporated the appropriate development of skills, as in the following example. During Year 7, every pupil completed six projects, each lasting half a term, on the themes of 'journeys', 'identity', 'positive images', 'art attach', 'survival' and the 'the power and the glory'. These drew on geography, history, religious education, dance, drama, art, and personal, social and health education. The pupils were able to assess their development against defined competencies, weekly or in individual lessons. As a result, they gained an understanding of their strengths and weaknesses which provided a powerful stimulus to learning and raising standards.
>
> (Ofsted 2008, pp. 9–10)

For other schools, a thematic approach meant that a major theme, such as the impact of rivers on environmental, social and economic development, was chosen and explored from a range of subject perspectives. Skills, knowledge and understanding within each subject were orientated around the chosen theme.

In all the schools that Ofsted surveyed, subjects were taught discretely for part of the time. From the perspective of the individual teachers, Ofsted noted that they:

Emphasised the importance of thorough and detailed planning that identified, unambiguously, progression in knowledge of the subject and the development of skills. They also identified clearly how, when and by whom the work would be assessed.

(Ofsted 2008, p. 9)

Approaches such as those identified by Ofsted in this survey were only effective when there was a high degree of co-ordination between a group of dedicated teachers or when they were initiated and sustained by a senior manager with a responsibility for the curriculum at the appropriate Key Stage. They are unlikely to happen by chance. The survey is quite clear that strong leadership at all levels is essential for successful curriculum innovation of this type.

However, at the level of the individual teacher and the work that is undertaken within that teacher's classroom, there is much more that can be achieved. This is primarily where this book will maintain its focus.

Moving forwards

As the various chapters unfold we will be examining how the development of an approach to cross-curricular teaching and learning can affect all aspects of a teacher's work. This will start in Chapter 2 with the principles and purposes for cross-curricular teaching and learning. It will draw on the work of Peshkin (1988) to prescribe the activities of cross-curricular teaching and learning to the teacher's wider sense of professional (and personal) identity, their understanding of their particular subject background and the context of their work.

The first part of Chapter 3 will outline the key elements of an effective pedagogy for cross-curricular teaching and learning from the individual teacher's perspective. The key point here will be that effective cross-curricular teaching extends beyond a mere consideration of the content of the curriculum and placing subjects together in arbitrary groupings to work with prescribed curriculum themes or cross-curricular dimensions. The second part of this major chapter will present ideas about the practice of cross-curricular teaching that span out from the work of individual teachers (and their developing pedagogy) to the collaborative approaches that are a requisite of good cross-curricular initiatives. It will conclude with a range of practical tasks that unite the various changes in an individual teacher's pedagogy that will be required with a wider school approach. The chapter will provide a series of practical steps to consider as you begin to envisage how such an approach could be implemented in your own curriculum and professional development.

Having established a broad framework for the principles of cross-curricular teaching and examined how this outworks through the construction of a skilful pedagogy and wider school-based pieces of curriculum reform, Chapters 4, 5 and 6 will take a more detailed look at a number of specific aspects of teaching and learning that can be developed through a cross-curricular approach.

Working from the starting point identified by Wertsch (1998) and Bruner (1996) that language can be conceived as a mediating tool through which teaching is delivered and by which learning is facilitated or constrained, Chapter 4 will take a detailed look at the language of cross-curricular teaching and learning. It starts with the focus on knowledge, language and thinking, before moving on to consider the development of an appropriate pedagogy for cross-curricular language development, including 'cross-curricular utterances' as a key principle for classroom use.

Chapter 5 will focus on the introduction and application of new technologies to processes of teaching and learning. Starting from a brief survey of recent initiatives and their impact on teachers' pedagogy (Somekh 2007), this chapter will consider ways in which ICT can play a mediating role in linking traditional subjects together in new ways. ICT has the potential to challenge pedagogical processes of teaching and learning and this will be the major focus of the chapter. Examples of hardware and software that implicitly promote cross-curricular ways of thinking will be analysed in light of the arguments presented in Chapter 4 about language and its essential role in the teaching and learning processes.

In Chapter 6 we will consider the processes of assessment and educational evaluation that need to be an integral part of the curriculum development process. Bolting on old approaches to assessment to new models of teaching and learning will not best serve the needs of teachers or pupils. Drawing on the work of Blanchard (2009), Whetton (2009) and Savage and Fautley (2007a), this chapter will briefly consider recent developments in educational assessment and apply them to the framework and model of cross-curricular teaching and learning presented in the previous chapters. It will argue for a mixed methodology of summative and formative assessment processes. This mixed methodology will serve two purposes. It will provide important data about pupils' learning to serve formal outcomes of learning (i.e. qualification frameworks and external awards), but, perhaps more importantly, will also empower teachers in their day-to-day work with pupils, allowing them to reflect on their implementation of new ways of cross-curricular working at the immediate level of curriculum design and classroom interaction.

Within this activity, the use of educational evaluation methodologies can help teachers explore the potential of cross-curricular approaches to teaching and learning. The second half of Chapter 6 will explore the benefits and practicalities of conducting small-scale pieces of educational evaluation of this type. By linking educational evaluation to a teacher's wider roles in curriculum development and assessment, this chapter argues that the burden on their time can be reduced. In this sense, the boundaries of assessment and evaluation may blur slightly and become embodied in the work of the skilful teacher.

Chapter 7 will draw a series of conclusions from the previous chapters. It introduces a number of new metaphors for cross-curricular teaching and learning and sets its conclusions in a consideration of where curriculum design will be heading over the next five to ten years. It will argue that the role of the skilful teacher will be an essential element for whatever shape or form education takes in the future. The principles and purposes of teaching and learning in a cross-curricular framework will only become more important to teachers' work and the education experiences of our pupils as this century progresses.

Summary

This chapter began with the setting out of three important key principles: first, that there is no curriculum development without teacher development; second, that subjectivity, whether that be related to the individual teacher or to a particular curriculum subject, is a garment that can not be removed but needs to be understood; and third, that the skilful teacher will embody a skilful pedagogy that is essential to good teaching and which can be developed and extended in new ways.

Having proposed a tentative definition for an approach to cross-curricular teaching and learning, we examined a number of contexts within which this has, or will, occur. These included a look back at the period of time surrounding the implementation of the first National Curriculum and a brief consideration of how primary schools have responded to similar issues. The current curriculum context was introduced and questions were considered about who was responsible for ensuring that cross-curricular teaching took place within schools.

The emphasis throughout these discussions has been on the function and role of the individual teacher and the knowledge, skills and understanding that they need in order to operate effectively within a heavily politicised period of educational reform. Making sense of national strategies and curriculum frameworks is not easy. But, rather than being dictated to by them, this book will take the view that they present opportunities for imaginative and creative approaches to teaching and learning which will not only inspire pupils but also inspire you to carry on teaching.

Part of that process is making oneself accountable to processes of professional development. For those readers undertaking initial teacher education, this would include reflecting on the Q Standards regularly and building your evidence base that demonstrates your effective meeting of them. For those readers already working as teachers, there will be strategies of performance appraisal and review, which involve core (C) standards, and require you to set targets and monitor your process through reflective cycles.

To assist with these processes, each chapter in this book, and the accompanying titles within the series, has considered how the text and activities within it have helped the reader meet the Q Standards for Qualified Teacher Status (QTS). A summary of the application of these standards to each chapter appears at the end of each chapter. We trust that you will find this a helpful way of applying your work in reading the chapters (and the completion of any of the activities within them) to your wider professional development.

Professional Standards for QTS

This chapter will help you meet the following Q standards: Q6, Q7a, Q8, Q11, Q14

Professional Standards for Teachers

This chapter will help you meet the following core standards: C6, C7, C8, C15, C16, C30, C40, C41

2

The Principles and Purposes for Cross-Curricular Teaching and Learning

Key objectives

By the end of this chapter, you will be able to:

- reflect on your own, intrinsic beliefs about your role as a teacher and the particular subject that you teach;

- hypothesise about the potential benefits and pitfalls of developing cross-curricular approaches in teaching and learning from your own individual and subject perspective;

- begin to make links between your own subject and other subjects through examining key concepts and processes that underpin them;

- justify a definition for cross-curricular teaching and learning;

- apply a range of research findings to establish principles and purposes for cross-curricular teaching and learning.

Introduction

> Courses and subjects that fail to reinvent themselves in the face of new circumstances are liable to decline or disappear.
>
> (Kirk, Macdonald and Tinning 1997, p. 273)

This chapter will establish a series of principles for cross-curricular teaching and learning from the teacher's perspective. Starting with the work of Peshkin (1988) it will investigate how the teacher's sense of professional and personal identity relates to their understanding of their subject and the opportunities to collaborate with others through a wider curriculum framework. It will do this by reflecting on two case studies drawn from the author's own experience of using Peshkin's work as a stimulus for reflective writing. Practical tasks will be presented that will allow the reader to undertake a similar piece of reflective analysis.

Following this piece of structured reflection, Peshkin's approach will be extended to consider the individual characteristics of subjects included within the curriculum. This will be done by looking at how Key Concepts and Key Processes, drawn from the recent implementation of the National Curriculum at Key Stage 3, can encourage teachers to begin to make productive links between subjects, and by using a case study written by an art teacher at the early stage of a cross-curricular project.

The chapter will conclude with a wider consideration of research studies of cross-curricularity in education. These help provide a broader canvas for the definition of cross-curricular teaching and learning, and also extend our understanding of the essential principles and purposes of this approach. Finally, these established principles and purposes will be related back to the definition provided in Chapter 1, and we will look ahead to the challenges of applying these ideas to construct a new classroom pedagogy, discussed in more detail in Chapter 3.

Getting the focus right

> One of the artifices of evaluation is to portray individuals but to invest them (and their lives) with meanings derived from the projects in which we observe them – like clothing dolls. . . . Instead of drawing a boundary around a project experience and reading individual lives within the context of the project, we need, just a little more often, to provide life experiences as contexts within which to understand educational projects.
>
> (Kushner 1993, p. 39)

Saville Kushner is one of the world's leading experts on educational evaluation. Over the years, he has worked on a range of projects exploring the nature of evaluation, how it can be done well and how participants within projects, as well as those observing them, can benefit from adopting a rich evaluative perspective.

Following on from Kushner's observation above, the danger that faces us is that we seek to develop an understanding of the principles and purposes of cross-curricular teaching and learning in isolation from the people that matter most in our study, that is, teachers and pupils. If we start with the educational project, in this case the curriculum requirement to develop a cross-curricular approach to teaching at Key Stages 3 and 4, and seek to understand this in isolation from those people involved in it, investing meaning and applying principles without respect to their wider life experiences, we will ultimately repeat the failures of previous educational initiatives. As we have seen in Chapter 1, the situation facing educators at this point in the twenty-first century is very similar to that facing educators twenty years ago. To avoid repeating the same mistakes, the challenge that this exemplification to cross-curricular teaching and learning takes is to start with teachers' life experiences and use this as the context within which to develop an understanding of the educational initiative. This, according to Kushner's ideals, would result in a greater understanding and ownership of the innovation from all sides.

Kushner's comments challenge contemporary thinking about curriculum reform and development, which are often remote to the lives of teachers, dictated through national policies with little consideration given to local contexts. But, as we explored in Chapter 1, some aspects of recent curriculum developments give teachers a real (and legitimate) opportunity to pursue these within the curriculum frameworks at Key Stages 3 and 4. The 'localisation' of the National Curriculum is a very important feature of QCDA policy (QCA 2008a). As we have discussed in Chapter 1, there can be no meaningful and lasting curriculum development without teacher development. Our focus, initially, has to be on teachers and how they are empowered to take ownership of curriculum policies and ideas and shape them for use within their individual classrooms and with their pupils. This perspective can open up many interesting questions. For example:

- How do my perceptions about my subject affect my choice of pedagogy and the opportunities for learning that I present to my pupils?
- How have my wider life experiences shaped my teacher identity?
- How do I know whether my teaching is successful? What are the terms or framework that I measure this against? Where have these come from?

Reflective Task 1

Before reading on, take a few minutes to consider these questions. Jot down a few notes in response to each one. You will need these later in the chapter.

These are all challenging questions for us as we start out in this chapter exploring the key principles and purposes of cross-curricular teaching and learning. Kushner's challenge to us is to seek, first, to understand education events through the context of our own life experiences. Kushner is well aware that such an approach is open to misunderstanding and the criticism of individualistic navel-gazing! But his writing boldly challenges us to take more account of our individual life histories. In that sense, it is impossible to ignore the personalising context that we all find ourselves in when considering the activities of teaching and learning:

Programs are subject to context as their meanings and significance are subsumed within personal lives.

(Kushner 2000, p. 58)

As an aside, it is interesting to note that in many writings about education this wider narrative is missing (Savage 2007a). Perhaps this is due to writers' wariness related to perceptions of what constitutes effective educational advice or policy and their roles within it. Or perhaps the educational community and its writers have caught a disposition to invest teachers and pupils with meanings derived from projects or initiatives rather then seeking to understand their inherent values and experiences first in any meaningful way. This needs to be reversed. The tables need to be turned.

In relation to the discussion on cross-curricular principles and purposes, it is clear where we will be starting.

Turning the tables

Developing an effective approach to reflection is key to a teacher's initial and ongoing professional development (Schon 1983, 1987; Watson and Wilcox 2000). Reflection has become a standard way in which teachers can 'become better acquainted with their own story' (Conle 2000, p. 51) and is rightly an integrated part of the UK government's professional standards for teachers (TDA 2007). Professional Standard Q7a states that anyone undertaking initial teacher education should be able to 'reflect on and improve their practice, and take responsibility for identifying and meeting their developing professional needs' (TDA 2007).

However, reflecting effectively on one's practice is a skilful activity in and of itself. It takes time to learn to reflect constructively, and this often requires coaching and support from sensitive mentors. After all, it is hard to know what you don't know! It is important to be self-critical and to provoke oneself. Uncritical reflection and a lack of self-interrogation are dangerous, as Johnson points out:

> The accounts teachers produce must be interrogated because those accounts are not 'out there' and fixed, waiting to be retold time and time again in the same manner.
>
> (Johnson 2002, p. 21).

Frameworks or tools to help teachers reflect on their work are commonplace. Any Internet search for 'reflective practice tools' will bring up multiple options. For our discussion, Peshkin's work on subjectivity provides a very useful framework that has the potential to link together teachers' wider views, their reflective practice and the 'project' of developing approaches to cross-curricular teaching and learning. It will also help in our wider objective of defining the principles and practices of cross-curricular teaching and learning.

Introducing Peshkin's I's

Defining 'subjectivity' as 'the quality of an investigator that affects the results of observational investigation' (Peshkin 1988, p. 17), Peshkin highlights the requirement for any observer of, or participator in, educational events to be 'meaningfully attentive' (Peshkin 1988, p. 17) to their own subjectivity as they conduct and reflect on their teaching activities. Peshkin describes subjectivity as a 'garment that cannot be removed' which has the capability to 'filter, skew, shape, block, transform, construe, and misconstrue what transpires from the outset of a research project to its culmination in a written statement' (Peshkin 1988, p. 17).

His research goes on to helpfully demonstrate this process through the identification of subjective 'I's' that he perceived and reflected on during an extended piece of educational research at Riverview High School in California. You can read more about this study in his book, *The Color of Strangers, the Color of Friends* (Peshkin 1991).

There are a number of important points here. First, the foundations for Peshkin's subjective I's are drawn from a range of sources, including:

- his own belief and value systems;
- his experiences of a particular environment, i.e. the town of 'Riverview';
- his ongoing experiences of life within the particular school;
- the wider community and the relationships that he, and other members of his family, established within that community.

Second, Peshkin categorises his subjective I's in two main ways:

- 'intrinsic subjectivities' that make up his whole reflective 'being', i.e. they are context-less (at least in basic ways, e.g. geographically);
- 'situational subjectivities' (Peshkin 1988, p. 18) that change from place to place, i.e. they are contextualised in some way.

The following two case studies show how Peshkin's intrinsic and situational I's can be applied in the development of one teacher. Following each case study, a series of activities designed to help you conduct a similar piece of reflective work will be presented.

Case Study 1: Defining intrinsic I's

Through a piece of structured reflection, I have identified the following intrinsic subjective I's that I believe have been an important influence on my work. They are presented chronologically, although the reader will quickly see that there are many overlapping, competing and conflicting dimensions.

1. The Musically Conservative I

This is, in a sense, the easiest 'I' for me to identify. It has existed for the longest and runs back in my memory to early childhood. It has its foundation in my training as a musician in the classical tradition, as a pianist from the age of five and a percussionist from the age of eleven. The strict disciplines of instrumental learning and performance practice are clearly etched in my memory alongside the immense enjoyment of being part of an orchestral group giving public performances. I grew

---

up to love the music of the Western classical tradition and, in many senses as a teenager, to despise the music of popular traditions.

2. The Musically Radical I

My Musically Radical I was more difficult to identify. Strange as it appears now, this I seems to have developed, to an extent, alongside the Musically Conservative I in my later teens. I remember an eccentric woodwind teacher at my sixth form college introducing my colleagues and me to a range of contemporary classical music. At first I did not understand the strange sounds that this music contained, but over the course of two years my musical palette began to broaden. This continued as a number of my friends began to compose experimental music of various types. As a percussionist, I was often called upon to perform these pieces and grew to love a broader palette of sound sources and textures.

However, like many performers, I was never that keen to engage in the act of composition itself. In contrast to my performing career, I had no formal tuition in composition beyond the stylistic pastiche exercises of Bach chorales and two-part inventions at Advanced Level. It was only as my piano playing developed alongside my interest in jazz that I began to learn to improvise and compose within this idiom. Ironically, the knowledge of music gained through my Musically Conservative I put me in a strong position to learn about and understand the harmonic and melodic features of jazz.

3. The Pedagogically Inclusive I

My experience taught me that there was only one way to learn about music. This was an exclusive and elitist activity available only to those who had sophisticated performance abilities and an understanding and appreciation of the Western classical tradition. But at some point, which I find it hard to put my finger on, I realised that there had to be another way into music that was less exclusive and elitist. This did not happen as a result of my own teacher training experience. In the gap between this last sentence and the previous one I have spent over an hour reading through my old assignments and teaching practice materials from my PGCE studies. I could not find any evidence in these materials of a change in my desire to teach music in any other way than in which I myself had been taught. There is one exception to this bleak picture that will be described below.

I believe that the development of my Pedagogically Inclusive I is tied up intricately with the establishment of the Technological Enthusiast I.

4. The Technological Enthusiast I

As a high school pupil I remember shying away from computers and seeking to adopt more traditional approaches to working with pen, paper, manuscript paper and conventional instruments. The strength of my Musically Conservative I meant that I had strong views about the types of music that I preferred and this led me to disparaging popular music and the ways in which it was produced. However, when I left music college in 1989 my brother gave me his old computer and I began to use it to record pieces of music. A friend and I fancied ourselves as songwriters and we made and recorded tracks with other vocalists. I used my musical notation skills to write arrangements for various people including the covers band that I played keyboards in.

It was as a young teacher at my first school that I began to appreciate the importance of technology in widening access to music for a different type of pupil from myself. My experiences of using technology had always been to reinforce and consolidate my musical practices in light of my Musically Conservative I. My Musically Radical I had been nurtured and fed through my undergraduate studies and, to a degree, through my PGCE. My Technological Enthusiast I spoke to me strongly during my early years of teaching and out of this melting pot I believe that my Pedagogically Inclusive I was born. Music education must be for all and not a few. I wanted to research and find ways to achieve this.

5. The Artistically Appeasing I

Through a lecture given during my PGCE course by a community musician, my view of what counted as 'artistic practice' was challenged at a fundamental level. Rather than focusing solely on artistic objects, he asked us to value the processes by which these objects were formed as well as the experiences contained within these processes. In many ways my career to this point had been about faithfully recreating artistic objects for others to enjoy and little attention had been paid to enjoying the process of making or recreating those objects. Yet I think that here are the seeds of my belief as a teacher that musical process is as important as musical product for our children. This cuts right against everything that I was taught and valued for many years. My musicality was judged against performance outcomes and I succeeded as a musician because my musical 'products' were considered acceptable.

This is why I have called this final subjective I my Artistically Appeasing I. My dictionary gives three definitions for the word 'appease':

1. to bring to a state of peace or quiet;
2. to cause to subside;
3. to pacify or conciliate, especially: to buy off (an aggressor) by concessions usually at the sacrifice of principles.

Whether within the classroom environment or the lecture theatre, I feel that I am appeasing many elements of my Musically Conservative I, bringing them to a state of peace or quiet. But this is not in the sense of buying off or giving concessions. There have been no concessions given or principles sacrificed. My

Artistically Appeasing I believes deeply in the genuine artistic practice of young people's classroom work at a philosophical, aesthetic and educational level. The ideals and beliefs of the Musically Conservative I are still present. I still love the music of the Western classical tradition and have sought to pass on that passion to my pupils in various ways. But I believe that the process by which these convictions have been appeased and, in a sense, broadened has made my approach to teaching more inclusive and tolerant of the various pathways by which pupils can come to know and understand musical knowledge and develop personal ways of expression.

These five intrinsic, subjective I's are summarised in Table 2.1.

TABLE 2.1 My intrinsic I's

INTRINSIC I'S	FOUNDATION	KEY IDEA
Musically Conservative I	Early childhood	Strict definitions of musical success; formalisation in the processes of musical development
Musically Radical I	Various, including performance opportunities during my sixth-form studies, the compositional work of friends and my own jazz studies	New sounds and structures; increasing palette of musical possibilities; extension and legitimising of new pathways drawn from the Musically Conservative I
Pedagogically Inclusive I	I've found this difficult to define, but it has led to a dissatisfaction with traditional music teaching methods as being exclusive and my seeking for more inclusive pedagogies	There are more ways into music (by which I mean the skills needed and the experiences one can obtain) than the way that I experienced myself
Technological Enthusiast I	Experience of music making with friends and others; kindled by intrigue and awareness of electroacoustic musical traditions at the University of East Anglia during my undergraduate studies	Technologies provide new ways to handle musical materials. They can change the whole nature of musical practices at a fundamental level
Artistically Appeasing I	Observation of teaching and my own teaching practice at my first school	The process of making music can contain as much of value as the final product of that music making

Practical Task 1a

Spend some time trying to analyse your own intrinsic I's. You can do this in a number of ways. This is a highly personal exercise. Reflect on the key notions or concepts that underpin your beliefs about teaching and learning in your specialist subject. Use your notes from the previous reflective task to help you here. Other processes of thought can help you define and refine your chosen intrinsic I's. Think through:

1. underpinning beliefs or philosophies (beyond the educational) about your subject and the impact it has had on your life throughout your childhood and formative years;

2. your own educational experiences and memories through formal and informal contexts (i.e. school, university, but also the home, local community, etc.);

3. conversations (or recollections of conversations) with key people that you have met who may have changed the way you think or feel about your subject;

4. your reading and the powerful ideas that this might have contained which may have impacted on you personally or educationally;

5. family or other relationships and how these may have shaped your personality and affected your teaching ability;

6. 'Eureka' moments from your own life experiences.

There will undoubtedly be all kinds of other sources for your ideas here too.

Labelling your intrinsic I's is difficult but important. Try to get down to the base level here and ensure that each 'I' has a distinctive 'flavour' or 'personality'. Putting ideas into categories can help with this process. Try to end up with four or five intrinsic I's of your own. This will help you in the next stage of the exercise.

For Peshkin, intrinsic I's are dominant voices in educational research. For us, Case Study 1 and the associated Practical Task have helped define key aspects of our own subjectivity in relation to teaching, learning and the associated concepts of a particular subject culture.

Moving onwards, Peshkin's argument is that these intrinsic I's come into play at key moments of innovation or change within our personal or professional lives. For us, this could relate closely to the development of approaches to cross-curricular teaching and learning.

As an example, the following case study explores how the intrinsic I's identified in Case Study 1 came into play at a particular moment in this teacher's career. At this particular point, the teacher was about to undertake a piece of educational research within his teaching. This required a deeper sense of reflection on the potential research focus and associated methodology. Through this consideration of intrinsic I's *in practice*, it was possible to define a range of 'situational I's'. These, in turn, related closely to a specific series of choices about the educational activities to include within the piece of action research (i.e. the particular 'situation').

Case Study 2: Defining situational I's

1. The Facilitative Curriculum I

At a very early stage in my career I began to realise that the curriculum was more than a written document or statement of learning objectives and outcomes. Within my initial teacher training I was taught to plan lessons and schemes of work with thought and consideration, specifying key learning objectives, choosing appropriate teaching activities and identifying possible outcomes by which I might know that my pupils have learnt something. The strict nature of this teaching model fell well within the realm of my Musically Conservative I. It was built on the belief that I could determine the pathways and processes of musical development for my pupils. I knew what was best for them, or so I thought, and I could plan for a range of teaching activities that would bring these supposed qualities out. What worked for me in my musical development would work for them in theirs. But even at the time of my training this all felt very deterministic and slightly at odds with what I considered was a key defining feature of artistic practice – namely unpredictable pathways of working and diverse musical outcomes.

This dilemma was exacerbated by my Technological Enthusiast I, which sought to consider the educational implications of moving technologies out of the music studio and into the music classroom. This was uncertain ground for me and required a new approach to curriculum planning and delivery.

The result of this conflict was the Facilitative Curriculum I that grew throughout my PhD studies. In its early development it was nurtured and given credence by my reading of work by Stenhouse and others. Stenhouse's vision of the classroom and the curriculum as opportunities for cultural development inspired me to think about and plan for a music curriculum, facilitated through ICT, that truly gave space for pupils to develop and learn about the 'culture of music' in ways that matched what I conceived to be authentic musical and artistic processes.

One particular question posed by Stenhouse became very important as I planned for these early studies of musical learning and teaching with new technologies:

> The problem of the curriculum can now be expressed as follows: what worthwhile curriculum content can we find as a focus for a classroom experience which will stimulate the pupils to an attempt to find for themselves standards which are worthwhile and viable in terms of their own experience of life?
>
> (Stenhouse 1975, p. 133)

This question challenged head on my conception of the curriculum as a closed spiral of 'creative' possibility managed and controlled by the teacher. Predetermined outcomes to an artistic problem, however helpfully presented by myself to the pupils, were second rate compared with Stenhouse's vision of classrooms as 'cultural laboratories':

> The classroom becomes a kind of cultural laboratory in which new face-to-face culture is generated at a humble level. The pupils are in fact not making a transition from one culture to another, but rather being provided with the opportunity to feed their own culture on the arts and sciences, and thus to build for themselves an enriched medium of communication and thinking. . . . The teacher ought to be a servant of his (sic) pupils, asking himself how his subject can make a contribution to the quality of their living.
>
> (Stenhouse 1975, p. 134)

I saw the establishment of a facilitative and empowering curriculum as one key ingredient in trying to create a classroom culture within which pupils could begin to make creative connections. I also realised that from the pupil's perspective the curriculum became embodied in my role as their teacher. I cannot remember any occasions when pupils asked to see my lesson plans. For my pupils, my own musical values, understanding and practice were what mattered.

The development of this Facilitative Curriculum I began to solve what I can now perceive as a conflict between my Musically Conservative I and my Pedagogically Inclusive I. My ability to redefine the curriculum as a facilitating environment for musical exploration and discovery through the careful use of ICT (as demanded by my Technological Enthusiast I) was central in this process.

2. The Embodied Curriculum I

Linked to the Facilitative Curriculum I is the Embodied Curriculum I. Whilst I sought to consider and plan projects that prioritised opportunities for pupils to re-imagine and enrich their musical thinking through the imaginative use of ICT, I quickly became aware that the quality of my relationship with my pupils was the most important ingredient in seeking to cultivate what I perceived as authentic musical practices with ICT. I had to learn to value pupils and place their experience of the curriculum centre stage in my thinking. To do this meant taking my focus away from the written or planned curriculum to a certain extent and placing it firmly on charting pupils' lived experiences of the curriculum, representing this in an authentic a way as possible through my written evaluations.

I describe this as the Embodied Curriculum I. As such, it reflects my desire to allow pupils to experience music at a deeper, more personal level than I experienced through my Musically Conservative I. It draws on aspects of my Musically Radical I, which saw, at that impressionable age of my mid-teens, that music was as much an embodied experience as a subject to be analysed and studied from afar. Similarly, it draws on my Artistically Appeasing I, which has taught me that the process of being involved in music can be as intrinsically valuable as the final product of that music making. I still believe that high-quality musical products are highly motivational for pupils and that they have an important part to play in their education. But as pupils begin to appreciate and embody curriculum processes their attention shifts from final product to an enjoyment of the activity of music making for its own sake. This has been a long journey for me to undertake, and one that I am still engaged in. However, at whatever stage of the journey I have found myself at I have been constantly aware that the influence of my Embodied Curriculum I has been central to my teaching and research process.

3. The Democratic Compositional I

Where does my belief in composition as a dominant force in music education come from? This question has puzzled me throughout my research. It is not that composition has played a large part in my own music education. I would not describe myself as a composer and, in many ways, would be uncomfortable about any public audition of my work. For me, composition has essentially been a private thing. So, apart from a requirement in the National Curriculum to teach composition, why overtly stress the importance of composition and use it as a central practice throughout my research?

I have thought long and hard about this. I believe it comes down to a strong dissatisfaction with my own experience of music education, which was privileged, elitist and, as discussed above, built entirely around notions of instrumental ability and performance skill. Many other pupils who I knew were not offered the same experiences and opportunities as I was. They grew to dislike music lessons and to see them as an irrelevance. But, as is the case with the majority of young people, music played a huge part in their wider lives. I succeeded through this model of music education but many others failed. This did not bother me at the time but it does now. There has to be another approach.

I believe that through the prioritising of composition I have provided a more democratic music education for my own pupils. My Technological Enthusiast I spotted an opportunity for change. At the start of the research process I was tentative about this. My Musically Conservative I was a strong force and I was tempted to fall back on personal experiences of music education that had worked for me. However, with the ongoing observation of other composers' work, and the support of key individuals, I was able to pursue and develop an alternative model of music education that had a focus elsewhere. Did this new prioritising of composition in my work provide a field of equal opportunities for pupils? Probably not, but it is a lot more level than it was before. I believe that my Technological Enthusiast I has been justified through the development of the situational Democratic Compositional I. More pupils have been able to succeed in this model of music education than did through the one that I experienced as a child.

Practical Task 1b

In the first part of this practical task (1a), you were asked to define a number of your own intrinsic I's. This task asks you to apply these within a particular context to create a number of situational I's.

Read the following series of quotations:

> School subject communities are neither harmonious nor homogeneous and members do not necessarily share particular values, subject definitions and interests.
>
> (Jephcote and Davies 2007, p. 210)

> The diverse memberships of school subject communities create conditions conducive to contest, conflict and tension, both within a subject and between it and other subjects where we need to understand the effects of interaction across a series of boundaries between subject subcultures.
>
> (Cooper 1983, p. 208)

> Courses and subjects that fail to reinvent themselves in the face of new circumstances are liable to decline or disappear.
>
> (Kirk, Macdonald and Tinning 1997, p. 273).

Imagine that you have been asked to collaborate with a colleague in another subject area on a short scheme of work to be taught within the normal timetabled arrangements at your school. You have agreed a focus for the scheme of work and are at the point of putting a few preliminary ideas together. This is a new 'situation' that you find yourself in. It will challenge your intrinsic I's in new ways.

Consider the following questions:

1. What advantages are there to the blending of the two subjects within the scheme of work? Do the subjects share any particular values or interests?

2. Are there any disadvantages that you can anticipate arising from the proposed collaboration? Which boundaries will be difficult to cross? Why?

3. What impact, if any, will your intrinsic I's have on the way in which you work with this colleague?

4. What key principles or ideas within your subject, and the way that you have conceived this within your intrinsic I's, will be affected by this collaboration? Will there be comprises to be made? Will your intrinsic I's be enriched through the collaboration? If so, how will these intrinsic I's need to be redefined? Given the new context for your teaching that has resulted from this potential collaboration, at what point will the application of your 'intrinsic I's' require you to move beyond

them and redefine the new notion as a 'situational I' instead? What will these situational I's be? Try to categorise and label them.

Extending Peshkin's I's

> School subjects provide a context where antecedent structures collide with contemporary action; the school subject provides an obvious manifestation of historical legacies with which contemporary actors have to work.
>
> (Goodson 1991, p. 118)

The concept of intrinsic and situational subjectivities (I's) provides a lens through which one can generate a more holistic view of oneself, one's beliefs and core values and how they might impact on one's teaching. But by considering the notion of an individual school subject these thoughts can be extended further. As Goodson helpfully comments, teachers within the secondary school work in a subject-based culture that is underpinned by a significant historical legacy. This can lead to fundamental differences of opinion about what should be taught within a particular subject, how it should be taught and how it should be assessed. Jephcote and Davies give a flavour of the complexity of the situation by picking up on Goodson's notion of the 'teacher as actor'; someone who has to work within different contexts or levels in order to present the subject as a meaningful 'whole' within the curriculum:

> Changing the curriculum is an outcome of contexts between actors in different arenas and at different levels. Its story needs to be told at a number of levels to reflect the membership and structure of subject communities and to provide a means of illustrating each level and their interconnectedness. At the micro-level accounts have been concerned mainly with teachers, school classrooms and subjects and at macro-level with processes of policy-making and its implementation. At the same time, the meso-level has been taken to comprise of subject associations, local education authorities and sponsored curriculum projects where there are mediating processes which provide means to reinterpret macro-level changes and to assess the range of new choices they present to subject factions.
>
> (Jephcote and Davies 2007, p. 208)

However, the problem becomes more difficult because, as the quotations in Practical Task 1b have shown, the assumption that school subjects are harmonious and homogeneous in their relationships with one another is also false. Subjects may have a range of competing values, definitions and interests (Jephcote and Davies 2007, p. 210) that could lead to conflict and tension, both within and across subjects (Cooper 1983, p. 208). Goodson and Mangen's (1998) concept of a 'subject culture' (p. 120) is instructive here. For them, subject cultures are the 'identifiable structures which are visibly expressed through classroom organisation and pedagogical styles' (Goodson and Mangen's 1998, p. 120). They are what make a particular subject unique and, in a simple sense, are what portray to pupils the sense that they are studying a particular subject at a specific moment in the school day.

Unpicking these subject subjectivities or cultures and relating them to one's own intrinsic and situational subjectivities is an important extension of Peshkin's subjective and situational I's. Key questions to ask at this point would include:

- What are the subjectivities that underpin an individual subject? How can these be defined and articulated?

- How do these relate to the teacher's own, declared, subjectivities about their role and purpose as an educator?

Practical Task 1b has helped you begin to answer these questions. But as you face new challenges within your teaching you will have to revisit these reflective processes again.

However, for many teachers at secondary level, the subject dimension and its associated 'ways of being' (Van Manen 1977, p. 205) define their practice at a fundamental level. Research in this area indicates that the opportunity to develop one's subject and teach others about it is one of the most important determinants of teachers' job satisfaction (Spear, Gould and Lea 2000, p. 52). Subject knowledge (by which one means the actual knowledge of the subject but also, implicitly, the way that the subject is presented and traditionally taught) is a strong, formative force on the beginner teacher. It can often consolidate (and can unhelpfully congeal) within one's practice and be taken for granted if an uncritical stance is allowed to develop.

In seeking to understand the subjectivities of one's own subject, and explore its historical legacy and its potential relationship to other subjects within the curriculum, it is helpful to consider the programmes of study for each curriculum subject (QCA 2008a). As we have seen in Chapter 1, these programmes of study present a statutory remit for cross-curricular collaboration. Looking for other links between subjects at the level of Key Concepts or Key Processes can also be instructive. As an example, the following case study looks at how an art teacher has reflected on creativity as a Key Concept within their subject area, resulting in a more informed collaborative cross-curricular approach.

Case Study 3: Creativity in the visual arts

As an art teacher, creativity is central to my work. I wouldn't be where I am today without it. Creativity is key to my own making practices. I try and utilise every opportunity to bring creative processes into my own teaching. The National Curriculum is helpful in this respect. At Key Stage 3, creativity is the first Key Concept for Art and Design. This is what it says:

There are a number of key concepts that underpin the study of art, craft and design. Pupils need to understand these concepts in order to deepen and broaden their knowledge, skills and understanding.

1.1 Creativity

a Producing imaginative images, artefacts and other outcomes that are both original and of value.

b Exploring and experimenting with ideas, materials, tools and techniques.

c Taking risks and learning from mistakes.

QCA (2007)

I really like some of the verbs in this definition: exploring, experimenting, producing. I also like that it mentions taking risks and learning from mistakes. This is really important in all artists' working practices.

Recently, I wanted to find ways to collaborate with other colleagues in my school. We'd look together at some of the cross-curricular dimensions but this didn't seem to inspire us very much. On the QCDA website I noticed that they had a tool for comparing subjects side by side. This got me thinking. Which other subjects had creativity as a Key Concept?

I was surprised to find that most other subjects did! I quite liked the definition of creativity in the programme of study for English:

a Making fresh connections between ideas, experiences, texts and words, drawing on a rich experience of language and literature.

b Using inventive approaches to making meaning, taking risks, playing with language and using it to create new effects.

c Using imagination to convey themes, ideas and arguments, solve problems, and create settings, moods and characters.

d Using creative approaches to answering questions, solving problems and developing ideas.

QCA (2007)

This seemed to contain similar ideas to those found within the Art and Design programme of study. It seemed to be encouraging a playfulness in using language that fitted well within my own views and the way that I work as an artist.

In contrast, the creativity Key Concept in the Music programme of study was a bit odd. It said this:

a Using existing musical knowledge, skills and understanding for new purposes and in new contexts.

> b   Exploring ways music can be combined with other art forms and other subject disciplines.
>
> QCA (2007)
>
> I liked the explicit link in part (b) to collaboration but this didn't seem to be about creativity to me (but I'm not a musician). It just didn't seem to chime with what I think creativity should be about.
>
>   In the end, it was great to collaborate with English and Music colleagues on a project that explored creative processes in lyric and song writing to produce a Year 7 album of songs (complete with artwork too!). I learnt a lot from the collaboration. The key, for me, was finding out about how different subjects could relate to each other. The QCDA website comparison tool was really helpful in that respect.

Reflective Task 2

Case Study 3 presents one teacher's account of how she began to make links to other subjects through the 'creativity' Key Concept within various programmes of study. What were the key motivations for the proposed collaboration from her perspective? How did her conceptions of her own subject link to the English and Music curricula and their approaches to creativity?

Looking beyond the individual teacher

Up to this point, this chapter has focused almost exclusively on the work of individual teachers and their relationship to their individual curriculum subjects. This is a vital and central plank of this book's key principles. However, the main task of this chapter is to define the principles and purposes for cross-curricular teaching and learning. To do this effectively, it will be important to consider and learn from a range of broader research that has been undertaken. Within the confines of this book, there are obvious limitations to this overview; but the following section will briefly consider some key research findings from the UK and Europe. This research supplements the historical overview presented in Chapter 1 by considering studies conducted in the last five years. This will also help provide a complementary perspective to that discussed above. Following this, the chapter will conclude with a reiteration of the definition of cross-curricular teaching and learning, together with a summary of the key principles and purposes.

Research review 1: Evidence from recent research within the United Kingdom

Commissioned by the QCDA, the Centre for the Use of Research and Evidence in Education (CUREE) has been analysing the impact of recent curriculum changes in

UK schools. Their map of research reviews (CUREE 2009a) presents some interesting evidence that will help us to develop our principles and purposes for cross-curricular teaching and learning. The key findings from their systematic review identified cross-curricular pedagogies as one aspect of teachers' practice that was facilitated or hindered by a range of issues. These were:

- the effectiveness of learning that is 'context based' (dealing with ideas and phenomena in real or simulated practical situations);
- the importance of connecting the curriculum with young people's experiences of home and community and the related, but also distinctive theme of parental involvement in children's learning in the home;
- the impact on pupil motivation and learning of structured dialogue in group work and of collaborative learning;
- the need to create opportunities to identify and build on pupils' existing conceptual understandings;
- the need to remove rigidity in the approach to the curriculum – to allow time and space for conceptual development, to encourage integration of cross-curricular learning;
- the need for excellence and professional development in subject knowledge – without which teachers would be unable to seize opportunities for curriculum innovation, particularly in relation to context-based learning.

(CUREE 2009a, p. 3)

Each of these issues is explored further in their review of individual studies (CUREE 2009b) and we will be returning to these in later chapters. But for now, it is worth reflecting a little on these overall findings. They present important clues in our search for principles and purposes for cross-curricular teaching and learning.

The first point to note is that cross-curricular approaches proved to be effective when they either were 'context based' (i.e. centred around a particular theme/dimension) or connected the school-based curriculum with young people's experiences more widely (e.g. in the home and the community). Second, the positive impact of this type of approach on pupils was noted in terms of their motivation, discursive language and potential to collaborate with each other. More negatively, the damaging lack of consideration to how this new approach would build on pupils' existing 'conceptual understanding' was noted. Turning this around, it will be important that new innovation in curriculum planning and development is constructively linked to pupils' current range of experiences and understanding [their 'folk pedagogy' in Bruner's terms (Bruner 1996)]. Third, and at the level of curriculum design, these types of approaches were facilitated by flexibility in curriculum design, by allowing 'time and space' for development. Finally, and perhaps most important for our ongoing discussion, the need for excellence in teachers' subject knowledge is prioritised. The research suggests that this is a vital precursor for curriculum innovation.

Research review 2: Evidence from the European context

The Consortium of Institutions for Development and Research in Education in Europe (CIDREE) produced an interesting European Union-wide report into cross-curricular themes in education (CIDREE 2005). Although this report deals primarily with the introduction of cross-curricular themes (e.g. personal, social and health education, citizenship education, etc.), it does identify a range of factors that influence the success or failure of a cross-curricular theme (either as a stand-alone component within a curriculum or embedded within existing subjects). The research surveyed twenty-seven countries using a variety of methods. This research identified a range of key problems in the implementation of cross-curricular approaches.

First, the most common obstacle to the successful introduction of cross-curricular approaches to curriculum planning was the pressure on school timetables and the overloading of the curriculum itself. As we saw in Chapter 1, these are common problems in the recent history of educational reform in the UK. The report emphasises that the role of the teacher is paramount in the successful implementation of cross-curricular approaches. But:

> Many teachers report a lack of self-confidence with respect to cross-curricular themes (Saunders *et al.*, 1995) or they feel themselves ill prepared in addressing these themes (Van Looy, 2002; Arnot & Wilkins cited in Kerr, 1999; Kerr, 2000; Inspectie van het Onderwijs, 2001). This inadequacy relates to both the lack of content knowledge and to the inability to employ a range of teaching and learning approaches appropriate to the theme (Kerr, 2000).
>
> (CIDREE 2005, p. 8)

To combat teachers' lack of experience or competence with cross-curricular themes or approaches, the report emphasises that teacher development was reported as the 'top priority' for schools in improving their provision. But, this was not easy either:

> However, even when teachers take part in in-service training relating to aspects of, for example personal, social and health education (PSHE), the impact of this training appears to be limited because teachers have insufficient time to put their training experiences into practice (Ofsted, 2001[a]).
>
> (CIDREE 2005, p. 9)

The report considers some of the reasons for these problems and identifies that, in contrast to traditional subjects, some of these themes 'lack academic traditions, research and development base' (CIDREE 2005, p. 9).

In terms of developing an appropriate pedagogy for cross-curricular teaching (our main focus in Chapter 3) the report has some interesting comments from a range of European perspectives:

> Research on the process evaluation of the introduction of cross-curricular themes shows that successful introduction requires the usage of active teaching methods which, according to many teachers, is difficult to realise (Stevens cited in Somers,

2001). . . . Furthermore, it seems that teachers often insist on the dominance of subject principles in structuring pupils' learning. This makes teaching the themes through including them in subjects very difficult.

(CIDREE 2005, p. 9)

As a specific example of this, the report identifies an issue related to language, our main focus in Chapter 4:

Particularly, the rules of use of 'talk' in different contexts seem to be one of the key problems (Whitty *et al.*, 1994). Buck & Inman (1993) advocate a form of learning which enables pupils to acquire knowledge through content which is both challenging and relevant and through learning processes which are active and experiential.

(CIDREE 2005, p. 9)

The extent to which teachers are able to co-operate and collaborate within a school was another important factor in stimulating cross-curricular activities:

There is a lot of evidence that co-operation between teachers and the involvement of all teachers of the same school are important conditions for successfully implementing cross-curricular themes (Van Looy, 2002; Estyn, 2002). However, this consultative structure is not always present in secondary schools (Inspectie van het Onderwijs, 2001) or there is a lack of communication culture (Somers, 2001). Furthermore, members of the school community who are asked to coordinate cross-curricular work in schools, often find it difficult to motivate colleagues and do not have the same influence on their colleagues as school directors usually have (Somers, 2001).

(CIDREE 2005, p. 10)

The nature and structure of educational resources were next to come under scrutiny. Here, the report criticises resources for a lack of advice about managing collaborative projects and a lack of coherence in the structure and approach:

Hargreaves (1991) states that the task to create coherence within the cross-curricular themes is being largely left to the teachers. This can be explained by the fact that some guidance documents provide insufficient advice as to how teachers might make these links. Moreover, guidance documents seem sometimes to intensify the difficulties since there is no coherence of approach across the different themes (Beck, 1996).

(CIDREE 2005, p. 10)

Assessment, which is the main focus of Chapter 6, was considered next. Here, the importance of an appropriate assessment methodology is raised:

Students feel that if an aspect of learning is not assessed, it implies that it is of low importance and low relevance to their lives (Walker, 2002). The pre-survey report for European Conference on the implementation of cross-curricular themes reveals that five countries mention the lack of evaluation as an aspect that undermines the status of the themes (Maes *et al.*, 2001). . . . The findings of this report clearly point to the importance of having identifiable evaluation systems to provide appropriate recognition and realization rules for work relating to cross-curricular themes.

(CIDREE 2005, p. 10)

Finally, and more briefly, the report was able to identify some positive features for the implementation of a cross-curricular approach. These are that cross-curricular approaches should:

- demand that pupils pull together appropriate knowledge from a range of subjects and relate it to everyday life;
- be characterised by an objective and open-minded approach to controversial issues with attention for the quality and quantity of evidence;
- use concepts as the intellectual building blocks and as essential aids to the categorisation, organisation and analysis of knowledge and experiences;
- use participatory and experiential teaching and learning styles;
- deal explicitly with questions and issues that enable pupils to explore fundamental aspects of our lives.

(CIDREE 2005, p. 11)

In relation to how schools can be managed effectively to achieve these aims, the report concludes by stating that effective schools are characterised by:

- having a vision and goals that are well described and with which all participants are familiar;
- aiming at both cognitive and personal and social development of their pupils;
- making decisions in a participative way;
- possessing a strong ability to self-assess and innovate.

(CIDREE 2005, p. 11)

The definition of cross-curricular teaching and learning

This book has defined cross-curricular teaching and learning in the following way:

A cross-curricular approach to teaching is characterised by sensitivity towards, and a synthesis of, knowledge, skills and understandings from various subject areas. These inform an enriched pedagogy that promotes an approach to learning which embraces and explores this wider sensitivity through various methods.

Having analysed the teacher's role and position in relation to their own and others' subjects, and considered, briefly, the wider research evidence, it is time to justify the choice of this particular definition. This will be done in two ways: first, by considering some of the key words in the definition; and, second, by drawing together some of the themes of this chapter in a list of principles and purposes.

Key words

1. Sensitivity, synthesis and skill

These are key words in the definition. They refer to the ways in which teachers should approach the knowledge, skills and understanding inherent within every curriculum subject. These are exemplified in curriculum documents but also have a historical legacy that is underpinned in various ways, not least in teachers' and others' conceptions about a particular subject and how it should be taught. Understanding this is a vital step that needs to be taken before moving into collaborative curriculum ventures.

These words also refer back to the act of teaching. In other words, they are important, informing teaching principles that impact on learning. Cross-curricular teaching is not about weakening and watering down subjects in any way. Rather, it is about the development of an enhanced pedagogy that a skilful teacher adopts for the explicit purposes of enhancing teaching and learning. This leads on to the second set of key words.

2. Enriching, embracing and exploring

The new, enriched pedagogy of cross-curricular teaching will embrace and explore the teacher's sensitivity towards, and synthesis of, the different knowledge, skills and understanding within curriculum subjects. For this to happen, there are at least two premises: first, teachers will need to understand their own 'intrinsic', and their subject's, 'subjectivities'; second, teachers will need to ensure that their subject knowledge is extended beyond their own subject areas. When this occurs, teachers will be in a position to develop a cross-curricular approach to teaching and learning that utilises a range of methods or techniques in line with the following principles and purposes.

Principles and purposes

In addition to the definition and the key words that it contains, the principles and purposes of cross-curricular teaching and learning that we have considered throughout this chapter include a range of other, generic principles and purposes. These are listed below in no particular order of importance.

The principles of cross-curricular teaching and learning

Cross-curricular teaching and learning is:

■ based on individual subjects and their connections through authentic links at the level of curriculum content, key concepts or learning processes, or through an external theme/dimension;

- characterised and developed by individual teachers with excellent subject knowledge, a deep understanding of their subject culture and a capacity to reconceptualise this within a broader context of learning beyond their subject, and with sensitivity towards other subject cultures;

- as much about the development of a skilful pedagogy as anything else;

- coherent in its maintaining of links with pupils' previous learning and experience;

- contextualised effectively, presenting opportunities for explicit links with pupils' learning outside the formal classroom;

- demanding in its use of curriculum time and resources, requiring flexibility and often needing the support of senior managers if collaborative approaches are to be implemented effectively;

- underpinned by a meaningful assessment process that is explicitly linked to, and informed by, the enriched pedagogical framework;

- potentially collaborative in its nature, requiring meaningful and sustained co-operation between subject teachers with support from senior managers.

The purposes of cross-curricular teaching and learning

The purposes of cross-curricular teaching and learning flow from an understanding of the definition and principles described above. As with the principles, these purposes benefit teachers and pupils alike. The purposes of cross-curricular teaching and learning are to:

- motivate and encourage pupils' learning in a sympathetic way in conjunction with their wider life experiences;

- draw on similarities in and between individual subjects (in terms of subject content, pedagogical devices and learning processes) and make these links explicit in various ways;

- provide active and experiential learning for pupils;

- develop meaningful co-operation and collaboration between staff leading to the dual benefits of curriculum and professional development;

- contribute towards a broad range of teaching and learning opportunities located within individual subject teaching, across subjects and in relation to specific external curriculum themes or dimensions;

- promote pupils' cognitive, personal and social development in an integrated way;

- allow teachers the opportunity to evaluate and reflect on their teaching and to be imaginative and innovative in their curriculum planning;

- facilitate a shared vision amongst teachers and managers through meaningful collaborations at all levels of curriculum design.

This chapter has sought to establish a principled basis for cross-curricular teaching and learning. In line with the key principles outlined at the beginning of Chapter 1, it has placed the individual teacher at the heart of this particular innovation. It has reflected on their role and value as an initiator of curricular design and reform. It has sought to understand the potential innovation from the teacher outwards, rather than invest the teacher with external meanings and priorities. Through the use of a particular reflective tool, it has explored a mechanism by which personal and subject-based sensitivities can be identified and explored. This process of self-interrogation is vital in order for meaningful collaborations to occur. Through this process, it is hoped that some of the peculiarities of individual subjects and associated pedagogies can be understood, acknowledged and, on occasion, moved aside in the pursuit of an enriched, cross-curricular pedagogy.

This work at the level of the teacher and their subject needs was then contextualised by a brief examination of wider, contemporary pieces of educational research from the UK and Europe. These studies, when placed alongside the broader historical overview in Chapter 1, have drawn together a useful range of insights into positive and negative attributes that affect the development of cross-curricular approaches to teaching and learning.

In light of these two perspectives, the definition for cross-curricular teaching and learning was examined and justified. A range of accompanying principles and purposes was also summarised.

The end of this chapter marks an important juncture in this book. In Chapters 1 and 2, we have explored the philosophical and theoretical approaches that could underpin cross-curricular teaching and learning. We have drawn on the wisdom of many educational thinkers and writers, as well as findings from substantial pieces of educational research, to assist our enquiries. Chapter 3 will be much more practical in its content. In it we will explore the components of a pedagogical approach to cross-curricular teaching and learning. By necessity, this will be generalist in tone, but there will be numerous examples of the approaches suggested from different subject areas.

Professional Standards for QTS

This chapter will help you meet the following Q standards: Q6, Q7a, Q8, Q10, Q14, Q22, Q23, Q25, Q29, Q32

Professional Standards for Teachers

This chapter will help you meet the following core standards: C7, C8, C15, C16, C29, C30, C40

3

The Pedagogy of Cross-Curricular Teaching and Learning

Key objectives

By the end of this chapter, you will be able to:

■ identify a range of issues that contribute to an effective, cross-curricular pedagogy;

■ make links between an individual subject-orientated pedagogy, an individual cross-curricular pedagogy and a collaborative cross-curricular approach;

■ utilise a framework for professional and curriculum development to assist developments in your own teaching practice;

■ reflect on the ideas and experiences contained within the book to this point, and make links to the second half of the book with its more detailed investigations of specific applications of these themes.

Introduction

It is schooling that has reduced knowledge to 'subjects' and teaching to mere telling.
(Alexander 2008, p. 141)

Chapter 1 introduced three key principles for teaching: first, that there is no curriculum development without teacher development; second, that subjectivity is like a garment that cannot be removed; and, finally, that skilful teachers embody a skilful pedagogy. Chapter 1 took up the challenge of addressing the first key principle in relation to this book's theme. It demonstrated how previously pieces of curriculum reform or innovation failed to build on the right educational foundation. Unfortunately, top-loaded initiatives and a lack of curriculum integrity failed to motivate teachers and inspire them to move outside their traditional subject boundaries. We discussed how a similar sense of 'initiative overload' is in danger of taking grip of schools as a new National Curriculum is implemented and significant pieces of curriculum reform at Key Stage 4 are gradually introduced.

Chapter 2 took up the theme of subjectivity and applied it to your developing teacher identity. It argued that only by understanding your own subjectivities and interrogating these through reflective analysis can you create the appropriate conditions for educational change or development. Through the development of a pun on Peshkin's use of the term 'subjectivity', it also explored how individual subject cultures are enforced through historical legacies and contemporaneous ideologies that, on occasion, constrict possibilities for curriculum development. Teachers have to work within these settings, searching for and refining subject boundaries. In a brief review of research surrounding cross-curricular approaches in education, we saw, curiously, how excellent subject knowledge is a major key in teachers' abilities to move beyond their own subject boundaries and create links to other subjects. We also considered a range of other principles of, and purposes for, cross-curricular teaching and learning that drew on our established definition.

However, if schooling is going to be able to be more than teachers 'telling' pupils about individual 'subjects', in Alexander's terminology (Alexander 2008, p. 141), my argument here is that there needs to be a major change in the type of pedagogy that teachers develop for all Key Stages and subjects in the secondary curriculum. So, in this chapter we turn to the third key principle of this book: skilful teachers embody a skilful pedagogy. We saw in Chapter 1 that pedagogy, as a term, is often misunderstood. We took definitions from Popkewitz, Bernstein and Bruner to make the point that, although pedagogy is something that teachers possess, it exists within a wider social context that includes pupils and, as we shall see in the following chapters, a range of other defining contexts including language and literacy (Chapter 4), technology (Chapter 5) and other educational elements such as assessment and evaluation (Chapter 6). Pedagogy is more than just a way of acting as a teacher. It involves a way of thinking and a way of knowing; it exists within a relationship of people, tools and ideas.

One of the most influential figures in recent discussions surrounding pedagogy has been Robin Alexander. As a Fellow of Wolfson College at the University of Cambridge and Director of the Cambridge Primary Review, his influence on educational policy has been significant in recent years. Alexander defines pedagogy as:

> the act of teaching together with its attendant discourse. It is what one needs to know, and the skills one needs to command, in order to make and justify the many different kinds of decisions of which teaching is constituted.
>
> (Alexander 2004, p. 11)

Alexander makes the key, and by now familiar, point that pedagogy is not the same as teaching. Pedagogy involves teaching, but it also involves an 'attendant discourse' that comprises knowledge and skills that inform and justify decision-making processes within teaching. Alexander's definition of pedagogy was, to use his term, 'hijacked'

(Alexander 2008, p. 174) in 2007 for the UK government's Primary and Secondary National Strategies, which state that:

> The National Strategies have developed the following working definition: pedagogy is the act of teaching, and the rationale that supports the action that teachers take. It is what a teacher needs to know and the range of skills that a teacher needs to use in order to make effective teaching decisions.
>
> (DfES 2007, p. 1/CD-ROM)

Alexander was not very happy about the appropriation and translation of his definition (Alexander 2008, p. 174), but it is a useful starting point for this important chapter on the pedagogy of cross-curricular teaching and learning. In particular, Alexander's two conceptions of 'pedagogy as discourse' and 'pedagogy as act' are worthy of contemplation. I will be using these throughout this chapter to frame our discussion about the development of a pedagogy for cross-curricular teaching.

Pedagogy as discourse

Pedagogy as discourse is conceived around three levels of ideas that relate to the classroom, the system (including policies that determine the system) and wider aspects of society and culture. All of these, Alexander asserts, 'enable, formalise and locate the act of teaching' (Alexander 2008, p. 174):

1. Classroom level: Ideas that enable teaching
   - *Students*: Characteristics, development, motivation, needs, differences;
   - *Learning*: Nature, facilitation, achievement, assessment;
   - *Teaching*: Nature, scope, planning, execution, evaluation;
   - *Curriculum*: Ways of knowing, doing, creating, investigating, making sense.

2. System/policy level: Ideas that formalise and legitimate teaching
   - *School*: Infrastructure, staffing, training;
   - *Curriculum*: Aims, content;
   - *Assessment*: Formal tests, qualifications, entry requirements;
   - *Other policies*: Teacher recruitment and training, equity and inclusion.

3. Cultural/societal level: Ideas that locate teaching
   - *Community*: The familial and local attitudes, expectations and mores that shape learners' outlooks;
   - *Culture*: The collective ideas, values, customs and relationships that shape a society's view of itself, of the world and of education;
   - *Self*: What it is to be a person; how identity is acquired. (Alexander 2007)

This concept shows how pedagogy is located in a range of contexts, all of which will, to a lesser or greater degree, impact upon it. In reading through the layers and elements within the extract, it is hoped that you will pick up on some of the themes already considered within this book. At a classroom level, these would include the curriculum and associated ways of knowing. As we have seen, these may well be significantly different within each subject. At the level of policy, pedagogy can be shaped within a discourse relating to assessment (our key focus in Chapter 6). But also, and interestingly for those working or studying within initial teacher education, Alexander identifies policy relating to teacher recruitment and training. Questions here may include how we select people for careers in teaching. Why should teaching be a graduate profession? Why do some providers of initial teacher education courses insist on certain degree classifications? Does having an 'expert knowledge of your subject' equate to a 2:1 or a first-class honours degree? Is that a good measure for being a successful teacher? At the cultural and societal level, conceptions about the self and community relate directly to our consideration of Peshkin's work in Chapter 2. It is imperative to understand where our identity as a teacher, and a subject specialist, has come from, and how, in order to make sense of new educational developments that we may find ourselves facing.

Pedagogy as act

These discursive components of pedagogy translate into a model of 'pedagogy as act' that contains three main categories: frame, act and form. This model outlines the key elements of each category, as shown in Table 3.1.

Within the form of an individual lesson, the framing and acting components of pedagogy come into play. A quotation from an earlier publication by Alexander reiterates this same point:

> The core acts of teaching (task, activity, interaction and assessment) are framed by space, pupil organisation, time and curriculum, and by routines, rules and rituals. They are given form and are bounded temporally and conceptually by the lesson or teaching session.

(Alexander 2004, p. 12)

TABLE 3.1 Pedagogy as act

FRAME	FORM	ACT
Space	Lesson	Task
Student organisation		Activity
Time		Interaction
Curriculum		Judgement
Routine, rules and ritual		
Tools[1]		

Notes

1 Added to Alexander's original table.

Source: Alexander (2008, p. 78).

This is where the pedagogical rubber hits the road. Decisions about issues such as how the space of a classroom is organised, the timings of lessons, the choice of activities or tasks, and the type and quality of interactions are all part of the 'pedagogy as act' concept. The majority of this chapter will consider this issue.

Reflective Task 1

Drawing on Alexander's work on 'pedagogy as act', reflect on the key elements of 'frame' and 'act' within the context of your subject. For each element, ask yourself questions about how these influence your subject pedagogy. Here are some examples:

Space

How is my classroom *space* organised? How does this affect the quality of the *interactions* that occur between my pupils and I?

Student organisation

What are the common strategies I have for *organising students*? What are the reasons for these? What would be the consequences of organising them in different ways (e.g. paired work instead of small group work)?

Time

How do I organise the *time* within a typical lesson? What are the common *activities* contained within the lesson? What proportion of the overall lesson do these take? What does this tell me about the priorities I have? Can I justify them?

Interaction

List the main types of *interaction* that occur within the lesson? These will not just be verbal. How do students interact with the *tools* I have chosen to use in the lesson (e.g. pieces of technology, textbooks, worksheets, etc.)?

Rituals

What are the *rituals* that are played out within the lesson? Where do these come from and are they productive? Is it within my power to change them?

Developing my pedagogy

The first major part of this chapter will construct a pedagogy for cross-curricular teaching from the individual teacher's perspective. As we have been discussing throughout the introduction to this chapter, the key point is that a sound pedagogical approach to cross-curricular teaching extends far beyond a mere consideration of the content of the curriculum or placing subjects together in arbitrary collaborative groupings. It has the potential to powerfully transform the pedagogy of the individual teacher who may be working in complete isolation from other colleagues. During this part of the chapter we will identify what the key components of this pedagogy will be, through work that has already been presented and reflected on through the various practical and reflective tasks, alongside case studies drawn from the work of other teachers.

The above reflective task has begun this process within the context of your own subject. Before we go on to reflect on this further, we will consider a range of examples of cross-curricular teaching through four case studies. These case studies have all been reported in formal, academic journals or have been part of recent government materials written to assist teachers in implementing the new secondary curriculum. The purpose of the case studies here is not to repeat their stories in full. Although the majority of these reports do recount collaborations between teachers within curriculum projects, the presentation of information from these reports in these four case studies will be deliberately selective and highlight aspects of their stories that relate directly to the development of an individual teacher's pedagogy. I would encourage all readers to find the original studies as they contain much more information that is very valuable but, unfortunately, we cannot consider here.

To reiterate, this individualised dimension of cross-curricular teaching and learning is under-researched. At this point, I am picking up on clues from the more common, collaborative projects that have been researched and applying these within my argument that significant changes in educational practice need to start with the work of the individual teacher.

The following pieces of research will be drawn upon:

1. Case Study 1: A case study exploring the way in which the pedagogies drawn from drama education affected delivery of the science curriculum (Dorion 2009).

2. Case Study 2: A consideration of common language learning strategies between English and modern foreign languages teachers (Harris 2008).

3. Case Study 3: An investigation into cross-curricular approaches drawn from history, RE and citizenship education (CfBT 2008a).

4. Case Study 4: 'Strange Fruit': A cross-curricular approach to teaching about the blues at Key Stage 3 between teachers of music, drama and dance (CfBT 2008b).

Case Study 1: Science through drama: A multiple case exploration of the characteristics of drama activities used in secondary science lessons

This study explored the forms, teaching objectives and characteristics by which drama was perceived to enable learning in science. The findings revealed that drama activities could convey a variety of topics. There was a greater scope for the teaching of abstract scientific concepts through mime and role play than through more traditional science pedagogies.

Three key findings emerged from the study:

1. There was a greater breadth of variety of drama in science objectives and topics described and observed.

2. Teaching and learning was perceived by the participants to be multimodal, with specific modes producing specific visualisations of abstract concepts.

3. Patterns of didactic, interactive, and dialogic discourse related to objectives concerning teacher control over the transfer of knowledge. (Dorion 2009, p. 12)

Given the nature of the study, the first of these did not seem that surprising. However, the second and third findings are particularly interesting for cross-curricular pedagogy. In terms of how this drama-infused approach to teaching science translated into a new pedagogy, the report identified a number of key elements.

1. Learning objectives

Learning objectives remained firmly within the domain of the science curriculum (i.e. to express science knowledge, to acquire abstract concepts, etc.). Drama was considered to provide a pedagogy that enhanced the affective features of learning, for example a sense of relevance and a community of learners.

2. Characteristics of lessons

Lessons incorporated social interaction, humour and a sense of fun, which pupils and teachers noted was atypical of their experience of traditional science pedagogy (Dorion 2009, p. 14).

3. Novel imagery

The use of novel or striking imagery was perceived as a means to develop pupil attention to scientific topics. As an example:

The teacher substituted the apparatus for the stretching of a copper wire with a scaled-up and theatrical apparatus for stretching one of the students. The teacher assessed later that the students had a greater understanding of procedural knowledge than through her traditional approach with a previous class.

(Dorion 2009, p. 14)

4. Humour

Humour was perceived by the teachers to be an important aspect of the 'atypical atmosphere' and enhanced the students' attention (Dorion 2009, p. 15). The report is not clear about how this related directly to the appropriation of a drama pedagogy within the science lessons.

5. Multimodality

Verbal, non-verbal and other forms of social interaction within the science lessons 'highlighted particular aspects of knowledge' (Dorion 2009, p. 15). Teachers spoke about a 'multimodal toolkit' (Dorion 2009, p. 15) from which they chose combinations of modes to focus particular features of knowledge.

6. Anthropomorphic analogies

Students noted that use of physical simulations made things easier to understand than the traditional approach of diagrams on a whiteboard.

7. Thought experiments

These physical simulations and associated anthropomorphic analogies empowered students' visualisation processes. As an example, while explaining an ionic structure, the teacher played the role of the nucleus and three students played the role of electrons. Another student commented that:

So . . . if we had like 20 more people, he'd have no control over the one that's furthest away.

(Dorion 2009, p. 16)

8. Discourse

Drama's potential to enable discourse and dialogue was a central characteristic across all activities. Through this teachers were drawn to the employment of patterns of talk and multimodal discourse that were atypical of the more traditional non-interactive/authoritative talk. Collaborative group work presented another form of discourse that gave students a greater degree of choice over the type of discourse to employ within their learning. This resulted in the 'democratisation' of the class and students perceiving themselves to be more autonomous in their learning:

The teacher might just have one idea but other students might have a different idea which would help you remember.

(Dorion 2009, p. 17)

In conclusion, the research stated that:

In a subject in which there tends to be little dialogic discourse (Scott *et al.*, 2006), drama may provide interventions to promote dialogic learning in relation to science-specific objectives. Drama's multimodal characteristics highlight imagination and embodied knowledge, the latter of which has gained in significance as education moves from primarily visual towards more 'virtual' worlds of learning. The drama activities in this study indicate that more use can be made of non-visual sensations in order to promote cognitive learning.

(Dorion 2009, p. 22)

Case Study 2: A consideration of common language learning strategies between English and modern languages teachers

This study aimed to encourage pupils to transfer common learning strategies between English and modern foreign languages. In particular, it sought:

- to explore the issues raised for teachers in creating opportunities for students to transfer language learning strategies;
- to investigate the extent to which government policies and the school cultures supported or impeded them;
- to investigate the impact of the resulting intervention on students;
- to draw on the findings with a view to identifying the optimum conditions for classroom-based cross-curricular collaboration where teachers from two subjects share pedagogic and subject-specific knowledge to create complementary opportunities to develop students' understanding of the language learning process.

(Harris 2008, p. 259)

The findings of the study are numerous, ranging from a critique of government policy in various areas to aspects that affect individual teachers' pedagogy. There are many tensions reported in the research for which there is not space to comment on extensively here. Rather, we will pick out the issues related to the teachers' pedagogy, the main focus of this chapter.

1. Curriculum design

The case study talks about the difficulties that both teachers had in seeking to combine elements of different teaching strategies that related to centralised government initiatives (e.g. the National Strategy).

2. Learning to learn

Both teachers were enthusiastic about the project's 'learning to learn' focus. This gave them a ready-made connection between languages and a range of approaches to support the development of students' speaking skills. As an example, the modern foreign languages teacher commented that:

> It was really novel for me to actually talk about the mood of the author. I guess the students are so used to oui/non, tick-box formats that they were at first a bit stunned by this one but then quickly got the idea and enjoyed it.
>
> (Harris 2008, p. 262)

3. Changing teacher's role

The English teacher noted a significant change in role. Rather than being a 'walking dictionary', she now:

> helps the kids work it out for themselves using the strategies. I mean making it explicit. And thinking about that, you, once you're used to that, that method of doing it, it definitely changes your methodology.
>
> (Harris 2008, p. 264)

The modern foreign languages teacher also reflected on the value of widening the scope of her lessons to include more meaningful tasks and content.

In conclusion, the study suggests that the cross-curricular approach adopted here 'can be a creative, productive process' (Harris 2008, p. 266). But the report spends just as much time identifying potential barriers to this type of process. These are summarised in the following statement:

> Conflicting Key Stage 3 policies coupled with an ever-increasing emphasis on performance measures create a school culture which leaves teachers little time for the cross-curricular collaboration necessary to make a positive impact on students learning. . . . The fostering of cross-collaboration requires a willingness to trust teachers to reach professional judgements and the development of structures and cultures within the school that allow them to do so.
>
> (Harris 2008, p. 266)

Case Study 3: Planning to lead or contribute to cross-curricular opportunities: RE, citizenship and history

In this case study the RE, citizenship and history departments of a small community high school collaborated to develop a project on the themes of diversity and identity. They wanted to devise a project for the summer term that would enhance their pupils' experience of cross-curricular work by drawing on different disciplines. By emphasising key concepts, processes and new ideas for content, the teachers hoped that they would be able to identify genuine links between citizenship, history and RE. A number of points are relevant for our discussion about the construction of a cross-curricular pedagogy.

1. The new secondary curriculum

The new secondary curriculum was a key starting point for these teachers. In particular, the focus on key concepts, processes and curriculum opportunities gave them a way to begin to connect together their thinking and ideas.

2. Timetabling arrangements

The school used a mixture of structures for the timetabling of these activities. These included discrete subject-based lessons alongside 'collapsed' timetable days in which pupils could work on a topic over an extended period of time.

3. School specialism

The school is a specialist languages college. This impacted on the nature of the cross-curricular work, with links being developed and exploited at a national and international level.

4. Differences between subjects

Key differences between the three subjects were identified during the initial process of collaboration. The teachers were keen to respect these. They suggested that each subject maintained a particular focus, for example:

- Citizenship: Pupils taking action and being involved in the community.
- History: Using and evaluating sources to investigate, identify and explain changes over time.
- RE: Investigating and explaining the importance of religions and beliefs in many people's lives.

5. A common approach, key question and outcome

All subject teachers agreed the establishment of an enquiry-based approach.

This included the formation of a key question that emerged through discussion between the staff. The focus question became: What can we learn from a study of the diverse groups living in Britain today? Finally, all staff agreed on a specific outcome (a film) to which all pupils contributed.

6. Cross-referencing

Teachers spoke about the benefit of cross-referencing each others' lessons on a regular basis. This was a conscious decision taken by the team and the considerable benefits of this were noted.

7. Resources

Project booklets were used and these contained assessment components that linked back to the three individual subject areas. Pupils were involved in assessing their work through self- and peer-assessment activities.

8. Senior management involvement

A senior manager at the school was consulted about the project. The manager's approval was crucial, particularly in obtaining the decision to include collapsed curriculum days within the project.

Case Study 4: 'Strange Fruit': A cross-curricular approach to the blues at Key Stage 3

This case study explored how teachers taught the blues to pupils in Key Stage 3 through an imaginative application and linking together of key concepts in the music, dance and drama curricula. It used 'Strange Fruit', a song sung by Billie Holiday based on a poem by Abel Meeropol, as a stimulus in each subject area. Key concepts and themes such as improvisation, syncopation and question and answer were explored in different ways in each subject. Through careful planning, explicit links were drawn between these subject areas and pupils were encouraged to build connections in their learning.

The case study sought to investigate a number of key questions:

- How has each area of the performing arts interpreted the stimulus of the blues?
- How have pupils responded to the stimulus and are they making links between music, dance and drama in ways that may not have happened before?
- How does pupils' creativity exhibit itself within each area of the curriculum?
- In terms of planning, how can the timetable be organised to facilitate this type of cross-curricular working? How is the process of planning lessons shared, negotiated or completed between different members of staff?

1. Artistic responses to a common stimulus

Each area of the performing arts interpreted the initial stimulus in a variety of ways. In drama there was a strong focus on the social/historical issues. In music there was an initial focus on personal expression and improvisation within a pre-determined structure. But each subject was underpinned by a range of common elements that emerged, through a natural process of discussion, amongst staff (e.g. improvisation, syncopation and question and answer). These have been used to plan lessons that link together key elements. This planning process was begun by individual subject teachers but shared through regular joint curriculum planning within wider departmental meetings.

2. The pupil response

Pupils responded favourably to the stimulus in each area of the curriculum. They were able to make links between the subjects and recognise both the similarities and the differences in concepts in a subtle way; for example, they were keen to explore improvisatory processes in music, dance and drama and relate key skills of experimentation, trial and error and risk taking in each subject area.

3. Linking pedagogies

All teachers commented on the increasing degree of ownership that pupils had taken over their learning in the unit. The joint approach to planning resulted in a practical, activity-based curriculum that challenged pupils to be energised and engaged with subject content, reflective about their previous learning and actively involved in exploring the blues (e.g. through hot seating in drama, melodic improvisation in music, or through the construction of transition movements in dance).

4. Collaborative planning and the pace of learning

The opportunities for collaborative cross-curricular work saved time for all the members of staff. They were able to build on each other's work in new ways. All of the staff noticed that the pupils were making links in intuitive ways within and between curriculum content. This was rare before. This has allowed staff to move at a faster pace through their wider curriculum materials.

Developing a cross-case analysis

Table 3.2 shows a summary of the key components from these four case studies. The majority of these relate clearly to the classroom level of discourse (see previous extract from Alexander 2007), although at points they extend into the levels of system/policy or culture/society, for example in teachers' acknowledgments of the recent developments in the National Curriculum. These cross-curricular components have

TABLE 3.2 A summary of case study key components

KEY COMPONENT	CASE STUDY			
	1	2	3	4
Central stimulus (question, resource, etc.)			×	×
Changing curriculum content		×	×	×
Common learning outcomes, products			×	
Common pedagogy			×	×
Common resources			×	
Community of learners	×			×
Flexible curriculum design	×		×	×
Humour	×			
Learning objectives	×		×	×
Maintaining subject differences	×		×	×
Metaphors	×	×		×
Modelling (physical, visual, virtual)	×			×
Multimodality	×		×	
New curriculum framework			×	×
Ownership of ideas	×			×
Relevance to other learning contexts	×			
Senior management involvement			×	
Shared technologies		×		×
Social interaction	×		×	×
Teacher role		×		×
Timetabling variations			×	
Widening discourses	×	×		

been grouped together under headings from Alexander's pedagogy as act (Table 3.1) to form a framework for a cross-curricular pedagogy (Table 3.3).

Following from this, Table 3.4 presents these components in a wider framework drawn from work presented in this book, together with a number of other ideas drawn from my own observations of cross-curricular teaching and learning throughout a range of schools across the north-west of England.

Reading through these case studies shows how individual teachers' subject-based pedagogies can be challenged and developed through cross-curricular initiatives. Although this is not always a comfortable experience, it is a significant and necessary stage in a process of cross-curricular-inspired teacher development. After all, as we have seen, there is no curriculum development without teacher development.

A pedagogy for cross-curricular teaching

In the following discussion, a number of the pedagogical elements presented in Table 3.4 will be taken, explored and applied to the development of an individual teacher's pedagogy. In doing so, we will be referring both backwards and forwards to other parts of this book.

TABLE 3.3 An emerging framework for a cross-curricular pedagogy

FRAME		FORM		ACT	
Space	Timetabling variations Senior management involvement	Lesson	Modelling Multimodality One part of a wider curriculum design	Task	Central stimulus
Student organisation	Encouraging sense of community			Interaction	Widening discourses Relevance Metaphors Humour Sociability
Curriculum	New frameworks Changing content Learning objectives Common learning outcomes Flexibility in design Maintaining subject differences			Judgement	Ownership of ideas Assessment
Tools	Common resources Shared technologies				

Source: Alexander (2008, p. 78).

TABLE 3.4 Components for a cross-curricular pedagogy

FRAME		FORM		ACT	
Space	Timetabling variations Physical factors (buildings, classroom layout)	Lesson	Learning objectives Explanations Questioning Modelling Multimodality One part of a wider curriculum design	Task	Central stimulus Inherent processes
Student organisation	Encouraging sense of community Flexible approaches to groupings Peer leadership and other roles			Activity	Who, what, where and how?

FRAME	FORM		ACT	
Time	Organisation of individual lessons Spanning lessons Homework		Interaction	Widening discourses Relevance Metaphors Humour Sociability
Curriculum	New frameworks Changing content Learning objectives Common learning outcomes Flexibility in design Senior management involvement Maintaining subject differences		Judgement	Ownership of ideas Broad range of assessment devices Educational evaluation of curriculum developments
Routine, rules and ritual	Traditional approaches to subject-orientated curriculum planning School conventions Historical legacies Individual subjectivities			
Tools	Common resources Shared technologies Discrete technologies			

Source: Alexander (2008, p. 78).

Routine, rules and ritual

Our time spent on considering these elements can be fairly brief. As the opening chapters of this book have considered, there are strong, often conservative, forces at work within traditional approaches to subject-orientated curriculum planning, the conventions of the school and wider educational policy. Change within school is often a slow process. But, as I have acknowledged, this is not necessarily a bad thing. We can all appreciate that there is much at stake.

The important point to emphasise here is that a new pedagogy for cross-curricular teaching will build on the routine, rules and rituals of your classroom practice and wider school context. This 'building on' will take a number of forms. In its most extreme form, it may see you replacing existing pedagogical elements within your teaching; less severely, you may be modifying your pedagogy by bringing in new features that will co-exist alongside existing elements of your practice; but, *and I think it is important to state this clearly*, there will be times in your teaching when the best way to teach will be through subject-specific pedagogical approaches. Whatever you choose – replacement, modification, co-existence or no change – the point is that you are making a pedagogical choice. In the first instance, the skilful element of the pedagogical choice relates to your perceptive analysis of the existing context (the routine, rules and rituals of your subject and school context). Second, the appropriate choice of pedagogical elements within that context can be made skilfully and thoughtfully (or not).

Curriculum

At each Key Stage within the secondary curriculum there are frameworks that teachers have to work within. National Curriculum requirements, GCSE specifications and new diplomas all have key ingredients that impact on the way that teachers work. Within our consideration of the development of a pedagogy for cross-curricular teaching, there are some key principles worth drawing out here.

First, a cross-curricular pedagogy will take a broader view of these frameworks, that is, one that extends beyond the traditional subject boundary. The introduction of new diplomas within the 14–19 curriculum has forced this issue on teachers in an obvious way. But, as we have seen, in the Key Stage 3 curriculum similar demands are made through the individual subject programmes of study. At a basic level, perhaps this broader view will be mainly associated with the content of other subject areas rather than their associated pedagogies (this will come below). So, we are not primarily talking about adopting elements of a drama pedagogy within a science lesson (as in Case Study 1), but rather about looking for commonalities across subjects in terms of content (such as in Case Study 4) or ways of addressing common issues (as in Case Study 3).

Springing from this wider viewpoint, the establishment of broader learning objectives within one's subject teaching will develop. This is a good example of a case in which 'co-existence' rather than 'replacement' is probably the best way forward. All teachers have a responsibility to their own subject, but a cross-curricular pedagogy will require teachers not only to be cognisant about other subjects, but also to plan for deliberate links between subjects when appropriate. Again, this is a skilful choice on the part of the individual teacher. There is a balance here, not just between what might be called the 'host' subject and any other subject, but also between the whole array of subjects that might be drawn upon within a piece of curriculum planning. At a subject level, aiming to create links between as many subjects as possible within medium- or long-term planning would be desirable. Lesson by lesson (i.e. within short-term planning), teachers will need to be much more selective. The explicit use of cross-curricular links to other subjects will also need to be balanced against the requirements to incorporate Functional Skills and PLTS as dictated within recent curriculum initiatives. As we will consider in our final chapter, this might necessitate the development of new curriculum models or frameworks.

It is worth stating some common advice about learning objectives here. One of the most frequent mistakes that young teachers make is that they write 'doing' objectives rather than 'learning' objectives. An example of a doing objective is: 'Pupils will construct a three-dimensional representation of the house from the given two-dimensional drawings.' This describes the doing, the activity. It does not describe the learning that the pupils are engaging with whilst doing the activity. In this imaginary scenario, the learning might relate to developing a sense or appreciation of scale, representation or projection through the activity of constructing an accurate three-dimensional house from the two-dimensional drawings. The learning objective might read: 'Pupils will develop an understanding of scale and representation through considering the relationship between three-dimensional and two-dimensional images.' The linked learning outcomes may go into more detail about the activity, together with anticipated differentiated outcomes in terms of the learning that has or has not occurred.

My argument here is that when learning objectives are construed as doing objectives then cross-curricular links remain difficult to establish. As a teacher not familiar with the design and technology curriculum, I would read the doing objective in the above example and wonder what the purpose of the drawing activity was. If I read the learning objective and saw the words 'scale', 'representation' and 'projection' then, as a teacher of music, I could begin to make all kinds of imaginative links to my own curriculum area. For example, I could begin to anticipate the benefit of drawing on pupils' knowledge of three-dimensional and two-dimensional drawing. As a term, 'projection' has a significant musical meaning that I could teach in a different way if I was able to make this kind of cross-curricular link with the design and technology curriculum. As we will go on to see in the following chapter, the use of metaphorical connections like this between subject knowledge is a powerful way of establishing cross-curricular elements within our individual subject pedagogies. But here, the writing of genuine learning, rather than doing, objectives will help establish cross-curricular links in a more authentic way. Focus on the learning, not just the doing.

Collaborative forms of curriculum development, although not the primary focus at this point within the chapter, are worth considering briefly here. As earlier chapters have shown, the construction of large, cross-curricular projects within school are seldom successful without the significant support of senior management teams. Similarly, flexible curriculum frameworks (e.g. the adoption of 'collapsed' curriculum days or cross-curricular weeks) require whole school commitment and should not be seen as a substitute for the kinds of approaches we are discussing here. But Case Study 4 shows a different way, something in-between the work of an individual teacher and the whole school initiative.

The departmental approach evidenced in Case Study 4 was particularly effective because it identified a common element in each subject and sought to exploit this, explicitly, at a particular point in time. This example came from the arts curriculum, but it could equally well have applied to the sciences or humanities. There are further benefits of this approach. First, interesting cross-curricular links may be more easily established with other subjects that are closer (philosophically and educationally) to your own subject. Second, and perhaps more pragmatically, the type of cross-curricular development evidenced in Case Study 4 took place through established departmental procedures and meetings. For the teachers involved, the departmental initiative was the kick-start they needed to begin the process of examining their own pedagogy more rigorously. Although not being on the scale of a whole school intervention, its localised, departmental focus enabled this collaborative form of curriculum development to have a significant impact. The teachers involved felt that they 'owned' the work in a way that larger initiatives may find difficult to achieve. The longer-term consequences and possibilities were also more closely related to their existing practice. Finally, the benefits of working on a piece of curriculum development with others that you know and trust cannot be underestimated.

Finally, in this important section on the curriculum elements that relate to the establishment of an individual, cross-curricular pedagogy, it is worth remembering, again, that individual subjects have their own routines, rules and rituals that need to be acknowledged. These have often shaped the very curriculum frameworks that we are considering here. I make no apologies for the repetition. Appreciating and valuing the historical legacies of individual subjects within the curriculum is a vital first step in establishing a meaningful cross-curricular pedagogy. If you are not sure what these historical legacies are, talk to your subject colleagues about why and how they do things. 'A little learning can be a dangerous thing' (Pope 1711) and a cross-curricular pedagogy should not be a synthesis of watered-down subject pedagogies.

Space

Before moving on to the vitally important consideration of the construction of a lesson and the cross-curricular pedagogical elements within this, I will give brief consideration to issues of space. For our discussion, space has two specific dimensions: curriculum space and physical space.

Curriculum space is allocated within timetables. The establishment of a timetable is a key informant and contributor to the notion of subject boundaries and specialisms. Teachers, pupils and parents expect subjects to be taught at a particular time and place, in a space designed for that subject (i.e. the science laboratory, the drama studio, etc.). As a parent, I have lost count of the times I have asked my son, 'What have you got today?' Subjects have become the organising component of the secondary school day and the benefits of this approach are obvious. However, as we have seen already, the downside of this is that boundaries between subjects have been built up to such an extent that cross-curricular ways of working, of the type I am proposing here, are almost entirely absent in many teachers' work. Larger-scale reconfigurations of the curriculum that avoid subjects being the sole organising principle of the school day are being experimented with by some schools [as an example, see the Royal Society for the encouragement of Arts, Manufactures and Commerce (RSA) Manchester Curriculum project (RSA 2009)]. However, this is far from normal in the majority of secondary schools.

Physical space refers, obviously, to the classroom spaces within which we teach. The processes of designing appropriate teaching spaces have been given significant architectural thought in recent years, particularly with the Building Schools for the

Future programme. There are many interesting stories of how new schools have been designed, together with innovative approaches to the design of individual learning spaces, from this project (Partnership for Schools 2010). But a quick survey of the types of learning spaces that a typical secondary school contains makes the point that particular subjects have specific requirements in respect of physical spaces (e.g. science subjects are taught in laboratories; physical education requires the use of outdoor spaces, etc.).

So, for our discussion here, the argument moves from issues surrounding subject content to that of subject pedagogy. It would be nonsensical to ask a science teacher to teach chemistry in a drama studio. Similarly, there is only so far that physical education can be taught in a traditional classroom setting. There are obvious and explicit requirements that both these subjects have (for laboratories and for the outdoors) that no one can, or should, deny. But there will almost certainly be pedagogical approaches within chemistry and physical education teaching that other teachers can benefit from learning about and adopting or applying within their teaching (through the replacement, co-existence or modification types of change that we discussed above).

As with previous pedagogical considerations, it is worth reflecting for a few moments on why the situation in schools, in relation to curriculum and physical space, is as it is today. There are undoubtedly elements of the current configuration of space that are desirable and educationally worthwhile. However, we should not let this limit our imaginations in conceiving how education could be delivered if things were arranged differently. This will become a key focus in Chapter 5 when we consider the application of particular technologies or tools in more detail.

Lessons

This is probably the most important context in which a cross-curricular pedagogy can be developed. In Alexander's terms (Alexander 2008, p. 78), the lesson is the 'form', that is, it is where things take shape within the 'frame' (several elements of which have been discussed above). This is related closely to elements contained within the 'act' (see Table 3.4), which we will be considering below. Within the curriculum framework, medium- and long-term planning can begin to promote and develop opportunities for cross-curricular links within individual lessons. Through our discussion of the following pedagogical elements, it will be important to remember that a cross-curricular pedagogy contains elements that are all part of an effective pedagogy anyway. I will not be going back to square one for each of them. Rather, I will attempt to draw on existing ideas and exemplify them within the context of generating a cross-curricular pedagogy of one's own.

1. Learning objectives and outcomes

Carefully planned learning objectives should underpin all lessons. Our discussion above highlighted the requirement for learning objectives to be about learning, and not about doing. It also emphasised that as learning objectives focus squarely on learning then the links between subjects will be easier to establish. In other words, learning is the common denominator that links all teaching, in every subject, together.

Here, I will take a slightly different but related line of thought. Within well-established lesson planning processes, learning objectives are normally linked to learning outcomes. In good planning processes, there is always a link between the objectives and the outcomes. Learning outcomes present an opportunity to formalise the cross-curricular links made through learning objectives. The outcomes of a particular learning sequence within a lesson will, in the majority of cases, be related to the particular subject being taught. However, there is an opportunity here to either add an additional cross-curricular outcome to the learning sequence or add a cross-curricular 'flavour' to an established, existing, subject-orientated learning outcome.

Furthermore, in many approaches to the planning of learning objectives and outcomes, differentiated strategies are used to try and predict the types of responses that pupils will make within a particular learning sequence. This has always seemed problematic to me (and I will explore why in Chapters 4 and 6) but, given that this is common practice, this seems an appropriate opportunity to try to envisage the ways in which pupils do relate together their learning from various subject areas. A number of the pedagogical elements that take place within this context of the lesson will focus on what you do as a teacher. The opportunity here is to use learning objectives and outcomes to assess what impact this new approach is having on the pupils. We will explore this in much more detail in the first half of Chapter 6.

2. Explanations

Explaining things is at the heart of every teacher's pedagogy. Good explanations are key to effective teaching and learning. The use of different types of explanations should allow a teacher to develop cross-curricular links in their teaching through the handling of concepts that relate to the knowledge, skills and understanding of different curriculum areas. In developing these, it is important to imbue them with an authenticity and respect for the other subject area. The inappropriate and careless handling of concepts can lead to confusion and misunderstanding. As an example, in Chapter 4 we will be considering the use of metaphorical devices as a key to expand the development of our curriculum idea and associated pedagogies. But metaphorical borrowings or interpretations carry risks with them. These risks can be mitigated by a responsible approach. For this reason, beginner teachers may find it helpful to script explanations to include within their lessons, ensuring that concepts related to their own and other curriculum areas are presented clearly, and that the use of any metaphors are handled in a way that enhances, rather detracts from, the anticipated learning.

However, explanations should not always depend on the spoken word. As we will see below when we consider modelling, the use of visual and other forms of communication can enhance the ways we explain things to our pupils.

3. Questioning

Like explanations, questioning is at the heart of every teacher's practice. As many other books illustrate (Terry and Churches 2009), questions are used for many different purposes and the skilful use of questioning strategy underpins many kinds of assessment. In Chapter 4 we will explore the use of questioning further through an application of the work of Bloom, Anderson and Krathwohl (Bloom 1956; Anderson and Krathwohl 2001).

4. Modelling and multimodality

Modelling can be a very effective element within a teacher's pedagogy. Good modelling demonstrates techniques to pupils in a way that enhances the opportunity for them to do something similar for themselves. It assists the process from pupils being dependent upon something (e.g. you, as their teacher, or another learning resource) to moving them towards a position of independence.

Effective modelling is normally accompanied by the teacher thinking out loud through a verbal commentary that accompanies their actions. This is often not as easy as it sounds. It is a little like the process of 'commentary driving', in which a car driver is required to give a full commentary about the process of driving a car. This process is a key component of learning to become an advanced driver. It is a particular skill that takes time to develop but, in the end, enables the driver to obtain an enhanced understanding of the environment which he or she is moving, or about to move, through.

So, in a general sense modelling involves thinking out loud, showing pupils how to avoid potential problems that may occur and giving them key messages to reinforce the learning objectives of the particular lesson. Modelling works because it often extends explanations, which tend to be dominated by the verbal, into the visual arena.

As we will see in Chapter 4, the opportunity for cross-curricular modelling will draw on the belief that pupils can know and feel things through all of their senses. The challenge is, therefore, twofold. First, to develop modelling in the light of lessons learnt from how teachers might model things in other subjects; second, to consider the development of further modelling techniques that build not only on what we can see but also on what we can hear, taste, smell and touch. This is one of the key elements in what has been called a 'multimodal' pedagogy (Jewitt 2008; Stein 2007).

5. The lesson as one part of a wider curriculum design and location

Finally in this section on the notion of the 'lesson', there is an obvious point that the lesson (and all that is contained within it) exists in relation to the medium- and longer-term planning that teachers undertake. To that end, a cross-curricular approach to teaching and learning will ensure that there is a degree of coherence in the short-, medium- and longer-term planning process. It will be important to ensure that there is both cross-curricular breadth and depth in the planning process at all levels. But there is a balance here that needs to be handled carefully.

Part of these considerations will be the opportunity to make links between teaching and learning that take place within and outside the classroom. Recent guidance has called for a greater degree of emphasis on the latter, as part of the Every Child Matters programme (DCSF 2009a). The chance to design opportunities for relocating learning when possible, and the creative use of homework activities, could all become important parts of an enriched, cross-curricular pedagogy.

Task, Activity and Organisation

Within the design of particular tasks or activities, teachers need to ask a number of key questions:

- Who is involved in the activity?
- What are they going to do?
- Where are they going to do it?
- How are they going to manage it?
- What is the central stimulus for the activity?
- How does it relate to the learning objectives I have established?
- What are the inherent processes within the activity that pupils will need to master in order to successfully engage with the task?

A cross-curricular pedagogy will ask similar questions but, as we discussed in relation to the teacher's development of modelling or multimodality, the answers that this approach might develop will draw on a broader repertoire of learning processes, styles or techniques. In Chapter 6 we are going to consider how one such example could impact on how teachers can develop a cross-curricular approach to assessment [through the adoption of a 'freeze framing' technique (drawn from the drama curriculum) (see Chapter 6, Case Study 1)]. Other creative borrowings from alternative curriculum areas will help extend approaches to the design of specific tasks and activities within your teaching.

The organisation of pupils within tasks is part of this process. Most subjects have a flexible approach to the ways in which pupils work together, using individual, paired or larger group tasks. Structuring roles within tasks is something that can be helpful and individual subject teachers may have different approaches to how this is achieved that can be usefully shared.

Generic devices for managing the roles of pupils within tasks or activities can also be applied and extended in a cross-curricular way. One example, the de Bono 'thinking hats', has been widely used in educational, counselling and business settings. In this 'system', each member of a group is identified with a particular coloured 'thinking hat'. The colour of the hat determines the type of 'thinking' they are allowed to contribute within the group itself, so the:

- White Hat calls for information known or needed;
- Red Hat signifies feelings, hunches and intuition;
- Black Hat is judgement, the devil's advocate or why something may not work;
- Yellow Hat symbolizes brightness and optimism;
- Green Hat focuses on creativity: the possibilities, alternatives and new ideas;
- Blue Hat is used to manage the thinking process. (de Bono Thinking Systems 2009)

Through the utilisation of this simple tool, a group of pupils can explore a particular concept or idea and tap into their collective thinking in a structured way. There are simple applications of this process in a cross-curricular pedagogy, which could see pupils asked to think about an issue with a particular subject perspective and contribute their thoughts from this perspective to the group as a whole.

Interaction

The types of interaction that occur within classrooms and the need to widen discourses in support of cross-curricular learning are the main topic for Chapter 4. In particular, the use of metaphors as a tool for curriculum planning and pedagogy will be discussed. But I was struck by the reference to humour in Case Study 1. Although it seemed a little unfair on the science colleagues referred to, it caused me to research the literature on this aspect of pedagogy. The literature enforces something that I suspect many of us know to be true from our own experiences of education: the use of humour creates a positive atmosphere, reduces anxiety and facilitates the learning process (Berk 1996, 1998; Hill 1988; Pollio and Humphreys 1996). Garner's call to H.A.M. it up in teaching made me chuckle (Garner 2005) and the observations contained within this are equally applicable to subject-based or cross-curricular teaching.

Tools

The tools that we choose to use within our lessons play an essential role in how we teach and how pupils learn. As an example, the use and application of ICT will be considered in detail in Chapter 5. Drawing on Wertsch's notion of mediated action (Wertsch 1998), we will investigate how ICT (as a type of 'tool') frames the processes of teaching and learning in a curricular way. The ideas explored within this chapter apply equally to other tools and resources that we may choose to use within our classrooms (e.g. the 'technology' or 'tool' of a pencil and paper will mediate teaching and learning in ways not dissimilar to that of a digital technology).

Judgements about Cross-Curricular Teaching and Learning

Issues associated with the ownership and judgement of ideas, the broad range of assessment devices that may be associated with cross-curricular pedagogy and the evaluation of cross-curricular pieces of curriculum development are all explored in detail in Chapter 6.

Practical Task 1

Choose one pedagogical element from those discussed above. Reflect on it further within the context of your own subject teaching. Try and identify a few opportunities in the coming weeks where you can extend your approach in light of some of the advice contained within this, and subsequent, chapters.

A bridge: Planning a process of professional development

This sounds like a lot of potential changes to one's pedagogy! It can feel quite threatening and perhaps you are wondering if it is worth the effort? I believe that it is. Developing a cross-curricular approach to your teaching will make you a more effective teacher. I believe it will also inspire and motivate your pupils within your subject.

However, a key founding principle of this book is that there is no curriculum development without teacher development. Whilst I do not want to get too distracted from this chapter's central theme, I think it is worth taking a slight deviation to consider a simple model for teachers' professional development. This will be followed up by a more extensive discussion related to educational evaluation (and the positive impact this can have on a teacher's professional development) at the end of Chapter 6.

There have been many studies of how teachers can improve their pedagogy (Altrichter, Posch and Somekh 1993; Edwards and Mercer 1987; Turner-Bisset 2001). For my purposes here, I will consider a model drawn from an interesting study of how a group of teachers' own professional development worked alongside a piece of collaborative curriculum development on which they were working. In this sense, this model serves to act as a bridge between the two parts of this chapter.

Leat, Lofthouse and Taverner's study (2006) explored the patterns in teachers' thinking and conceptualised the conditions that supported the actions and interactions of a particular group of teachers who were seeking to implement what has become known as a 'thinking skills' curriculum. However, the focus of the study was not the piece of curriculum development itself, but rather the processes that the teachers went through as they developed their practice. From this analysis, the authors present a six-phase model, which is shown in Table 3.5.

The obvious question for our discussion is at what point should this process of a cross-curricular perspective to teaching and learning be introduced and encouraged? I think there are different answers that can be given to this question, depending on the teacher involved and the purpose of the piece of curriculum/professional development.

Teachers in the early stages of their careers should be encouraged to adopt a broad, cross-curricular perspective to their work as soon as possible. This should begin during their initial teacher education courses and carry across into their induction year. Although notions of subject knowledge and its application within pedagogy are contestable (Parker 2004; Parker and Heywood 2000), most graduates coming into secondary education will have degree-level knowledge in a related subject area to that which they are proposing to teach. The strategies for teaching in what might be called a centrifugal way, that is, outward looking in terms of subject knowledge, should be embedded strongly within the process of initial teacher education.

Teachers who are further ahead in their careers have the benefit of experience and, providing that this has not resulted in complacency in terms of ongoing professional development, this should allow them to enter this model at a higher level. However, as with any change to one's pedagogy, it is likely that concerns will be felt when new approaches are implemented. Therefore, teachers within this category may encounter

TABLE 3.5 A six-phase model for cross-curricular and professional development

PHASE	KEY FEATURES
Initiation	Motivational aspects for proposed piece of curriculum development
	Analysis of beliefs about teaching and learning
	Identification of any external benefits for undertaking the development
Novice	Initial stage of teacher planning and classroom experimentation
	Anxiety in planning lessons and preparing resources but this can be overcome quickly
Concerns	Initial enthusiasm hits a buffer as the requirement for more detailed knowledge about pedagogical elements (e.g. an approach to questioning) becomes apparent
	Self-doubts may emerge
	Questioning the perceived benefits in relation to the amount of effort involved
	Significant shifts in one's belief about teaching as the self-evaluation processes begin to challenge traditional thinking
Consolidation	Issues and concerns raised in the previous phase are resolved through collaboration and other external forms of support
	Collaborative and comparative nature of the exercise helps staff maintain their energy and commitment
	Sharing practice and related coaching is a significant benefit at this point
	External benefits (e.g. studying for a higher degree) help staff here
Expansion	Individual classroom practices begin to make links across curricular subjects and with external themes
	New practices gradually become embedded within routine practices
	Further study aids this process
Commitment	Shift in teacher identity brought about by the opportunity to reflect on experiences and clarify beliefs
	New practices embedded and no going back
	Teachers become strong advocates of the innovation and sustain it in their own teaching

Source: Leat, Lofthouse and Taverner (2006).

significant challenges as subject-centred approaches to teaching and learning give way to cross-curricular approaches.

To conclude this short diversion, it is worth moving the focus away from the individual teacher for a moment and considering the wider, school-based systems that are needed in order to encourage and support this type of professional development. O'Brien and MacBeath provide a helpful summary of these:

- development will only be effective within a supportive, co-operative ethos at least at some level (school, department or classroom), but preferably at all levels;

- those responsible for development must have a genuine understanding of the context in which teachers work – as teachers perceive it;
- teachers need to be recognised as people at different stages in their personal and professional life cycle.

(O'Brien and MacBeath 1999, p. 70)

Working as a teacher can be a solitary experience at times. One of the benefits of this type of professional development linked to curriculum development is the opportunity to make productive links with other colleagues. This can be a powerful and motivating force and I would encourage all readers to seek to collaborate with other supportive colleagues. This will have benefits for your own professional development and also the wider curriculum developments that a cross-curricular approach to teaching and learning facilitates.

Collaborative approaches to cross-curricular teaching and learning

The pedagogical approaches described thus far could be broadly described as 'teaching inside out', that is, starting from the work of the individual teacher and their associated subject and teaching outwards to encompass the content and pedagogy of other subjects in a sympathetic but enriching way. In Chapter 7 we will explore this 'inside out' approach through the metaphor of centrifugal teaching. But, as we have seen, reported examples in the educational research literature are few in number. The corollary to this approach, which I might tentatively describe as 'teaching outside in', would be related to the more common approach of providing a collaborative framework for teaching and learning in a cross-curricular way. This is the approach that many schools have adopted in response to the recent changes in the curriculum at Key Stages 3 and 4. Reports of this type of curriculum development provide important insights into pedagogical aspects that relate closely to the issues that we have discussed above. To this end, I do not see these approaches as being different. Teaching 'inside out' and teaching 'outside in' are two sides of the same educational coin. The skill will be deciding which approach to adopt for a particular purpose.

The second, much briefer part of this chapter will present ideas about the practice of cross-curricular teaching that spans out from the work of individual teachers (and their developing pedagogy) to the collaborative approaches that are a requisite of good cross-curricular initiatives. To facilitate this process, key lessons from a range of interesting school-wide and collaborative curriculum projects will be considered. These are drawn from four briefer case studies:

1. Case Study 5: Constructing a new Key Stage 3 curriculum (Campbell and Kerry 2004).

2.   Case Study 6: Communication across the curriculum and in the disciplines (Dannels and Housley Gaffney 2009).

3.   Case Study 7: Sustaining effective literacy practices over time in secondary schools (May 2007).

4.   Case Study 8: Working together? Partnership approaches to 14–19 education in England (Higham and Yeomans 2009).

Case Study 5: Constructing a new Key Stage 3 curriculum

This study provides an interesting insight into a whole school review of the Key Stage 3 curriculum at Brooke Weston College (Campbell and Kerry 2004). The features of this new curriculum were:

- a reduction of the Key Stage from three years to two years;
- a fundamental reshaping of the curriculum to a thematic structure that spanned Years 7 and 8;
- the construction of new learning resources within an online 'Learning Library' that allowed programmes of study and individual lessons to be easily stored and retrieved;
- a quality assurance mechanism embedded within the curriculum development cycle.

The timing of this study is informative. The date of the published outcome (2004) is prior to the most recent iteration of the National Curriculum. As a school proclaimed by Ofsted to be a 'leader amongst state-funded schools' (Ofsted 2001b), it is easy to see aspects of Brooke Weston College's approach in the recent National Curriculum framework. As part of the 'process concerns' part of their study (Campbell and Kerry 2004, p. 403), a number of pedagogical elements were identified as being successful drivers for change. These included a commitment to cross-curricularity, a reappraisal of the use of time in the construction of the curriculum framework, empowering technological solutions to curriculum management and the construction of new learning resources, and a new focus on team teaching. Alongside these changes, the report emphasises how new features of curriculum design have worked alongside traditional strengths within the school, including a 'distinctive differentiation system' (Campbell and Kerry 2004, p. 403). Looking ahead, the authors suggest that future curriculum developments need to move beyond matters of content (i.e. they will challenge pedagogy) but that they also need to acknowledge a school's distinctive ethos and expertise.

Case Study 6: Communication across the curriculum and in the disciplines

This American study of 'communication across the curriculum' (Dannels and Housley Gaffney 2009) is interesting on a number of fronts. First, it provides a useful, alternative perspective to the predominantly UK-centric focus of this book. Second, it is based in higher education and so it takes us outside our predominantly Key Stage 3 and 4 focus. Third, it is based within a 'subject' that is different from the majority of traditional subjects or themes that make up our curriculum frameworks: communication studies.

The authors have reflected on the last 25 years of education in the United States and provided a synopsis of scholarship in relation to the teaching of communication across the curriculum. They identify three broad approaches to cross-curricularity: cross-curricular pro-activeness, cross-curricular scepticism and cross-curricular curiosity. These are investigated in some depth and, broadly speaking, cover much of the material that we have considered in previous chapters.

The conclusion of the study has some interesting pedagogical applications for a collaborative, cross-curricular approach to teaching and learning. It argues that a renewed approach to empirical rigour within subjects will enhance the opportunity for cross-curricular developments. This resonates strongly with our discussion of the CIDREE study (2005), which pointed out that effective cross-curricular approaches to teaching and learning were more likely when a teacher's subject-specific knowledge was strong. The research here identifies several features of theoretical work and research that have built new 'sub-disciplines' within the field of communication studies. These have developed and been applied within the work of educators who have continued to refine their subject knowledge and associated pedagogical approach, together with a reconsideration of the ways in which students may learn, within these new frameworks. This enquiry into a progressive and development pedagogy that accompanies the process of subject, and curriculum, development is extremely helpful.

Despite not being an expert in any sense within this particular area of the curriculum, one of the key features of this study for me was that the curriculum subject seemed to be alive in some sense. It was the subject of enquiry for researchers and teachers as they sought to develop its content and practices (in a theoretical sense) and then apply this rigorously within a subject-orientated and cross-curricular framework. There is also honesty in their account. They remained, at the end of the study, within the cross-curricular curiosity 'camp':

> The danger of moving forward with a mindset of cross-curricular advocacy is that we run the risk of altering the pedagogical, administrative, and scholarly course of countless disciplines.
>
> (Dannels and Housley Gaffney 2009, p. 142)

This is a welcome call for conservatism and a responsible approach to curriculum development.

Case Study 7: Sustaining effective literacy practices over time in secondary schools

Continuing with studies carried out outside the UK, this study drawn from New Zealand secondary schools explores the implementation of literacy across the curriculum (May 2007). It argues that effective literacy practices need to be established, consolidated and sustained for effective cross-curricular change to take place.

One of the key features of this study was the link between the cross-curricular change (in this case in relation to the development of literacy across the curriculum) and the process of teachers' professional development. Through an extensive mapping process, each of the three stages (related to establishing, consolidating and sustaining effective literacy practice) show how teachers' work within these schools is challenged, supported and developed in specific ways. Within this brief summary of the research it is not possible to identify these in detail, but issues such as the resources required for teachers' professional development activities are identified, alongside changing practices of assessment and differentiation, and the establishment of new teaching resources. Additionally, structures for the peer mentoring of teachers and the opportunity for teachers to work together in each others' classrooms were highlighted as key components of change.

This study highlights the significant whole school changes that are required for a major shift in cross-curriculum development of this type. It reaffirms the view that curriculum development at this level requires not only a high level of support from senior managers, but also a shared commitment to change amongst the whole staff. It is also not going to develop overnight; the study suggests that a five- to six-year time period for change is more realistic.

Case Study 8: Working together? Partnership approaches to 14–19 education in England

Although it falls slightly beyond our primary focus, this is an informative and helpful study to consider here (Higham and Yeomans 2009). The development of educational partnerships is a key feature of the new diplomas recently introduced in the Key Stage 4 and 5 sectors. In addition, many individual subject programmes of study at Key Stage 3 include the requirement to make links to external groups or agencies.

The study outlines the various opportunities and pitfalls of partnership working. It provides a framework for the analysis of educational partnerships, including their strategies for inclusion, engagement, focus and scale (Higham and Yeomans 2009, p. 10). On the basis of this framework, it suggests that the 'orientation' taken by the partnership to its collaborative venture is central to its success or failure. An overly 'technical' or 'instrumental' collaboration is less likely to be sustained over the longer period than a more committed collaboration that builds on individual partners' own values, educational aims and circumstances (Higham and Yeomans 2009, pp. 11–12).

In perhaps the study's most interesting finding, it is suggested that national policy (which, as the authors demonstrate, in itself is not consistent) is strongly mediated by locally contextual factors resulting in networking opportunities that are highly dynamic and subject to change. These include:

- competition and collaboration between local partners;
- institutional autonomy and selective collaboration;
- personal missions and the individual career opportunities for networking professionals.

For all these reasons, the study suggests that a key element of a successful approach to partnership working in this sector is to have a highly responsive and reflective group of practitioners within an organisation.

Bringing it together

This chapter has explored a range of issues associated with the development of a cross-curricular pedagogy. It has focused primarily on the work of the individual subject teacher and looked at how they can develop and adapt their pedagogy to facilitate a cross-curricular approach. Teaching 'inside out', or centrifugally, is a metaphor that we have used to describe this approach. This will be developed further in Chapter 7. I have argued that this approach is by far the most productive in developing what I might call an authentic cross-curricular pedagogy. In contrast with recent government initiatives and calls for cross-curricular dimensions within the curriculum, this approach does not rely on large-scale, collaborative approaches between staff. Rather, it reinforces a bottom-up approach to teacher development in line with the principles of this book.

This is not to say that collaborative approaches to cross-curricular development are not worthwhile. They are. My own experiences as a teacher (e.g. in the opening, personal narrative in Chapter 1) confirm this. But to depend on these as a pre-requisite for action would be unhelpful. I would encourage all teachers to share and discuss ideas about the development of their cross-curricular activities. One of the roles of senior managers in schools should be to support and develop platforms for these types of discussion between colleagues. More widely, teachers should be encouraged to tell their stories of curriculum developments to wider audiences and it is the role of policy makers to value, promote and find ways to facilitate this kind of curriculum storytelling.

Postscript

The end of this chapter marks the midpoint of the book. It provides an important point of reflection for the reader. What follows in Chapters 4, 5 and 6 is a more detailed discussion and investigation of particular aspects of cross-curricular teaching and learning (language, technology and assessment). We will return to, and exemplify more fully, many of the ideas that we have discussed in this chapter in what is to come.

Professional Standards for QTS

This chapter will help you meet the following Q standards: Q10, Q25 (although it will touch on many other of the Q standards)

Professional Standards for Teachers

This chapter will help you meet the following core standards: C10, C29, C30 (although it will touch on many other of the C standards)

4

The Language and Literacy of Cross-Curricular Teaching and Learning

Key objectives

By the end of this chapter, you will be able to:

- analyse the role of language as a mediating tool through which cross-curricular teaching and learning are facilitated;

- understand the link between language, knowledge and thinking and how these relate to and implicate educational processes, including how a subject is represented and provides potential links to others;

- consider the use of metaphorical language as a key to broadening cross-curricular approaches to teaching and learning;

- develop strategies for utilising cross-curricular utterances as a key element of teacher talk;

- apply key ideas raised throughout the chapter to common uses of language and literacy within the classroom context.

Prelude to Chapters 4, 5 and 6

Having established a broad framework for the principles of cross-curricular teaching and examined how this applies to the construction of a skilful pedagogy and wider school-based pieces of curriculum reform, this chapter, and the following two, will take a more detailed look at a number of specific aspects of teaching and learning that can be developed through a cross-curricular approach. This chapter is focused on the language and literacy of cross-curricular teaching and learning; Chapter 5 analyses the impact of information and communication technologies; and Chapter 6 moves on to consider assessment and educational evaluation. In contrast with the previous chapters, these three chapters can be considered as more detailed, explorative approaches to key, common elements of all teachers' pedagogy. As such, I hope that they provide a broader rationale for further studies on the development of cross-curricular teaching and learning.

Introduction

The aspiration that every teacher should be a teacher of language has a long history. It can be traced back as far as 1921 to the Newbolt Report (Board of Education 1921) and has been renewed periodically by government and others (Marland 1977; QCA 2000, 2001). As an example of a cross-curricular initiative, perhaps these calls have resulted in some of the most promising cross-curricular links between subjects within secondary schools. After all, although we are not all teachers of English, language and literacy are common elements in the teaching of all subjects within the secondary curriculum. If a common approach cannot be found here, perhaps it is unrealistic for it to develop anywhere else.

This chapter will begin with a brief survey of collaborative approaches to curriculum development that have used language and literacy as a core ingredient within their cross-curricular approach. Its premise is that language can be conceived as a mediating tool through which teaching is delivered and by which learning can be facilitated.

The cross-curricular potential for language and literacy

There have been several studies and examples of the ways that language has been used as a stimulating, collaborative tool for cross-curricular curriculum development between teachers (Alexander, Walsh, Jarman and McClune 2008; CIDREE 2005; QCDA 2009b). These have emphasised that 'teachers are implementing cross-curricular and interdisciplinary initiatives, but rhetorical imperatives can translate into superficial realities' (Alexander, Walsh, Jarman and McClune 2008, p. 1). Unfortunately, this is becoming an underlying theme of this book. As we saw in Chapters 1 and 2, at times of initiative 'overload', teachers often prioritise those areas of curriculum development that are perceived as essential and other areas fall by the wayside. We also noted how in the most recent reform of the National Curriculum (QCA 2007) there was a statement regarding compulsory development of cross-curricular approaches within every curriculum subject's programme of study. But the requirement to teach collaboratively through cross-curricular dimensions was non-statutory. This mixed message is not helpful and it is hoped will be clarified in future policy announcements.

However, the cross-curricular potential of language and literacy is noteworthy and, perhaps because it is recognised as being important by the majority of teachers, has resulted in a number of interesting cross-curricular, collaborative ventures. As an example of one effective piece of work in this area, the 'Making Science: Making News' project is outlined in the following case study.

Case Study 1: 'Making Science, Making News'

The 'Making Science: Making News' project, funded by the Particle Physics and Astronomy Council and based at the School of Education, Queen's University Belfast, ran from 2004 to 2006. It was an ambitious, cross-curricular and community-focused initiative. Its aim was to encourage schools to establish partnerships with local newspapers with the intention that their pupils research and write astronomy-related articles for publication. Participating in the project were seven schools ranged geographically across Northern Ireland to permit each of them to link up with a different local newspaper. There were three grammar schools (two all boys and one all girls), three secondary high schools (two mixed and one all boys) and one integrated school (mixed). The pupils, almost 180 in total, were in Year 10, which in Northern Ireland is their third year of post-primary schooling and the final Key Stage 3 year (ages 14–15). The science and English teachers who taught the Year 10 class collaborated to run the project during timetabled lessons.

There was an ideal plan of how it was envisaged that the project would proceed and this was adhered to in its broad outline by the schools, although obviously small variations arose because of local circumstances. The principal involvement of the university researchers was to arrange the links with outside agencies – the visiting scientist, the local newspaper and one of its journalists. Seven leading research scientists from the School of Mathematics and Physics at Queen's University or from Armagh Observatory were linked with the schools. The scientists offered several topics on which they would be prepared to talk to pupils and the science teacher decided which topic they thought was most appropriate to their context. Eventual topics included: the Hubble telescope; the moons of Jupiter; solar winds; potential asteroid impacts; gamma ray bursts. Astronomy-related topics were favourably received by the teachers because, while some knowledge of space features on the KS3 syllabus, not all science teachers are comfortable with teaching it.

The scientist then provided the school with a 'press release', giving a general introduction to the topic, explaining its importance and perhaps citing some websites where further information could be found. This permitted advance preparation for the scientist's visit; this groundwork was done in both science and English classes from their subject perspectives. The pupils studied the press release, discussed the relevant issues and planned questions to ask the scientist.

A journalist then visited the class and, to help the pupils get into role, they were issued with attractive 'press passes' and a notebook and pencil. The journalist advised the pupils on how they might make the best use of the press release and assisted them in preparing for the scientist's presentation and question-time – 'press conference' and 'interview'. The journalist also reviewed the major features of newspaper articles – headline, graphics, structure, etc. The journalist's visit was followed by the scientist's visit, giving a short talk on the selected research topic and then answering questions. The challenge then was for the pupils to work together as a news team to find out more about the topic and to present all that they had learned, through text and graphics, in an attractive, interesting and newsworthy way. This work occupied a number of science and English lessons. The final articles were forwarded to the editor of the local newspaper, who selected from the material received for publication. When the school phase of the project was complete, the university researchers administered a pupil questionnaire and interviewed all the participating teachers. They also obtained all the articles written by the pupils. In addition to the literal 'hard copy', therefore, there was considerable information on the effectiveness of the project, pupil attitudes to it, and the kinds of learning that resulted from it. (Extract from Alexander, Walsh, Jarman and McClune 2008, pp. 26–7)

Reflective Task 1

Read through Case Study 1. What were the features that made this a successful collaborative cross-curricular project? Were there any potential worrying or problematic features that you noted? What lessons can be learnt for your own emerging practice in this area?

In my analysis of Case Study 1, I was struck by a number of enriching elements within this work that signalled a successful approach to collaborative cross-curricular development. The links that schools made with other professional groups (scientists and journalists) were central to the pupils' experiences and framed the curriculum activities in a helpful way. From the teachers' perspectives, the benefits in terms of their own subject knowledge, especially from the science perspective, were noted. This confirms my belief that there is no meaningful curriculum development without corresponding teacher development. I was intrigued by the comment that the groundwork for the scientists' visits was carried out within curriculum time but through each individual subject's perspective. From this platform, pupils were able to work in both their English and science lessons on the production of the news item. This respect and accommodation for individual subject perspectives within a cross-curricular project was interesting. This element of mutual respect and accommodation is an important one that we will return to and examine in much more detail in the following chapter.

From the point of view of the researchers, the project provided a range of outcomes that are a useful starting point for our discussions.

First, they assert that the combination of literacy and subject discourses can be learnt and practised, 'but to do so it is necessary to go beyond a narrow skills agenda' (Alexander, Walsh, Jarman and McClune 2008, p. 33). In particular, they cite the transformation of the science curriculum through this project in terms of the 'real life' elements that the collaboration with English facilitated, for example communication and the media. These links to wider life experiences were emphasised further in the research:

> Science is embedded in life activities and the animation of these activities in the classroom is seen here to be crucial to engagement with science. English/literacy has been the vehicle by which this distinction has been made, that is by lifting 'science' from an exclusive focus on its content or 'skills' to a consideration of how it is applied not just to real-world problems but by real people in specific situations. Science needs not only to be located in 'real-life' activities but also to be seen to be part of life. Pupils do not do science and then communicate it, but discover it as part of a process of curiosity, engagement, problem-solving and reciprocal communication. Science teachers thus see that role-play, group work and presentations are not just communication or English activities to be consolidated in the science classroom but form a crucial aspect of science education.
>
> (Alexander, Walsh, Jarman and McClune 2008, p. 34)

In this study, then, there seems to have been a transformation in the traditional pedagogy associated with the science curriculum through both the engagement and collaboration with the English teachers and the real-world scenarios considered during the project. This also reaffirms an important lesson related to planning and learning objectives referred to on a number of occasions in Chapter 3. In this project, the learning objectives clearly did move beyond the subject-specific skills base (i.e. avoiding the trap of the 'doing' objectives rather than the learning objectives) and focused on learning that spanned across subjects into the 'real life' activities within the project.

Second, this seemed to be an example of genuine cross-curricularity in which subject specialisms and discourses were respected and built upon. There was a genuine sharing between professionals at all levels that sparked interest amongst teachers, scientists, journalists and pupils.

Finally, the case study's conclusions present a worrying angle that we will need to consider carefully:

> Projects that aim to replace subject autonomy with ongoing involvement are likely to be over-ambitious and misplaced. Subject disciplines have their own purposes and discourses, and collaborative projects such as the one described above should respect the integrity of the domain of the other. There can be no cross-curricularity without distinct curriculum content. Subject domains were established not by ex-cathedra decree but by the processes of historical and social development. Subject learning evolved to meet educational needs and to provide routes and maps for learners. Effective cross-curricularity constructs new paths to make new connections but does not seek to ignore broad highways worn by custom and use leading to known destinations.
>
> (Alexander, Walsh, Jarman and McClune 2008, p. 34)

This balance between the historical development of subjects within the curriculum and cross-curricular projects of this type is something that we have discussed in previous chapters. As you may have noticed, it is becoming a recurring theme throughout this book. But this case study presents a timely reminder that any new pieces of curriculum development need to be cognisant of broader educational themes or cultures. In planning approaches to cross-curricular teaching and learning, an over-reliance on ongoing subject collaborations of this type is unlikely to achieve significant changes. In this sense, having the odd 'cross-curricular day' in which traditional teaching timetables are collapsed is going to have only limited ongoing benefits. They are just too intensive and consuming to be done regularly and too haphazard in the development of individual teachers' pedagogy to be sustained throughout their teaching. The distinctiveness of subject curriculum content is an essential starting point for new approaches and collaborations. One-off projects of this type need to engender commitment from teachers and empower them to make changes to their own classroom practices in light of the pedagogical and learning issues that have been raised. As a reminder of this important point, reconsider Case Study 4 in Chapter 3. This departmental arts cross-curricular project provided the initial stimulus that the teachers needed to begin to make significant changes within their own pedagogy. Without this loop back into a teacher's individual pedagogical practice, the ongoing development of a cross-curricular pedagogy will not be nurtured and sustained beyond one-off project work of this type.

With that note of warning, we will return to the theme of this chapter. Collaborative approaches to language and literacy have proved to be useful doorways into cross-curricular teaching and learning. But if we are to avoid the pitfalls discussed above, a broader consideration of language and its influence on the process of planning for teaching and learning is going to be needed. This will provide a platform for the development of a teacher's richer, subject-based cross-curricular pedagogy and it is to this that our attention will now turn.

Language as a focus for planning cross-curricular opportunities

Language is a common element in all curriculum subjects. This is not to say that individual subjects do not have a particular or specific discourse that needs to be acknowledged. As I discuss below, acknowledging these specific subject discourses will be an important strand in building a broader cross-curricular pedagogy. However, there are a number of key ways in which language mediates teachers' engagement with their own subject. One of these ways is illustrated through the process of planning.

As we discussed in Chapter 3, effective planning is based on the setting of appropriate learning objectives and outcomes, choosing and structuring suitable teaching activities and defining strategies for differentiation and assessment. Within the planning process, language has a specific role to play at a number of levels. At a macro level, the division of the curriculum into subject areas has itself resulted in artificial distinctions in language usage, with certain language types or words seen as belonging to a particular subject or discipline. At the meso level, within specific subjects the language patterns and prevailing types of discourse mediate teachers' and pupils' engagement with particular concepts or forms of knowledge, how they are interacted with in learning sequences or presented in a lesson structure. Finally, at the micro level of the individual classroom, the types of language and talk that accompany these learning sequences will exhibit elements of various discourses, including the subject culture and its associated patterns of language use, the formal or informal language types that teachers and pupils adopt, and more besides.

But at each of these levels, language has a provisionality and ambiguity that is at the core of its importance as a tool for thinking and learning:

> The fact that language is not always reliable for causing precise meanings to be generated in someone else's mind is a reflection of its powerful strength as a medium for creating new understanding. It is the inherent ambiguity and adaptability of language as a meaning-making system that makes the relationship between language and thinking so special.
>
> (Mercer 2000, p. 6)

By becoming aware of this inherent ambiguity, teachers can begin to play with language within the planning process in a productive way. This could affect the way they plan their own subject teaching as well as any potential cross-curricular approaches that they want to develop. The richness of language, and the possibilities for multiple meaning making, can be exploited for educational benefits in a range of contexts. Mercer gives us an obvious example from the English curriculum perspective:

> When we are dealing with complex, interesting presentations of ideas, variations in understanding are quite normal and sometimes are even welcomed; how otherwise could there be new interpretations of Shakespeare's plays, and why else are we interested in them? I am sure that my understanding of Pinker's book, despite the clarity of his writing, will not be exactly what he might have intended or expected, and I know that I will not make quite the same interpretation of it as other readers. I expect that many authors are frequently dismayed to discover that readers misunderstand their 'message'; but they should not necessarily take this as failure on their part. The act of reading any text relies on the interpretative efforts of a reader, as well as on the communicative efforts and intentions of the author.
>
> (Mercer 2000, p. 5)

The same issues would be true for the majority of subjects. The key point here is to consider how the quite normal and expected variations in thinking that occur when using language as part of planning, or more widely within the classroom, can be built upon to develop a more extensive cross-curricular perspective.

Practical Task 1

Spend a few minutes listing some of the key language that underpins your own subject. What are the key words (nouns, adjectives, verbs, etc.) that you will expect pupils to know and use at the end of Key Stage 3, Key Stage, 4, etc.? Where have these language 'types' come from?

Think through some of the lessons you have taught recently. Try and identify when you used some of these key terms and how they were introduced within the lesson. Were they accompanied by explanations? Did you focus teaching activities around them? Can you identify any ambiguities within your use of language that can be developed or exploited for a cross-curricular pedagogy?

Using metaphors to provide connections across the curriculum

Metaphors are a language 'type' that has some potential in helping teachers make links across traditional subject cultures. Lakoff and Johnson (1981) define a metaphor as 'understanding and experiencing one kind of thing in terms of another' (p. 5).

This definition is built on the notion of a metaphor being able to capture the essential nature of a particular experience and relating it to something else. To that end, metaphors are a perfect language type for our discussion about cross-curricular pedagogy. 'Understanding' and 'experiencing' are also active words that resonate strongly with processes underpinning Eisner's (1987) argument for multiple forms of representation and knowing. In another key similarity with Eisner, Lakoff and Johnson insist that metaphors are not solely based in language. Metaphors, in their definition, can include any expression or thing that is symbolic for a person. This would include non-verbal behaviours, pieces of artwork or something in a person's imagination. In other words, anything a person sees, hears, does, feels or imagines can be used to help them think or reason through metaphors:

> In all aspects of life, . . . we define our reality in terms of metaphors and then proceed to act on the basis of the metaphors. We draw inferences, set goals, make commitments, and execute plans, all on the basis of how we in part structure our experience, consciously and unconsciously, by means of metaphor.
>
> (Lakoff and Johnson 1981, p. 158)

The use of metaphors as tools for teaching and learning has a long history. According to Gorden (1978), one can chart the use of metaphor (and the related concept of analogy, which, he suggests, is merely an extended metaphor) back to Greek myths, religious texts and fairytales, which all help readers (or listeners) learn expected conduct. Hoffman (1983) estimated that the average English speaker uses over 3000 metaphors every week as part of their natural language use, and Bowers (1993) goes as far as suggesting that all human thinking is metaphorical in some way. It is interesting to reflect for a moment on the number of metaphors that relate to learning itself (e.g. switching on a light bulb, planting a seed, etc.).

According to Lakoff and Johnson's definition, metaphors describe one experience in terms of another. As a teaching and learning tool, metaphor can help a teacher relate something that is unfamiliar to pupils to something familiar. This gets to the Greek root of the word metaphor – *metapherein* – which means to transfer. Metaphors can also be used to specify and constrain our ways of thinking about the original experience. This influences the meaning and importance one can attach to the original experience, the way it fits with other experiences, and the actions that one can take as a result. Pedagogically, this may or may not be problematic. Glynn and Takahashi (1998) do report that metaphors need to be handled carefully within educational situations. Incorrect use of metaphors can lead to greater confusion. Teachers must make sure that the coherence of the metaphor is accurate and clear. There is a responsibility for the teacher, within the classroom setting, of choosing the appropriate metaphor and using it in a way that promotes clear communication.

For our discussion about developing approaches to cross-curricular teaching and learning, the use of metaphor as a key strategy presents a range of opportunities for curriculum and pedagogical development. There are various established models for this type of general activity building, including the 3C model (Create, Connect and Combine). We will revisit this approach below.

Waters' (1994) work on productive metaphors is worthy of study and application within this context. His study of metaphors centred on art-making processes in various digital fields. But, as we will consider, these can be usefully applied to the context of cross-curricular teaching and learning. His 'Toolbox of Productive Metaphors' is divided into four main sections:

1. Basic Concepts.
2. Strategies of Reduction.
3. Strategies of Connection.
4. Strategies of Contextualisation.

Although he acknowledges that these distinctions are artificial, this four-part structure does represent a helpful framework within which the metaphors can be explored. Waters' work is extensive here, but, for our purposes, in each section I have chosen four metaphors to briefly explore. Each metaphor is presented and defined through a quotation from Waters' work. Following this I have added my own interpretation of the metaphor, which I hope will prove helpful to your own work in applying metaphors to the teaching of your own subject area in the following practical task. These personal interpretations of the metaphor may contain ideas of how the metaphor might be represented (within particular subjects), questions about the metaphor and how it might be interrogated to produce links between subjects, or just immediate, reflective responses to the possibility of the metaphor and its application to pedagogy. They are by no means conclusive (so please do not read them as such), and are merely included to help prompt your own thinking about how the metaphor can help you understand or experience one thing in terms of another. In Waters' own words:

> What is offered here is a toolbox of productive metaphors; keywords which are not in any current sense discipline-specific, although they have originated in a specific practice. . . . They are all intended as projects for further investigation and personal annotation. The incompleteness is therefore intentional; an invitation to continue, to add, to argue.
>
> (Waters 1994, pp. 75–6)

1. Basic Concepts

System

> Any complex series of connected parts of things, whether material or not; any set of devices or processes which function together.
>
> (Waters 1994, p. 77)

Identify some of the 'systems' within your subject. What kind of behaviours do these systems exhibit? How are they structured? Are they hierarchical or networked (latticed)? How do objects, ideas or materials behave within the system? At what level is this system similar to systems in other curriculum areas? Do they overlap? Can they be networked?

Resolution/definition

> The resolution of an experience or a system is the relation of the size of its components to that of the whole. In a high resolution experience, the grain or individual elements of the representational medium chosen do not impinge on the definition or distinctiveness of the represented object.
>
> (Waters 1994, pp. 78–9)

Resolution/definition is about a relationship between individual components and the whole. It could relate to geographical elements such as maps or photographs which contain numerous graphical or actual elements that relate together to form a landscape or ecosystem; there are artistic dimensions such as the choice of colours and their interaction in a painting; it could be translated as the way in which we view particular objects, events or time periods in a historical narrative, focusing in on particular moments or zooming out to capture wider societal, political or cultural movements. Zooming could become a productive metaphor in its own right. Microscopes zoom in and out on things providing greater or lesser definition of an object. Narrative structures within poetry allow the writer to zoom in on a particular object, event or person, describing it in greater detail and enhancing its meaning when compared with the surrounding text.

Transformation

> Dynamic change. Change of two or more characteristics or behaviours simultaneously. Interaction of two or more processes.
>
> (Waters 1994, p. 79)

Transformation is a powerful metaphor in any aspect of learning. Pupils' minds are being transformed by new experiences. Experiences that we have planned and taught about many times, will be experienced as if 'for the first time' by your pupils. This needs to be cherished. How do things transform within your subject? The amount of pressure on a paintbrush can transform an otherwise bland line; gradients transform a landscape and these can be represented through contour lines on maps; the shapes made by individuals and groups of dancers transform in front of our eyes. Do elements transform when they are placed together and combust? Transformation and process have close links and impact on all subjects. What about yours?

Play

Play in its many forms is one of the closest forms of performance activity. Yet such exploratory behaviour is undervalued and suppressed in most areas of human activity beyond childhood.

(Waters 1994, p. 80)

Does your subject encourage a sense of play? What would this involve? What is playfulness and how does it relate to learning? Are some pupils, or subjects, more playful than others? If play is undervalued and suppressed within education, how could your subject seek to value and utilise it more? If play involves making mistakes and failing, how can you teach your pupils to fail well? What would they learn from that? If playful learning is the answer, what is the question? (Heppell 2010)

2. Strategies of Reduction

Editing

Editing is selecting, moving things around, deleting or erasing, cutting and pasting.

(Waters 1994, p. 83)

As a process, editing is a vital skill. It applies to every curriculum area but is something that needs to be encouraged because it seems, from my experience, that pupils like to avoid it. Pupils like to produce things; perhaps the sense of achievement is tied up in the final object that they produce. How can this process be slowed down so that the pathway towards the final object of their learning is appreciated more fully? How can editing be encouraged as part of a playful process of engagement within your subject? How can you keep the opportunities and options for choices open for longer rather than forcing pupils down a particular route (perhaps for expediency or to save time)?

Masking

The original sense of masking: covering the face to disguise, amuse, terrify or protect; and all other senses, share the idea of information lost because of the intervention of a second object.

(Waters 1994, p. 84)

What masks are we wearing? How do they disguise who we are, what we value and what we might have lost? Are our subjects masked in any way? Why? As a mechanism of reduction, what have we lost through this masking process? Was it important and should we try and get it back? If our subject masks are lowered for a while, will we find more in common than perhaps we first thought?

Iteration

> Iteration is a strategy for moving towards a required goal as quickly as possible. It relies on repeatedly attempting whatever is being done, and selecting those outcomes which most closely meet the goal.
>
> (Waters 1994, p. 85)

Iterative processes can be found in various curriculum areas. Mathematicians use iterative processes to help in averaging and estimating; scientists use them to help generate hypotheses; artists sketch and doodle; musicians jot ideas down through improvisations. Repeatedly attempting something is not worthless activity in and of itself, providing it becomes part of a creative and intellectual process. It creates mental and physical patterns that become part of how we act, think or feel within an activity. How can all this be valued more?

Excavating/uncovering

> These are strategies which result in discovery/rediscovery as a result of the removal of a concealing layer of material or activity.
>
> (Waters 1994, p. 86)

This conjures up the image of an archaeologist in my mind. Or a forensic scientist? Brushes, spades, gentleness, rigour, patience and a keen eye are required by both of these occupations. In an obvious, physical sense, geographers, geologists and artists all excavate and uncover things (maybe through studying landscapes and rocks and working with oil paints), but what about the rest of the curriculum? How do processes of excavation impact on your curriculum area? What do you need to remove in order to discover something new?

3. Strategies of Connection

Diffusion

> Diffusion is the activity which results in an object or behaviour becoming more widespread than previously. It is also a metaphor of the increasing social connection or dissemination of a process.
>
> (Waters 1994, p. 87)

My first thought here is of gases. They diffuse under certain conditions. But other things diffuse too. I have an image of ripples on a pond, diffusing outwards towards the edge. Sound diffuses differently depending on the acoustical properties of a space. Is it about multiplication in some sense? But it could also be about replacement, because sometimes the thing that is diffused changes so much that nothing of the original is left behind (at least, not in our consciousness). Replacement might be another productive metaphor worth exploring.

Looping

> Loops are merely regular repeated cycles. Loops operate in any medium. They have much to do with narrative, acting as an essential component of memory or recall.
>
> (Waters 1994, p. 88)

Loops are a key musical device found all over the world, for example in Indonesian gamelan music and many Western popular musical styles. Loops seem linked to patterning. This is something that is found in the teaching of textiles (e.g. Islamic textiles such as prayer mats have incredible loops/patterns in their design). The idea of regular, repeated behaviour underpins many sports. The strokes you need to play tennis well (forehand, backhand) have an obvious loop physically (in their shape) but also need regular, repeated practice in order to execute them efficiently. This requires the player to build up muscle memory because, in the pressure of the game, there is little time to 'think' about what one is doing. Narrative loops help create mental patterns that aid one's understanding of story, its characters and action.

Ghosting

> Ghosting is a technique drawn from time-based media. The idea is that one person leads and the others follow as near to simultaneously as possible. The 'leader' has to be aware of the extent and speed to which the 'ghosts' can follow. The ghosts also have to listen and respond with incredible speed and suppleness.
>
> (Waters 1994, p. 89)

As a child, I remember playing follow my leader in the primary school playground. Sometimes, a whole group of us would follow the leader around the playground in a long line, watching and copying their every movement. As a game, I have seen drama teachers use similar techniques in their warm-ups. In contemporary parlance, ghosting is a form of identity theft in which somebody takes over the identify of a deceased person. You also occasionally get ghosted images on a television (a kind of motion blur) when the signal is not received fully or the technology is working too slowly.

Mapping

> In addition to the widely understood cartographical sense of making a representation of a geographical surface, indicating its features, there is an equally significant metaphorical sense of the term from mathematics, this referring to the association of each element of one system or set with that from another system or set.
>
> (Waters 1994, p. 87)

In an obvious sense, mapping something involves investigating it thoroughly and representing it in a particular form. In another sense, it is about translation, taking the properties or proportions of one structure and using them to determine the structure of something else. Therefore, the mathematical results of an equation might be used to determine a new type of musical scale; the contour analysis of a particular landform becomes a starting point for a piece of art.

4. Strategies of Contextualisation

Reading/interpretation

> An extended sense of the term 'reading' can be usefully related to an extended sense of the work 'text'. In acknowledgement of the cultural and historical contingency of any 'reading', such 'readings' are regarded as being in contention, competing for attention. In practice, most individuals tend to favour what is experientially a single, albeit continuously evolving, sense of what something means in order to be able to negotiate, at least temporarily, share meanings with other people.
>
> (Waters 1994, p. 89)

Reading is central to the majority of subjects. But we read in different ways. We read or interpret a book, an image, a musical score, an advertisement. These all involve (and imply) different sets of skills and result in different understandings. One person's reading will vary from another's. This is because we do not read or interpret something as a blank canvas. We contextualise what we read and interpret against our previous experiences. We have to negotiate and share our meanings of things to gain a consensus. Sometimes, a lack of consensus is the best outcome. It gives us our personality. So, what are the links between reading a text, an image, a film or a piece of music? What are the skills that underpin these related activities? As teachers, how are the processes that we undertake within our pedagogy to elicit and develop our pupils' understanding related? There is much of value here for a cross-curricular pedagogy.

Recontextualisation

> Recontextualisation involves moving something from a position to which it, or those experiencing it, has become accustomed, to another position. Of course this position may be conceptual rather than spatial.
>
> (Waters 1994, p. 90)

This book is about recontextualisation! As teachers, we have the power to move ideas around and this is one of the major challenges this book is promoting. It is also a key to this whole concept of productive metaphors acting as prompts for cross-curricular language development and wider pedagogy. Specifically, what happens to a literature text when it is recontextualised within a different genre – the theatre, a film or musical? When objects are moved they take on a different dimension. 'Play Me, I'm Yours' shows this clearly. In this art project Luke Jerram (2009) relocated pianos within different urban environments (skate parks, bus stations, industrial estates) and left them there for the local communities to use as they saw fit. Pianos, once the object of the pianist, take on a different dimension as they are used in whatever way the local community wants. What would this look like for familiar objects within schools, within your classroom or other communal spaces? What impact would this have on pupils' learning inside and outside the classroom?

Displacement

> Absence, displacement, change, loss, alienation. All these are related in some way. Perhaps the most creatively useful form of displacement is that of moving to another society to feel the 'fish out of water' effect; to temporarily escape one's complicity in one's own culture.
>
> (Waters 1994, p. 96)

Experiencing life as 'another' can be life changing. 'Reflecting Others' (Savage and Challis 2002) gave pupils the opportunity to see and feel life in a young offenders' institution through the exchange of digital media. As a metaphor, this could have powerful historical or geographical interpretations. There are obvious scientific connotations too. Displacement could be about personal and cultural identity. But it could also be a way of considering change, whether personal, societal, political or cultural. What is gained, what is lost and how are people/ideas alienated or empowered when displacement occurs?

Narrative/journey/line/story/travel

> The act of getting from one place to another, not only geographically, but also conceptually and metaphorically.
>
> (Waters 1994, p. 94)

This metaphor presents numerous possibilities. Everyone is involved in a journey of some sort. Personal narratives collide in relationships, communities, school and society. How are the stories of these narratives told? Whose do we value? In another vein, the narrative of a story, an event, a historical artefact, a character's dilemma in a play, the belief system of a tribe, all need telling or representing in some way. Within educational systems, is the learning journey treasured and valued as much as the experience of actually getting somewhere, reaching your end goal?

Applying metaphors to cross-curricular teaching and learning

As a linguistic device, the metaphor is a powerful tool in linking together the content and pedagogy of different subject areas. The presentation of Waters' (1994) work in the previous part of the chapter has begun the process of identifying and applying a range of potential metaphors that can span across subjects and be used by teachers to create links, both at the planning stage and in the production of cross-curricular language for use in the classroom (a topic that we will return to below).

In applying metaphors to develop cross-curricular approaches to teaching and learning, there are various methods to aid one's thinking. The approach that I am going to present here is paraphrased on a model produced by Eikenberry (2009) and adopted by the North American Simulation and Gaming Association (NASAGA; 2009). The 3C model provides a helpful structure for applying metaphors to learning contexts. It is based on two premises – first, that the brain works by building connections and associations between concepts and ideas; second, that the brain remembers more easily things that are unusual or novel. The three-stage model incorporates the following three steps: Create, Connect and Combine. This model will be introduced in a practical task that will help you apply metaphors (either those drawn from Waters' work, described above, or your own) to the teaching of a lesson that introduces a new concept to your pupils.

Practical Task 2

1. Create

- Determine which lesson you want to focus on. Make sure you allow yourself plenty of time to complete this element of the planning process.

- Write down all the key elements of the topic that you want to cover during the lesson. This would include trying to sketch out some key learning objectives and outcomes for the lesson.

- How do you want to teach this? Think about the type of teaching or learning activities that you might want to incorporate within the lesson. It would also include examples you might use in the explanatory parts of the lesson. Write down any ideas you have in simple, non-jargon/technical language. This will help you see potential metaphors more easily. You can afford to be quite experimental here. Do not rule out ideas at this stage.

- At this point you are going to begin to compile a list of metaphors for use within the lesson. Go through the list of key elements that you have constructed. What do these remind you of? Use free association techniques to help here. How did you remember these elements when you were learning about them? This is a creative process and some of the ideas may be odd, strange or incomplete. This does not matter at the moment. Write them down anyway.

- Do a random association exercise. This would include:
  - Create a random list of words (there are lots on the Internet) or choose one of the productive metaphors discussed above;
  - Select a word from the list;
  - Is the word you have chosen like one of the key elements that you are wanting to teach? Perhaps it is not? One word may not give you an immediate connection. But it may lead you to another word that does spark an idea.

- Capture your ideas by making short notes. The random words you are using may become the metaphor you ultimately want to use in your lesson;
- Repeat this process by picking another word from the random word list.

■ From all your notes to this point, pick one or more of the really promising ideas. Perhaps you have identified different possible metaphors for different pieces of lesson content, or perhaps you have an overall metaphor for the lesson. The key point here is to try and make a provisional decision about what you want to implement within the lesson. Make sure you are enthusiastic about it! If not, repeat the process but choose a different key element.

You are now ready to move onto the next stage.

2. Connect

In this stage you are going to make connections between the key elements of the lesson and the metaphor(s) that you are going to adopt within the lesson.

Compare the metaphor idea with the lesson content. Write down the potential metaphor and some general elements of that idea. Compare these with the ideas about the lesson content. Ask yourself the following questions:

■ How are the general elements of each connected?

■ How are they alike? Are there any key differences?

■ Can you use phrases from the metaphor to describe parts of your content?

■ Are there key differences that you will need to be aware of, and possibly make learners aware of?

■ Are there any potential confusing elements related to the metaphor, or the way that you have applied it, that will stifle the instructional use of the metaphor in your lesson?

3. Combine

The final important stage determines how you are going to combine or integrate the metaphor within the flow of the lesson. This will have implications for your use of language, the design of any teaching resources to accompany your lesson and, perhaps, any accompanying assessment framework or processes. The following questions and answers, from the NASAGA (2009) materials, may help you build on your ideas. But, as they point out, they are only suggestions, and you may find yourself diving off into completely different directions. Just remain focused on the learner experience in the lesson and try to plan for the best possible approach to teaching in this cross-curricular way with metaphors that you can.

- Can I introduce the metaphor before the lesson, perhaps in a previous lesson or in a previous homework task? Maybe your metaphor will become a theme for the lesson. In preparation, pupils could be encouraged to bring something, wear something, be thinking of something related to the metaphor in advance of the lesson. This may raise your pupils' level of anticipation for the lesson and have beneficial results.

- How will I introduce the metaphor to the group? In this example, perhaps you have chosen a metaphor for a specific purpose during the lesson rather than as a general theme (as in the above example). In this case, you might want to use the metaphor in the explanatory part of the lesson. If you can help pupils construct a mental framework for the metaphor then this will help them piece together new content against this framework at a later part of the lesson. Of course, visual or kinaesthetic frameworks are excellent at doing this. Try and make use of these, including any interactive (physical or virtual) elements that you can prepare, as often as possible.

- What could I do visually to enhance the connection between my content and the metaphor? As mentioned in the previous answer, there are many options here. Using the wall space in the classroom can help (see Savage 1999 for one example of how this was done to good effect). Put up graphics or pictures of the metaphor or its component parts. Use a theme on any presentational and class materials that you prepare for the lesson to accentuate the metaphor.

- What other senses can I use to solidify the metaphor? Think about other senses beyond sight. How can pupils engage their sense of touch (perhaps through a model or toy), smell (actual or related) or hearing (sound effects, other noises)? I remember watching a lesson about musical form that included binary, ternary and rondo forms (basically an AB, ABA and ABACA structure respectively). The trainee teacher brought this to life by making a basic hamburger in front of the class. Binary (AB) became the bottom half of the bun and the burger; ternary (ABA) placed the top of the bun on the burger; rondo involved placing another burger and top of the bun on top of the existing 'ternary' burger (it ended up looking like a Big Mac!) I am not sure what it tasted like, but it smelt good and I am certain the pupils remembered their musical forms for a while.

- How can I reinforce the metaphor in the conclusion of the lesson? Make sure that you reinforce the metaphor through repetition at the end of the lesson, by referencing it in your plenary and using it to help structure questions that relate to the new content taught alongside the metaphor. Ask pupils to summarise the new content, using the metaphor and any associated frameworks as a guide.

Eikenberry uses a metaphor of his own to reinforce the importance of metaphors as learning devices that can link together subjects and ideas in a helpful way:

When building a house, the right techniques and building materials will lead to a solid house. When we build our learning events using strong metaphors and analogies we improve the structure and stability of the learning. Our job as trainers, facilitators and designers is to help our learners be successful. Strong metaphors and analogies do just that.

(NASAGA 2009, p. 4)

Teacher talk and the enriching possibilities of cross-curricular language

All teaching involves action. Most teaching involves language, spoken and written. Of course, this is a fundamental dimension to many human activities and, as such, the actions that activities contain have been subject to considerable analysis. Wertsch's work is particularly helpful to our specific context of cross-curricular teaching and learning. He defines the task of this type of analysis as being:

To explicate the relationship between human *action*, on the one hand, and the cultural, institutional, and historical contexts in which this action occurs, on the other.

(Wertsch 1998, p. 24) [his italics]

Wertsch calls the link between action and the various contexts within which it is being exercised as 'mediated action' (Wertsch 1998, p. 24). Mediated action has a range of characteristics, which we will look at more closely in Chapter 5. For now, it is worth stating that all human action is mediated action. Mediated action takes place in a particular context (or scene), against a particular backdrop, with particular characters involved (known as 'agents'), using particular tools and interacting with particular sets of ideas and assumptions. All of these features mediate the actions we take, sometimes explicitly and sometimes implicitly, sometimes internally and sometimes externally.

Wertsch's concept of mediated action has a useful relevance as we come to look at the spoken word. Here, Wertsch defines language as being a cultural tool and speech as being a form of mediated action. Following a similar theme, Bakhtin exemplifies the spoken word as being a series of 'utterances' that are:

The *real unit* of speech communication. Speech can exist in reality only in the form of concrete utterances of individual speaking people, speech subjects. Speech is always cast in the form of an utterance belonging to a particular speaking subject, and outside this form it cannot exist.

(Bakhtin 1986, p. 71)

In Bakhtin's analysis, utterances are not solely produced by individual speech subjects and unconstrained by other factors. They need to be viewed within a context, or network, of other factors. Some of these are potentially repeatable and others will not be. As he explains:

Behind each text stands a language system. Everything in the text that is repeated and reproduced, everything repeatable and reproducible, everything that can be given outside a given text (the given) conforms to this language system. But at the same time each text (as an utterance) is individual, unique, and unrepeatable, and herein lies its entire significance (its plan, the purposes for which it was created). This is the aspect of it that pertains to honesty, truth, goodness, beauty, history. With respect to this aspect, everything repeatable and reproducible proves to be material, a means to an end. This notion extends somewhat beyond the bounds of linguistics or philology. The second aspect (pole) inheres in the text itself, but is revealed only in a particular situation and in a chain of texts (in the speech communication of a given area). This pole is linked not with elements (repeatable) in the system of the language (signs), but with other texts (unrepeatable) by special dialogic relations.

(Bakhtin 1986, p. 105)

Therefore, any analysis of the spoken word (utterances) needs to be understood in relation to the wider language system (the cultural tool). This will contain important features that implicate the utterances made.

For the purposes of our discussion about how teachers can develop the use of their language to promote cross-curricular learning, the concept of 'speech genres' (another term developed by Bakhtin) is informative. Speech genres are not forms of language, but rather are typical 'types' of utterance with a particular kind of expression inherent within them. Bakhtin's view is that speech genres correspond to various different types of situations, for example teaching, and that these affect the style and presentation of utterance as well as the choice and meaning of individual words within this. He continues:

Speech genres organize our speech in almost the same way as grammatical (syntactical) forms do. We learn to cast our speech in generic forms and, when hearing others' speech, we guess its genre from the very first words; we predict a certain length (that is, the approximate length of the speech whole) and a certain compositional structure; we foresee the end; that is, from the very beginning we have a sense of the speech whole, which is only later differentiated during the speech process.

(Bakhtin 1986, pp. 78–9)

Some examples of speech genres that relate to teaching and learning will be given below.

Language systems in teaching

Wertsch's and Bakhtin's work can help us get to grips with the types of speech that underpin typical teaching episodes. At a higher level, the language systems of teaching have been established through curriculum frameworks such as the National Curriculum (which could be viewed as a historical and cultural construct relating to what teaching should be about), examination specifications, frameworks for initial teacher education and continuing professional development, such as the Professional

Standards for Teaching, and other, general public discourses. Of course, all these elements exist in a state of flux. Yes, many of them are written down in policy documents but their interpretations are not fixed and are subject to negotiations between policy makers, practitioners and others.

However, following the example given by Bakhtin, these language systems are behind the formation of speech genres that have been developed and shaped over time. In our context, is it worth asking what the speech genres that underpin our teaching are?

Speech genres and utterances within teaching

Defining speech genres is not a precise science. A cursory analysis drawn from the arguments about cross-curricular teaching and learning presented through this book so far reveals that there may be three key and closely related genres of speech that relate to our discussion.

First, there is what I would call a 'whole school' genre of speech. This is the language that is used to portray a school's ethos, vision and aims. It is something that is used by schools to communicate with pupils, parents and the local community, particularly in developing aspirations about the school, its function and its role. It has a key role in framing school policy and the outworking of this in terms of approaches to school discipline, equal opportunities and other whole school dimensions.

Second, there is a 'generic teaching' speech genre. This concerns the language of instruction, motivation, facilitation and assessment. It is the common framework of ideas that surrounds subjects within the secondary curriculum, their programmes of study, aims and objectives. This speech genre extends across all schools to some extent.

Finally, there are the 'individual subject' speech genres. These are closely related to the whole school and generic teaching speech genres, but are extended and enriched through a subject's distinctive language system. Individual subject speech genres draw on the language system of the subject as construed within the educational context, but also from the wider historical and cultural traditions of the subject, which have informed that educational context over the years. The individual subject speech genre will contain a range of technical vocabulary, concepts and processes, which, although drawing on standard language systems, are imbued with significance and meaning that tap into that subject's roots. As we have seen through our discussion on metaphors, unpicking some of this language presents key opportunities for cross-curricular thinking and teaching.

This tripartite language framework underpins the 'utterances' that teachers make in the classroom. It informs and mediates not only the choice of words, but also the ways in which they are said and the intentions with which they are imbued. As Bakhtin, in one final quotation, comments:

> There are no 'neutral' words and forms – words and forms that can belong to 'no one'; language has been completely taken over, shot through with intentions and accents. For any individual consciousness living in it, language is not an abstract system of normative forms but rather a concrete heteroglot conception of the world.

All words have the 'taste' of a profession, a genre, a tendency, a party, a particular work, a particular person, a generation, an age group, the day and hour. Each word tastes of the context and contexts in which it has lived its socially charged life; all words and forms are populated by intentions.

(Bakhtin 1981, p. 293)

Reflective Task 2

Spend a few minutes reflecting on the various types of language that you use in your classroom. Can you identify the three types of speech genre that have been presented above: whole school, generic teaching and individual subject?

Focus further on the individual subject speech genre. This is likely to dominate large parts of your teaching. What are the subject-based words and forms of speech that you find yourself using? In Bakhtin's words, can you identify elements of the 'taste' of your particular subject in these words or forms of speech? What are the subject's 'intentions' that underlay your utterances? What are the contexts from which these words and forms of speech have derived?

Developing cross-curricular utterances in your teaching

One of the key components in an approach to cross-curricular teaching and learning will be your ability to develop and use what we will call cross-curricular utterances. Cross-curricular utterances are words and forms of speech drawn from subjects outside of your own. These will need to be appropriated within your teaching in particular ways (which we will examine below). As an opening point, it is important to state that in a fundamental sense there is an inauthenticity attached to this approach which needs to be clearly acknowledged. But this should not paralyse us into inaction.

As an example, read through the following case study that explores the notion of a 'digital native' and 'digital immigrant' in relation to the production and consumption of music. Whilst reading, looking out for references, both metaphorical and actual, to language and speech.

Case Study 2: Digital natives and immigrants

Teaching and learning in schools is changing dramatically. These changes are part of a much larger social and cultural change driven by many factors, including the use of digital technologies. But the changes go beyond the technological tools themselves. The students have changed as well, maybe not physically but in other important ways. It is hard to overestimate this change. Prensky puts it like this:

Today's students have not just changed incrementally from those of the past, nor simply changed their slang, clothes, body adornments, or styles, as has happened between generations previously. A really big discontinuity has taken place. One might even call it a singularity, an event which changes things so fundamentally that there is absolutely no going back. This so-called singularity is the arrival and rapid dissemination of digital technology in the last decades of the twentieth century.

(Prensky 2001, p. 1)

Prensky draws a useful comparison between those who are 'natives' of this digital revolution and those who are 'immigrants' (Prensky 2001, pp. 2–3). Digital natives are 'native speakers of the digital language of computers, video games and the Internet', whereas digital immigrants have been 'fascinated by and adopted many or most aspects of the new technology but always retain, to some degree, their "accent", that is, their foot in the past' (Prensky 2001, pp. 2–3). Although these distinctions are contentious and have been debated amongst educators (Owen 2006), for the purposes of this study the hypothesis was that 'digital natives' are working with new technologies in ways far beyond the experience of many 'digital immigrants' who dominate the teaching profession at the current time.

There are numerous examples of this in contemporary society. One major example concerns the way that music is produced, marketed and shared through digital tools and devices. The power of the Internet allows users immediate access to, and purchase of, music from many genres, styles and traditions. Similarly, producers of music exploit the immediate and communicative potential of the Internet to artistically shape their output. Paul Korda, in an interview with Kroeker, stated that:

File-sharing's effect on music for me, as an artist, is currency. If I record a song today about a current subject, people can hear it tomorrow, given the wide-reaching effects of the Internet. It's the richness of the here and now, bringing new ideas to life, producing them and releasing them to the people. Currency is what technology is all about, and you either move into the future with the here and now, or you live in the past.

(Kroeker 2004)

The price of technologies that allow users to create, perform and share music has fallen so greatly that it is now possible to produce music of extremely high technical quality in the home environment with a modestly equipped personal computer. Indeed, many powerful musical tools that were previously housed within the realm of the professional recording studio are now available freely over the Internet. This has had an impact on the types of spaces that music can be produced within and how this is done. Théberge (1997) has discussed the domestication of the recording studio and indicates that the home studio is essentially a private space, both physically (often in a bedroom or basement) and acoustically, with headphones being used as an 'instrument of isolation' (p. 234).

These developments continue to move on apace. Yet the consequences of young people developing their musical skills in this private and isolated world of technologically mediated musical activity for the shared and public world of classroom music has been neglected (Savage 2007b).

Prensky's notions of the digital native or immigrant have been widely debated within educational circles. His assertion that the majority of university students are digital natives has been questioned by some (Salavuo 2008). But the point here is to pick up on the reference to 'accent' in the above case study. Prensky used this term to describe the digital immigrant's approach to the use of new technologies. Although they may try hard, according to his theory they cannot shake off the 'accent' of their previous ways of working. They have, in Prensky's terms, one foot in the past which it is impossible to move.

For our discussion on how the development of cross-curricular utterances may help develop a broader approach to cross-curricular teaching and learning, I have started with a negative. In seeking to make explicit links to the subject-specific speech genres of other subjects, you will always have an accent from your own subject area that it will be difficult, if not impossible, to give up. I believe that this is part of the subject 'subjectivity' that we discussed in Chapters 1 and 2 which, as Peshkin (1988) states, is difficult to remove (p. 17). But, on reflection, perhaps this is not such a negative point to make. After all, an approach to developing a language and vocabulary that promotes cross-curricular teaching and learning should not be about blandness and mediocrity, something that makes all teachers look and sound the same. The preservation of our subject 'identity' and 'voice' should remain an important priority in ensuring our distinctiveness as teachers is not lost.

That said, there are a number of ways in which all teachers could usefully develop an approach to cross-curricular utterance that will, when done with respect and sensitivity to one's own subject culture, assist in the promotion of a cross-curricular approach to teaching and learning.

Consistency in handling the generic teaching speech genre

The first strategy in the development of a cross-curricular language in the classroom will be seeking to develop consistency with the generic teaching speech genre. In other words, if you are able to use the general language and vocabulary of teaching in a way that builds on pupils' experience of this in other subjects and areas of the curriculum, you will, by default, ensure that the teaching within your subject resonates with their wider educational experiences.

The problem with this is that, after their initial teacher education, teachers seldom, if ever, get the opportunity to visit other colleagues' classrooms (in their own subject, let alone other subjects!) and so this sense of consistency may be hard to judge. But this does not detract from the general point. If there is a consistent approach to the general teaching speech genre then pupils will make links, quite naturally, across and between subjects in constructive ways.

As an example, consider the use of the terms 'level' and 'target' in respect of pupil attainment. Imagine a situation in which, in one subject area, the levels in attainment are regularly used. In fact, they are used so regularly that within this subject they have written sub-levels to ensure that pupils' progress can be carefully monitored week by week. When pupils enter the classroom, there is a large display on the wall showing each of the levels and sub-levels, together with examples of how they develop their knowledge and understanding from one sub-level to another. As well as this, as a regular feature of each lesson pupils receive feedback from the teacher about their progress, with individual pieces of work being given a sub-level and a target being set for how it can be improved. The use of the words 'level', 'sub-level' and 'target' are an inherent part of this teacher's individual subject speech genre.

In contrast to this approach, but in the same school, a teacher in another subject has a different view about the usefulness of 'levels' and 'targets' within the context of individual lessons. For this teacher, the levels of attainment are a summative tool, something to be used at the end of each year as a way of reporting back to parents about a pupil's progress over a longer period. This teacher finds the use of levels, sub-levels and targets as part of the language and vocabulary of an individual lesson an anathema. Therefore, his choice of language relating to the assessment of individual pupils is very different. It is more exploratory and, to his mind, less mechanistic. It allows pupils a greater degree of freedom to grapple with ideas and processes rather than having to fit within predetermined models of knowledge and how these might be acquired.

Issues relating to assessment are normally contentious. I have used this example not because I want to celebrate one approach and denigrate the other. Rather, I want you to consider what the consequence of this use of language would be for the pupils who happen to be taught by both teachers. In one sense, this is quite a trite example that concerns a common educational process that all subjects have to adopt in some shape or form. There may be quite valid reasons why assessment is carried out differently in different subjects. But if these teachers were to attempt to establish cross-curricular utterances that draw upon each other's subjects and the language that underpins them within the classroom context, it may be that the discrepancies in their language use could become an unhelpful resisting force.

Approaches to technical language and vocabularies

Second, it is important that all teachers acknowledge the technical language and vocabulary sets that underpin subjects other than their own. Although a metaphorical approach to language may be helpful in identifying areas within planning that encourage cross-curricular links to be made, it will be important for all teachers to use key technical language accurately and responsibly. To do otherwise is to undermine the work done by other colleagues and shows a lack of mutual respect for other subject cultures.

At a pedagogical level, there are bound to be interesting 'borrowings' between subject cultures related to the handling of different language types or vocabularies. This is explored further in the following brief practical task.

Practical Task 3

For this task it will be necessary to work with colleagues from as many other subject areas as you can find!

For each subject area represented, write down two key technical terms that are unique to that subject area. Choose one term from the list and 'teach' it to the group using your standard, subject-based pedagogy. As you are being taught by your colleagues about their key terms, try and identify key elements of their pedagogy. To what extent are they different from you own? Are there any similarities?

Once everyone has taught one of their terms to the group, share your views about the pedagogies that have underpinned the introduction of the key terms. Identify any subject-specific as well as any common approaches.

For the final stage of the exercise, take your second key term and try teaching it to the group using one pedagogical feature drawn from a colleague's approach. In your own mind, compare and contrast the approach. If it works well, try it out in your own teaching in the near future.

Using cross-curricular utterances with questioning strategies

Many books that discuss elements of pedagogy and language talk about questioning strategies. As we have already discussed in this chapter, because pupils will know more than they can tell (Polanyi 1967, p. 4), the development of your questioning skills is particularly crucial. Skilful questioning will help you and your pupils interrogate their understanding of a particular topic. One of the most useful starting points for this is Bloom's taxonomy (Bloom 1956), a classification and labelling system of six categories of thought. Research carried out by Bloom and his team at the time found that 95% of teacher questions were at the lowest level. His classification system was revised nearly fifty years later by Anderson and Krathwohl (2001). Like Bloom, they present a hierarchy of thinking with 'creating' being at the apex of higher order thinking (Table 4.1).

For our discussion, it is interesting to hypothesise about the distinction between subject-orientated and cross-curricular dimensions of these cognitive activities. At a basic level, it appears that 'remembering' and 'understanding' could be easily applied to subject-based teaching and learning in an unproblematic way. But from the 'applying' level upwards, there seem to be more extensive opportunities for cross-curricular links, utterances or questions to be developed. In these categories, pupils are being asked to use their understanding for a particular purpose and reflect on this through a process of analysis. Of course, this could be orientated towards a specific subject, but there are opportunities here for the subject knowledge to be applied and understood elsewhere. The challenge associated with this application and analysis process would provide a useful added stimulus at this level that would probably motivate many

TABLE 4.1 Anderson and Krathwohl's taxonomy

TAXONOMY DESCRIPTOR	COGNITIVE ACTIVITY
Creating	Come up with original ideas
Evaluating	Make judgements about effectiveness
Synthesis	Use multiple understandings
Analysing	Reflecting on understanding
Applying	Use understanding
Understanding	Demonstrate they know something
Remembering	Recalling information

Source: Anderson and Krathwohl (2001, p. 27).

pupils. Things become more explicit when we reach the 'synthesis' level of cognition. Here, multiple understandings become important. Again, whilst a subject orientation would clearly work, there are opportunities for metaphorical links to be made with other subject areas. Perhaps these could then form part of any evaluative activities that are to be undertaken. Clearly, by the time we reach the 'creating' phase of cognitive activity, the opportunities for pupils to come up with original ideas in a free way that span across subjects will aid originality.

One common approach adopted to develop these questioning skills (and to avoid the easier option of always asking questions aimed at the 'remembering' and 'understanding' phases) is to make explicit use of question stems within your teaching. The list given in Table 4.2 will give you a good start as you seek to make more explicit links with the knowledge, skills and understanding underpinning other subject cultures through your own pedagogy.

Acknowledging the potential of language and literacy as common mediating devices that span subject cultures is vitally important for all teachers. Using language skilfully in the classroom is a key, generic teaching skill that teachers, at every stage in their careers, need to continually develop and refine. The potential of cross-curricular language as a tool for skilful subject teaching and cross-curricular teaching (although by now the distinctions between the two should be less obvious) is significant. This chapter has looked at a range of approaches, including handling propositional language, metaphorical language, speech genres and cross-curricular utterances. Through these approaches, it is hoped that a richer pedagogy for cross-curricular teaching and learning will emerge. This will take time to develop and, of course, it will emerge in relationship with a wider pedagogical approach (considered in detail in Chapter 3).

But language and literacy are just one part of a much broader context of teaching and learning within our schools. Our attention will now turn to another area that has exploded in significance in recent years – the development and use of ICT within teaching and learning.

TABLE 4.2 Question stems

Remembering	Describe . . .
	Describe what you are doing . . .
	Show me what you are doing . . .
	Can you remember how to . . .
	Identify . . .
	Can you recall . . .
Understanding	What is the idea behind this . . .
	Can you show me an example where you . . .
	What differences are there . . .
	What is going on at this point . . .
	Can you demonstrate ...
	Explain . . .
	Illustrate . . .
Applying	How will you go about . . .
	What will you do to . . .
	Can you think of (or show me) an instance where . . .
	How will you carry out . . .
Analysing	How might it have been different if . . .
	What happens in the bit when you . . .
	Can you explain what went on as you were doing that bit where . . .
	Compare that with . . .
	Can you distinguish between that and . . .
	Are you able to describe how you . . .
Synthesis	What would happen if you were to put your ideas together with hers . . .
	What would happen if you changed that bit where . . .
	How could you do this differently . . .
Evaluating	What was successful . . .
	What changes might you make . . .
	Can you justify why . . .
	How do you feel about . . .
	Why do you think that . . .
	Are you able to suggest how . . .
Creating	Can you come up with a solution where . . .
	Are you able to devise . . .
	Can you generate . . .
	How about a different response . . .
	What would that look like if . . .
	What would that sound like if . . .
	How would that be made up . . .
	Can you produce . . .

Source: Adapted from Savage and Fautley (2007b).

Professional Standards for QTS

This chapter will help you meet the following Q standards: Q4, Q17, Q23, Q25c

Professional Standards for Teachers

This chapter will help you meet the following core standards: C4, C17, C29d

5

ICT as a Mediating Tool for Cross-Curricular Teaching and Learning

Key objectives

By the end of this chapter, you will have:

- studied research related to the future of education and the role of ICT within it, and considered how future curriculum models might be developed that are genuinely cross-curricular and mediated through ICT;

- considered the choice and use of pieces of ICT to design and develop opportunities for cross-curricular teaching and learning;

- used techniques drawn from socio-cultural theory to help analyse and reflect on the use of ICT as a teaching and learning tool within a cross-curricular context;

- developed basic strategies for finding out more about ICT and developing your own skills with it;

- planned how to make your future teaching with ICT more effective.

Introduction

Modern technologies permeate every aspect of our lives in the twenty-first century. They present us with an opportunity to transform the ways in which we communicate, share ideas together, teach and learn. Technologies can also help us develop our thinking about subjects and curricula, reshaping our views about the principles and purposes of teaching and learning. On occasions, learning in the 'real' world, outside of the formality of schools and classrooms, is sometimes portrayed as more transparent and boundless. Without the discrete notion of subjects and curricula, learners can navigate their way seamlessly amongst and in-between subject knowledge, which, in a more formal setting, might be more difficult to achieve. Of course, such bald parallels are based on false assumptions and a narrow understanding of what happens within both contexts. But modern technologies can offer the opportunity to change. I repeat, they have *the potential* to challenge our way of thinking about subjects, curricula, teaching and learning. But this is not something that happens automatically. It requires a deliberate sense of engagement and, as with any aspect of educational practice, the critical and reflective user of technology stands a better chance of understanding and implementing effective technological change within their particular field. As this chapter unfolds, it will encourage you to become this more critical and reflective user of technology, both in the way that you use technology as a tool in your own teaching, which I hope will become increasingly cross-curricular in its 'flavour' and scope, and in the way that you design opportunities for your pupils to use technology to assist their learning. These dual aspects are reflected in the government criteria for effective teaching and learning with technology.

The Q Standards talk about the use of ICT in a number of ways. First, they emphasise the importance of your own ICT skills (Q16). This is why there is a specific skills test in ICT. Second, they also discuss the importance of your teaching enabling pupils to develop their own ICT skills. Like numeracy and literacy, these are not the preserve of ICT teachers alone. All subject teachers are required to develop these through their subject (it is part of the Functional Skills strand of the new secondary curriculum). But neither of these concerns is our main focus in this chapter. Here we will be primarily focused on Q17, which states that you will 'know how to use skills in literacy, numeracy and ICT to support your teaching and wider professional activities' (TDA 2007). This 'translation' of ICT skills and application of them in support of your teaching is an essential strand in the development of your teaching abilities. More specifically, this chapter will consider ways in which ICT can play a mediating role in linking traditional subjects together in new ways. It will also consider ICT's potential to challenge subject-orientated pedagogical processes of teaching and learning.

The introduction and application of new technologies to processes of teaching and learning have been widely researched and evaluated (Somekh 2007). It is not the purpose of this chapter to revisit all these ideas but, as has become apparent in previous chapters, a brief review of some of the referenced materials would prove beneficial for any reader unfamiliar with these developments. Here, one research project will be used to frame the broader agenda of using technology as a key component within an approach to cross-curricular teaching and learning.

'Beyond Current Horizons'

One of the most recent, and extensive, pieces of research into the future of education and technology was recently completed. 'Beyond Current Horizons' was a two-year project that drew together over 100 academics from disciplines as diverse as computer science, demography, psychology and sociology of childhood, and involved contributions from over 130 other organisations and individuals from industry, practice, policy and research. The aim of the 'Beyond Current Horizons' research project was:

> to explore the potential futures for education that might emerge at the intersection of social and technological change over the coming two decades. Its purpose is to map out current and emerging socio-technical trends, the critical uncertainties in our understanding of future socio-technical developments, and the challenges or opportunities that such developments might offer to educators.
>
> (DCSF and Futurelab 2009, p. 3)

The research was commissioned in 2007 by the Technology Futures Unit at the Department for Children, Schools and Families (DCSF). It had a broad remit to inquire into possible future trajectories for socio-technical change and to seek to understand what society might look like in 2025 in order to anticipate the demands that will be placed on the UK's education system.

To assist its research methodology, the programme developed four principles that built on a review of the existing fields of futures research and educational futures, theoretical gains from social studies of technology and insights from educational philosophy. These four principles are briefly summarised in the following sections and provide a useful context for the implications of the research for education. But in relation to this chapter's main theme, they also provide a useful focus to help us start imagining alternative uses of technology to support cross-curricular approaches to teaching and learning.

Principle 1: Educational futures work should aim to challenge assumptions rather than present definitive predictions

As the Director of the 'Beyond Current Horizons' project commented:

> Researching the future cannot simply be a case of producing a set of predictions of what 'will happen' as though this were beyond the intervention of individuals or societies. Nor can it simply be a case of discussing what we 'want' or 'will make' happen, as though there were no prior contexts to shape our actions.
>
> (Facer and Sandford 2010, p. 76)

Rather, the 'Beyond Current Horizons' researchers quote Bell (1997), who proposes that futures research can best be understood as an attempt to explore the relationships between 'possible, probable, and preferable' futures. This involves asking 'what can or could be (the possible), what is likely to be (the probable), and what ought to be (the preferable)?' (p. 73). But before seeking answers to these questions, the first task of any exploration of possible futures must be to critique the assumption that there is an inevitable future to which we must simply adapt or resist.

Within the context of our study, it is important to bear in mind that any imagined future curriculum models are similarly contextualised by assumptions, contexts and actions that are known to us today. Bell's questions are as relevant to proposed cross-curricular developments as they are to future uses of technology in education.

Critiquing the assumptions, contexts and actions that we take today in relation to current curriculum development and our pedagogies is a vital first step. The materials presented in the early part of this book have begun that process. Similarly, as you turn your consideration to your use of ICT in your subject teaching, it will be important to maintain this questioning and enquiring mindset. As we all know, technology moves on apace and things that we find hard to imagine today may well become the norm within the near future. Therefore, we need to continually question our assumptions about the future of education within this changing landscape. There are twin dangers here: first, assuming that change will not happen; second, assuming that it will happen more quickly that it does.

Principle 2: The future is not determined by its technologies

The twin dangers of assuming too much or too little are evident if one takes a retrospective view of the impact of technology in different fields. Although the history of technology is saturated by stories of unfulfilled visions (e.g. a paperless world), it is also dominated by stories of visions being realised more quickly than anticipated (e.g. the human genome project). Technological determinism in any form is worth avoiding in seeking to reconceptualise our pedagogy and practice. Facer and Sandford comment that:

> The sociology of technology, actor network theory, socio-cultural psychology, and post-structural critical theory, however, all make visible the complex relationship between technological development and social change. Although there are different positions on this spectrum, these perspectives imply an understanding of social change as a co-production of technical, discursive and social factors.
>
> (Facer and Sandford 2010, pp. 76–7)

Within our study, it is by now apparent, I hope, that technology has only one part to play in developing an approach to cross-curricular teaching and learning. An important part of this chapter will be to focus on how technology relates to those other areas that we have considered throughout this book, not least the wider development of your pedagogy in this area (Chapter 3), your developing use of language (Chapter 4), assessment and evaluation (Chapter 6).

Principle 3: Education has a range of responsibilities

The 'Beyond Current Horizons' programme saw education as responsible for:

- qualifying learners to take on certain roles (requiring the development of knowledge and competencies);
- socialising learners to participate in wider community, family and social contexts;
- equipping learners to develop their own sense of selves, identity and agency.

(DCSF and Futurelab 2009, p. 18)

The programme drew on a range of values implicit within the UK educational policy context. This included the underpinning aims of the National Curriculum as described in every subject programme of subject, namely:

The curriculum should enable all young people to become:

successful learners who enjoy learning, make progress and achieve;
confident individuals who are able to live safe, health and fulfilling lives;
responsible citizens who make a positive contribution to society.

(QCA 2007, p. 7)

It also drew upon wider historical and cross-cultural perspectives that made visible the diverse purposes and goals of education in evidence in various societies at different times (Biesta 2007).

The key point here is that, when one is thinking about change in a future educational context (e.g. the development of your cross-curricular pedagogy), it is important to understand how broader changes both within and outside education might relate to these proposed changes (in educational practices or the use of particular technologies), questioning and challenging our assumptions about the wider purposes of education. These might include processes of personal and social interaction, how individual and community identity are formed over time, or how the practices of creativity and imagination might develop over the coming years. All of these elements are key components of the early chapters. The founding principles of this book (outlined in Chapter 1) are as relevant here as anywhere.

Principle 4: Thinking about the future always involves values and politics

Conceptions about, and visions of, the future are powerful rhetorical devices (Facer and Sandford 2010, p. 77). Individuals or groups often use them to pioneer change. There are many examples one could give from the world of politics and education. At the time of writing, the UK is facing a general election. Both main political parties have argued about the nature of the curriculum that is on offer to pupils. Many writers have noted that the subject-centred curriculum may have outlived its usefulness (Bennett 2009) as other themes vie for place within timetables (e.g. personal finance, domestic violence or sex education). Other commentators and politicians argue for a more rigorous approach to the inclusion of traditional subjects within curriculum frameworks and see any weakening from this as an 'erosion of standards' (Gove 2008).

Re-imagining an approach to cross-curricular teaching and learning will, like the 'Beyond Current Horizons' project, need to empower individuals and groups to make decisions about possible future educational approaches and about the values of and aspirations for the future that underpin them. As we saw in Chapters 1 and 2, simply legislating for these approaches with a 'top-down' mentality clearly does not work. Initiative overload is as dangerous today as it was when the National Curriculum was first introduced (Sergeant 2009). Similarly, senior management decisions to force teachers to work together in collapsed curriculum days (or weeks) are not a meaningful response to the opportunity to develop authentic, rich cross-curricular pedagogies that will permeate teachers' practice throughout the year.

So, rather than simply coercing teachers towards certain pre-determined actions in the design of curricula or their pedagogy, there needs to be a careful exemplification of the origins and values underpinning the initiative being presented. This exemplificatory process needs to be accompanied by the creation of opportunities for teachers to debate and discuss the educational purposes for, and philosophy underpinning, cross-curricular approaches to teaching and learning. Teachers need to have a meaningful say in this ongoing debate, challenging and critiquing ideas so that the future shape of curriculum initiatives has a greater degree of shared ownership and, it is hoped, a wider impact. I hope that throughout the course of this book the reader has obtained a clear understanding of this particular vision for cross-curricular teaching and learning.

To summarise the important principles from this piece of futures educational research, the technologies that we propose to use in our teaching are very likely to develop over the coming years, but their impact will be dependent upon the social context, value frameworks and educational agendas that they are brought into and work alongside. New curriculum initiatives such as the development of cross-curricular approaches to teaching and learning will make different demands on teachers in their choice and use of these technologies. We will explore these below. It is vital that we maintain a critical stance in relation to these issues. Technologies do not hold all the answers to all the potential educational challenges that we will face. They are one part of a web of influences on the work of teachers. Their use is mediated by other important and powerful factors that need to be held within a careful balance. The relationship between new pedagogical approaches, and the role that technology might play within them, is often a delicate and fragile one that needs to be understood and reflected on within the context of the activity itself. This is another reason why there is no curriculum development without teacher development. Developing that reflective 'eye' and being alert to the changing practices within your own teaching are particularly important with these powerful, mediated tools. This will become a major focus as we turn to strategies to evaluate cross-curricular teaching and learning in the second half of Chapter 6.

Auditing your ICT usage

As we have discussed in the opening to this chapter, the use of digital technologies has been an important part of teaching and learning in schools across the UK over the last twenty years. But the provision of technology across schools can be patchy. New technologies have made a significant impact in some schools but less so in others. This can be the result of decisions made by senior leaders within the school in respect of funding priorities. But there are also significant differences between subject areas. These are often down to the decisions made by individual teachers about subject content, pedagogy and the choice of particular tools (resources) for teaching and learning.

In seeking to develop as a teacher and respond to the opportunities of cross-curricular teaching and learning, it will be important to consider the choice and application of digital technologies, because they can play a key role in facilitating links between traditional subjects. In particular, one will need to look beyond one's own subject (and the associated subject subjectivities associated with it) to a broader selection and use of technology. As a start, complete Practical Task 1, which asks you to focus in on your own subject usage of technology.

Practical Task 1

Audit your use of technology within your own subject area. This will include your use of pieces of technology within your formal teaching role. It will also include your pupils' informal use of any technology. In respect of your teaching, you could do this in a number of ways:

1. Survey your schemes of work or other medium- to long-term curriculum plans. Make a list of all of the pieces of technology (hardware and software) that you would use;

2. Designate a short period of time (two weeks) and keep a list of all of the pieces of technology that you use during that period within your teaching.

As a supplement to this audit, if you work within a departmental setting with other colleagues, why not take the opportunity to ask them about their use of technology and add their suggestions to your audit.

In respect of your pupils, you could consider the following questions:

1. What screen-based technologies do pupils use to develop their ideas about the subject?

2. What other non-screen-based technologies do they use?

3. How do pupils choose the technologies they use, and who or what else do they connect with through these technologies in support of their informal learning?

Reflect on the list of technology that you have collated. Categorise the items into 'general' tools (e.g. a digital camera) and 'subject specific' tools (e.g. a piece of software that allows pupils to explore Egyptian artefacts).

ICT and subject cultures: Developing cross-curricular exchanges with ICT

Practical Task 1 is relatively straightforward. It deliberately begins the process of analysing your use of ICT within your own subject area. This is probably where you are most comfortable. But, of course, the central thesis of this book is that a cross-curricular approach to teaching and learning should be empowered through a synthesis of knowledge, skills and understandings from various subject areas. This synthesis will exhibit itself in an enriched pedagogy which will promote an approach to learning that embraces and explores your own and other subject areas in a more holistic way. The argument of whether ICT can facilitate this process in any meaningful way has still to be explored. It is to this that our attention will now turn.

The notion of subject subjectivities or cultures was introduced in Chapter 2. Goodson and Mangen (1998, p. 120) define subject cultures as being 'identifiable structures which are visibly expressed through classroom organisation and pedagogical styles'. Put simply, subject cultures are the means by which a pupil knows that they are doing a specific subject at a particular point of any given day. Recent research at the University of Bristol has investigated how ICT can mediate across subject cultures. As a first step, it investigated four major dimensions across which subject cultures might differ significantly in respect of their relationship with ICT. These were:

- *'Sunk costs'* refers to the material and symbolic investments teachers have consciously or unconsciously made in conceptions of the content of the subject, its purpose, how it should be taught.
- *Modes of learning.* This refers to the characteristic processes, demonstrations and outcomes of learning within the subject culture. Equally taken for granted are what counts as success in the subject, how it is achieved and how it is known.
- *Relationship to Wider Contexts.* Subject cultures are differently situated in terms of their wider contexts and how they relate to them. The most important of these contexts are the National Curriculum and the subject's place in the pecking order of the school, both of which may impact critically on their access to and use of ICT.
- *Relationship between Technology, Pedagogy and Content.* This is the most directly relevant dimension and constitutes in some respects the sum of the others. It has been usefully seen as made up of four principles: 'teachers first; complementarity (with existing practices); workability (efficiency); and equity.

(University of Bristol 2010a)

Through the construction of Subject Design Teams, teachers and researchers collaborated together to share and discuss related research, classroom experiences, software and equipment. Sub-groups of these teams then worked together to develop learning initiatives that:

- centred on key areas within a subject domain
- incorporated a range of technologies as appropriate
- incorporated ways of taking into account students' existing knowledge
- focused on the development of a community of inquiry
- focused on learner-centred and knowledge-centred environments
- focused on problem-solving and creativity

(University of Bristol 2010b)

The findings of this study are presented online through groupings of materials produced by each Subject Design Team (University of Bristol 2010b). But a particular area of relevance for our discussion here is the influence of the teacher in incorporating ICT within their pedagogy. Yet, as we have seen throughout this book (and this will become a recurring theme in the accompanying titles within this series), using ICT to build bridges between subjects is not simple because there are a range of powerful, historical forces that mitigate against this. As John comments:

> At the core of this 'cultures in tension', the idea that the particular discourses that have dominated the educational landscape for more than a century and a half have been thrown into sharp relief by the rise of digital technologies.
>
> (John 2005, p. 471)

This tension can result in subject areas retracting and consolidating, and ICT skills being situated as part of a wider generic and functional agenda for education. In reflecting on his research within the 'InterActive Education Project', John's conclusions explore the use of a metaphor (trading zones) through which subject cultures can begin to build bridges in a cross-curricular way through the use of ICT. In the following extended quote from his paper, this metaphor is firstly introduced and then applied to our theme:

> Of central importance, however, were the ways in which the crucial 'borderlands' between the subject and ICT became transaction spaces or what Galison (1997) terms 'trading zones' where exchanges and intense collaborations took place. In Galison's (1997) book, *Image and Logic: the material culture of micro-physics*, we are able to watch the fascinating trading that takes place between the various sub-cultures of physics (theoreticians, experimentalists and engineers) and how the various traditions underpinning the sub-cultures remained intact inside the collaborations that went on among them. These collaborations produced two competing instrument cultures – image and logic – which ultimately joined. Taking his lead from anthropology, Galison (1997) observed how exchanges between sub-cultures can be compared to the incomplete and partial relations which are established when different tribes come together for trading purposes. Each tribe can bring things to the 'trading space' and take things away; even sacred objects can be offered up and exchanged. This trading process also gives rise to new contact languages which are locally understood and co-ordinated.
>
> The metaphor of 'trading zone' highlights the transient, evolving and incomplete nature of the relationship between subject sub-cultures and ICT. . . . To occupy a 'trading zone' does not mean abandoning one's 'sacred' disciplinary 'home' nor allowing the 'profane' to dominate the exchange; rather it respects subtle negotiation and accommodation (Wertsch 2003; Claxton et al., 2003) processes that encourage multiple and modified identities to emerge over time.
>
> (John 2005, pp. 485–6).

Reflective Task 1

John's argument is that trading zones of this type are characterised by certain attributes which, when fostered and developed by those involved, lead to various transfers or transactions taking place. It is worth reflecting on this argument further. In particular, the exemplification of the metaphor contains several elements that can help our thinking:

1. The element of exchange is at the centre of John's thesis. Who is involved in the exchange? What are they exchanging? When and where does the exchange take place?

2. John highlights the notion of value. What is the value of the things that are exchanged? How has that value been ascribed? How does this value affect the way in which the item that has been exchanged is acted on, or with, and understood?

3. John emphasises the provisional nature of these transactions. It is part of an evolutionary process of change within which the affordances and constraints of the situation and the ICT within it will continue to facilitate or limit the nature of future interactions or exchanges. How does this happen? How can the positive facilitative aspects be enhanced within an educational exchange of this type, and the negative limited features be minimised?

4. Finally, John's discussion argues for mutual respect in respect of all parties involved in the exchange. The process of exchange does not equate to an abandonment of one's founding principles or philosophies. Rather, through a process of subtle negotiations and accommodations the opportunity for new modified ideas can be facilitated. How can respect be maintained in cross-curricular educational exchanges? What accommodations need to be made by parties involved in these exchanges to ensure that fundamental subject principles are respected?

ICT mediated cross-curricular exchanges or interactions of the type John is anticipating are something that we can all aspire to developing. At their peak, they may lead to an opportunity for new language or discourse of cross-curricular teaching and learning to emerge, locally situated and, perhaps, of value to and understood by only those directly involved (but no less educationally valuable because of this). But this will happen only when the items that are being exchanged are of value. There are plenty of low-value exchanges being carried out between subject cultures in schools' responses to new curriculum frameworks such as the National Curriculum at Key Stage 3. These are characterised by pieces of curriculum development that merge subjects down to their lowest common denominators, which underplay the well-established strengths of subject cultures and replace them with hastily constructed curriculum components or competencies, and which disempower teachers and cut short the development of their own, unique cross-curricular pedagogy through imposed, disrespectful and crass curriculum exchanges. In contrast, high-value cross-curricular exchanges will result in meaningful curriculum development because they are centred on attributes that underpin ongoing teacher development.

I would suggest that, in a similar way to what has been proposed in respect of integrating ICT within schools, for this high-value cross-curricular exchange process to work, schools are going to need time to adjust, explore and engage with these transactional processes between subjects. Of course, Chapter 1 highlighted the lessons from previous attempts to implement a broader cross-curricular approach to teaching and learning. Time was precisely one of the elements that was missing from those early attempts. However, my argument here is that much of the work needed to facilitate this cross-curricular exchange mediated through ICT is situated within the individual teacher's pedagogy (my third key principle for this book; see the opening of Chapter 1). To that end, if you can see the value of an activity as both beneficial to your ongoing professional development and important for curriculum development there is a greater opportunity for engagement, exploration and implementation with smaller-scale, classroom-focused applications of these ideas.

Practical Task 2

This task will require you to work with a colleague within a subject area different from your own.

In our application of the findings from the 'InterActive Education Project', we have developed the notion of cross-curricular exchange mediated through ICT. Working with a colleague from another curriculum area, you are going to explore how these exchanges might be developed through an analysis of two factors that will implicate your teaching and learning: first, where you teach; and second, teacher- or learner-centred approaches using ICT within subject teaching.

For each factor, complete the exercise independently from your colleague. Following completion, meet together and discuss your responses. Try to identify any common elements. Which elements could form the basis for cross-curricular pedagogical exchanges?

1. Compare and contrast the ways in which you might teach your subject in two different locations, e.g. your own classroom and a specialist computer room. What difference does the location make to the pedagogy that you can adopt within your teaching? How are the opportunities for meaningful cross-curricular exchanges encouraged or constrained within each setting? More generally, how does the location of ICT resources affect teaching and learning within your subject?

2. Compare and contrast your approach to a particular sequence of learning with a piece of ICT with that to a similar piece of learning without. What differences do you notice? In particular, focus on the ways that you and your pupils would use the piece of ICT in the first approach. What are these replaced with in the second approach? Have you been able to identify any differences in your pedagogy within these two approaches? Which do you feel is more effective? Why?

To summarise, traditional subject cultures need to be acknowledged. They are an important component of the teaching and learning context that all teachers face. ICT presents an opportunity for mediation between these subject cultures. This can be done effectively or ineffectively. The notion of cross-curricular exchanges between subjects, mediated through ICT, is desirable but these exchanges need to be based on mutual respect between subjects, acknowledging the provisional nature of their transactions and, preferably, containing items of value. These ideas are challenging and will need time to be implemented fully. But there are approaches that can help you develop a more analytical approach to working within and beyond your subject area. The next part of this chapter will revisit one important concept that can help us to do this better: mediated action.

ICT and mediated action

The previous section of this chapter focused on the development of cross-curricular exchanges mediated by ICT.

Wertsch's notion of 'mediated action' was introduced briefly in Chapter 4 in relation to language and its use as a key component in cross-curricular teaching and learning. But Wertsch's own exposition of the theme of 'mediated action' draws on many examples of technology, including the QWERTY keyboard. Another one of these is rather surprising and comes from the athletics field.

Pole-vaulting has a long history (Rosenbaum 2009). The first known pole-vault competitions were held during the Irish Tailteann Games, which date back as far as 1829 BC. The sport was an original modern Olympic event in 1896. Central to the sport of pole-vaulting is the pole! As such, Wertsch uses it as an example tool, a type of technology. But in the history of pole-vaulting, this tool and the materials from which it has been made have been the source of many problems for the sport.

Early poles were made of wood. They were probably just large sticks or tree limbs. In the nineteenth century competitors used wooden poles, but these were replaced by bamboo (lighter) prior to the Second World War. Subsequent developments saw the emergence of metal poles (stronger). Today, the modern athlete has the benefit of carbon-fibre and fibreglass composite poles (which are lighter, stronger and more flexible). Despite the changes in the materials used to make the pole, the aim of pole-vaulting has remained the same: to get over the highest possible barrier. In 1896, the first time that pole-vaulting was included in the Olympic Games, William Hoyt won with a leap of 3.30 metres; the current world record of 6.14 metres was set by Sergey Bubka in 1994.

Wertsch's more detailed account of these developments charts the various rivalries and factions within pole-vaulting that emerged at transition points surrounding the adoption of new poles (Wertsch 1998, pp. 27–8). At one point these even included the possibility of breakaway groups favouring particular types of poles, and accusations that users of new types of poles were cheating. The history of pole-vaulting itself distinguishes between the various 'eras' of particular poles (On Track and Field 2009).

As a tool, Wertsch argues, the pole is essential to pole-vaulting. It mediates the action between the athlete (the agent) and the goal of hurtling over the barrier at the highest possible height (the context). He goes on to explore, through the use of socio-cultural analysis, the relationship between human actions and the cultural, institutional and historical contexts in which these actions occurs. In our context, teachers or pupils are the 'agents' (to use Wertsch's terminology), the 'cultural tools' are the technologies we are choosing to use, and the context would be, at least in a simple application of his work, the classroom or other learning spaces where pupils can work informally. Wertsch calls the interplay between agents, tools and contexts 'mediated action'.

Wertsch's key message here is that all human action is mediated action. Applying this to our discussion, all teaching and learning involves mediated action. Our teaching is mediated by the tools that we choose to use; our pupils' formal and informal learning is mediated by the tools they choose to use. As we saw in Chapter 4, these tools will include our language, but they will also include things such as the curriculum framework we are working within, a chosen pedagogy that we choose to adopt or, as we are discussing here, particular pieces of technology. The educational goals that we, or pupils, establish exist within this wider conceptual framework of mediated action. So, just as you can jump higher in pole-vaulting with certain types of poles, you can aim for different educational goals through the effective use of some technologies or tools. Similarly, it may be possible to aim for more challenging and complex teaching and learning if the technologies or tools that you have chosen to use take care of basic, lower-level functions or issues. The point here is that these tools exist within a wider relationship of teaching, learning and cognitive processes. The teacher's key role will be seeking to exploit the possible educational affordances offered through these relationships.

Wertsch goes on to list the ten key principles of mediated action. These are summarised in Table 5.1, together with a further sentence of explanation taken from later in his book that will aid your understanding of the concept.

The argument here is that by analysing the technologies we are using in our subject area through the concept of mediated action we will be able to build a firm foundation from which we can extend our teaching approach towards a cross-curricular model. As we have seen in Chapter 3, this will include working from within our subject and drawing on other curriculum areas, as well as making explicit collaborative links with other curriculum subjects or curriculum dimensions (we might call this teaching 'inside out' and teaching 'outside in'). Case Study 1 provides an interesting example of this, drawn from the theory surrounding online learning.

TABLE 5.1 Wertsch's ten principles of mediated action

1.	Mediated action is characterised by an irreducible tension between agent and mediational means	Cultural tools are powerless to do anything. They can have their impact only when an agent *uses* them (p. 30)
2.	Mediational means are material	The external, material properties of cultural tools have important implications for understanding how internal processes come into existence and operate (p. 31)
3.	Mediated action typically has multiple simultaneous goals	Mediated action is often organised around multiple, and often conflicting, goals due to the fact that the goals of the agent do not map neatly onto the goals with which the mediational means are typically associated (p. 34)
4.	Mediated action is situated on one or more developmental paths	Agents, cultural tools, and the irreducible tension between them, always have a particular past and are always in the process of undergoing further change (p. 34)
5.	Mediation means constrain as well as enable action	Mediated action can be empowering and enabling. But it can also 'constrain or limit the forms of action we undertake' (p. 37)
6.	New mediational means transform mediated action	The dynamics of change caused by introducing new cultural tools in mediated action are often quite powerful and all too easily escape notice (pp. 42–3)
7.	The relationship of agents toward mediational means can be characterised in terms of mastery	The emphasis is on how the use of particular cultural tools leads to the development of particular skills rather than on generalised abilities or aptitudes (p. 46)
8.	The relationship of agents toward mediational means can be characterised in terms of appropriation (i.e. taking something that belongs to others and making it one's own)	Appropriation always involves resistance of some sort. Cultural tools are often not easily and smoothly appropriated by agents. Some form of resistance or friction is the rule rather than the exception (pp. 54–5)
9.	Mediational means are often produced for reasons other than to facilitate mediated action	Most of the cultural tools we employ were not designed for the purposes to which they are being put (p. 59)
10.	Mediational means are associated with power and authority	Where is power and authority situated? A focus on mediated action and the cultural tools employed in it makes it possible to 'live in the middle' and to address the socio-cultural situatedness of action, power, and authority (p. 65)

Source: Wertsch (1998).

Case Study 1: The pedagogical applications of ICT: An example from the theory of online learning

To illustrate one of the approaches to the selection, use and analysis of ICT in teaching and learning through mediated action, we are going to consider a specific example of ICT use that spans across individual subjects: the construction of an approach to online learning. Approaches to online learning is something that has grown exponentially in recent years. Recent developments in schools have seen every pupil having access to a virtual learning environment of some sort. This has not been without its problems, partly because the theory that underpins online learning has not really been applied with the degree of rigour needed to effect substantial change. As a result, online learning environments are often used as a 'bolt on' to traditional curriculum tools or opportunities, rather than being transformational in any meaningful way. Anderson and Elloumi (2004) present this theme in their interesting study. But first, they recognise the socio-cultural links between learning online and other approaches:

> Learning and teaching in an online environment are, in many ways, much like teaching and learning in any other formal educational context: learners' needs are assessed; content is negotiated or prescribed; learning activities are orchestrated; and learning is assessed.
>
> (Anderson and Elloumi 2004, p. 273)

They quickly move on to consider some of the key differences that an online learning environment can provide:

> However, the pervasive effect of the online medium creates a unique environment for teaching and learning. The most compelling feature of this context is the capacity for shifting the time and place of the educational interaction. Next comes the ability to support content encapsulated in many formats, including multimedia, video, and text, which gives access to learning content that exploits all media attributes. Third, the capacity of the Net to access huge repositories of content on every conceivable subject, including content created by the teacher and fellow students, creates learning and study resources previously available only in the largest research libraries, but now accessible in every home and workplace. Finally, the capacity to support human and machine interaction in a variety of formats (text, speech, video, etc.) in both asynchronous and synchronous modalities creates a communications-rich learning context.
>
> (Anderson and Elloumi 2004, pp. 273–4)

As an aside, there is an interesting reference in the above quotation to the power of the Internet in providing access to the knowledge base of 'every conceivable subject' including that created by teachers and pupils. This, as we will see below, is not without its difficulties. But, in a final quote from their work on online learning, Anderson and Elloumi consider the role of the teacher in this type of environment:

In a work on teaching presence, Anderson, Rourke, Archer, and Garrison (2001) delineated three critical roles that a teacher performs in the process of creating an effective teaching presence. The first of these roles is the design and organization of the learning experience that takes place both before the establishment of the learning community and during its operation. Second, teaching involves devising and implementing activities to encourage discourse between and among students, between the teacher and the student, and between individual students and groups of students and content resources (Anderson, 2002). Third, the teaching role goes beyond that of moderating the learning experiences when the teacher adds subject matter expertise through a variety of forms of direct instruction. The creation of teaching presence is not always the sole task of the formal teacher. In many contexts, especially when teaching at senior university level, teaching presence is delegated to or assumed by students as they contribute their own skills and knowledge to the developing learning community.

(Anderson and Elloumi 2004, p. 274)

The article presents an interesting example of how teaching and learning in an online learning environment can be analysed. It has been chosen for discussion here because many of the defining characteristics of mediated action are apparent. As an example, the authors demonstrate how learning in an online environment is not discreet or separate from learning in a traditional classroom. There are patterns of behaviour on the part of the teacher and pupil that will be similar. The communicative patterns that occur within traditional and online learning spaces will also have common features. To that extent, the journey of teaching and learning from traditional classrooms into online spaces is one that needs to be charted carefully by those involved (Wertsch's fourth characteristic of mediated action). By doing this, a fuller understanding of the cognitive processes that teachers and learners will bring into that new space (the second characteristic of mediated action) will emerge.

Moving on to the role of the teacher, Anderson and Elloumi recognise that, as in a traditional learning space, the teacher 'presence' is an integral part of the design of, and opportunity for, learning within the online learning environment. This is related not just to the virtual interactions that will occur within the online learning space between teachers and pupils, but also to the design and the functionality that the space itself affords. Notions of power and authority come into play here (the first and tenth characteristics of mediated action). The decisions that the designer of the online learning space has made will be felt by all users. This can prove problematic, particularly when the affordances of other online spaces (e.g. spaces used for social interaction or entertainment) may be preferred by users, or seen as more facilitative. The visibility or invisibility of the teacher within the online space (in terms of its design and use) will be an important component of how pupils learn within that space.

Reflective Task 2

Wertsch provides a very rich framework of ideas to consider in relation to the use of ICT in teaching and learning. In the following exercise, you are going to be asked to choose a particular piece of ICT that you identified in Practical Task 1 and answer a range of questions about it (the tool) and your (the agent) use of it in the classroom (the context). In doing so, you will be considering how your action as a teacher is being mediated.

Choose a particular piece of technology that you have used in your teaching. This could be a piece of hardware or software. Using the questions in Table 5.2 that relate directly to Wertsch's ten characteristics of mediated action, construct a wider understanding of the impact that the piece of technology may have on the processes of teaching and/or learning. You are undertaking a socio-cultural analysis of your use of a particular tool through mediated action! If possible, find another student or colleague who is using a similar piece of technology in their teaching and compare your approaches. You will find differences. Why?

Mediating technologies across the curriculum

The tools of socio-cultural analysis can give you powerful insights into how you choose, design and use particular pieces of technology in your work. As we have explored, the use of a particular piece of technology implicates and mediates the action that is taken with it. The early part of this chapter has sought to develop an understanding of this socio-cultural perspective from the standpoint of your own subject. It is now time to extend this approach to other areas of the curriculum. As we have discussed in Chapter 3, this can happen in two ways. Whether you are seeking to extend your own pedagogy through the adoption of a more cross-curricular approach (teaching 'inside out'), or to work collaboratively with other colleagues (teaching 'outside in'), the same issues will emerge. Certain tools will offer a range of affordances for cross-curricular teaching and learning. One of the keys points here is learning how can one assess the value of these.

Using common tools across subject areas

First of all, and perhaps most obviously, there will be a range of common tools that are in use across multiple subject areas within the school. Technologies such as digital video cameras, digital cameras, presentational software and word processors are good examples of these. As these technologies are in wide use, they present a good opportunity to explore a broader, cross-curricular approach to their use.

As an example, we will consider one of these tools, the digital camera. As a generic tool (i.e. one not designed with a particular subject in mind) this piece of technology has many potential affordances across a range of subjects. It is also a technology that many pupils will be familiar with through incorporation of its functionality within mobile phones. What are the consequences of this within our teaching?

TABLE 5.2 Key questions for Reflective Task 2

WERTSCH'S KEY POINT	KEY QUESTIONS
1.	How do you use a piece of ICT? How does your use of it give it 'power'? What type of power results and how is that power evidenced within the classroom?
2.	How does the external property of a piece of ICT affect the internal mental processes by which we use it? How are these mental processes informed and developed as we begin to use the particular piece of technology?
3.	Does the piece of technology, and its particular uses, fit neatly within the teaching context that you are using it for? Do you have to 'force' it to fit or do its design and function work naturally with the process of teaching and learning you are seeking to develop?
4.	What is the 'history' of the particular piece of technology that you are seeking to use? How might this affect your use of it today? Can you anticipate any problems? How might the technology develop further, particularly as you apply it within the teaching and learning context?
5.	How does the piece of ICT enhance the opportunities for teaching and learning in your subject? How does it constrain them?
6.	What evaluative or assessment processes can you build in to your use of the piece of ICT to ensure that you are fully aware of the impact that it is making in the classroom?
7.	What are the specific skills you are hoping that the piece of ICT will facilitate? What would 'mastery' of the technology look like, in terms of your teaching or your pupils' use of it?
8.	If 'appropriation always involves resistance of some sort', what does the use of a piece of technology resist against? What causes the friction? How could this be 'smoothed out'?
9.	Questions here relate to (3) and (8) above. How many of the technologies that you are using were specifically designed for the educational context? Even if they are, do not presume that they will fit naturally within your classroom context. What preparatory work can you do to ensure a 'best fit' in relation to the other cultural tools that are at work?
10.	What are the competing sources of 'power' and 'authority' at work within your classroom? How does the power and authority associated with a piece of technology play out with these other sources?

Within the curriculum planning that you are doing, it will be important to ask what role you perceive the digital camera will play. It may be used as a device to collect digital materials (e.g. photographs of a geographical feature; documentary evidence from a historical artefact; or sample material for an artistic project). But the digital camera might be used for assessment purposes (e.g. to provide evidence of pupils' group work in a drama or dance activity). Or it might have a more formative assessment use, as part of pupils' peer or self-assessment within a collection of reflective data within an e-portfolio of evidence for physical education. The digital camera may also be the focus of a project itself within the design and technology or art curriculum.

Here, pupils may be learning how to use a digital camera more effectively, or studying technical issues such as the use of different exposure settings or artistic issues such as how to frame a photograph or the use of different perspectives.

It would also be beneficial to explore with pupils what roles they envisage the digital camera might play. The different perceptions that people have about a particular tool will shape their potential use of it. In theoretical terms, mediated action shows us that the affordances of a tool (i.e. the beneficial processes that it facilitates) are as much about the agent's perception as they are about the actual tool itself. In our example, if we want to get the most out of the digital camera as a tool within our teaching, it will be important to acknowledge not only that its use spans across many subjects (and different teachers will have different perceptions of its usefulness and application) but also that the perceptions of pupils, as agents within the learning process facilitated by mediated action, will shape the educational possibilities that it affords.

This broad range of activity across the curriculum, but all supported by this one piece of technology, presents a good opportunity for developing a cross-curricular approach within your teaching. Although you might not be an expert in using a digital camera yourself, it will be important that you are aware of the range of work that is going on, and that you prepare yourself to make the links with other curriculum or educational uses of the technology explicit in your work with the pupils. For example, if you are asking pupils to use the camera as a means to collect evidence for an assessment that you are undertaking, try to adopt a similar routine for the collection and storage of the digital photographs that might be used elsewhere. Perhaps pupils have been taught a system for naming the resulting digital files within their ICT lessons. Make sure that you are aware of what this is and use the same system within your lessons. In art lessons, pupils may have considered aesthetic issues related to framing a photograph, the impact of light or colour on a particular shot or how objects are placed together for an expressive affect. Whatever subject you may be teaching, try and ensure that pupils are using the technology in ways that reinforce their learning with the same tool in other subject areas. This cross-curricular approach should seek to make it easier for pupils to transfer experience and expertise from one subject area into another, rather than creating boundaries that limit this type of knowledge exchange. In this way you will be reinforcing lessons that pupils have received from other teachers in a helpful manner.

Finally, do not forget that many pupils will have experience of using this piece of technology in their wider lives. Perhaps not many of them will be expert photographers, but most of them will use their mobile phones as digital cameras and will be enthusiastic about their use of these to document their attendance at sporting or entertainment events, or to take pictures of their friends and social activities for use on social networking sites. This presents us with an opportunity to link to broader uses of this type of technology. Instead of asking pupils to write down their homework task, why not consider letting them take a picture of the whiteboard instead? Rather than asking pupils to search through Google Images illustrations for a piece of project work, why not ask them to devise and shoot their own image using their mobile phones and bring that into school or upload it to an appropriate folder on the school network?

The example of the digital camera can be extended to other pieces of common technology used in all subjects. Although some subjects may claim a greater 'hold' over a piece of technology, exploiting the various uses of a common tool across a range of subjects within your own subject teaching can be a straightforward way to bring an extra, cross-curricular element to your teaching.

Using subject-specific tools in new ways

As part of Practical Task 1 you listed the common types of technology that are in use within your subject area. Having done that, you categorised them into generic and subject-specific tools. As we have seen, generic tools used across various curriculum subjects can provide a useful stimulus for a cross-curricular approach within a specific curriculum subject. Can subject-specific tools be used in this way too?

At first, this may not seem so obvious. If a particular technology is focused in one particular subject area, surely it cannot be easily translated into another? But this approach is putting the cart (the technology) before the horse (the subject). Outside of the educational system, with its subject divisions, there are often creative overlaps between areas of knowledge and the tools that support them.

Several examples can be given. By their nature, these examples are more subject specific than the example given above. The point here is not to go into a lot of depth about these specific subject contexts, but rather to make some general principles that can be taken and applied to whatever subject area you represent. More specific subject examples will be followed up in the companion titles within this series.

Within the music curriculum there are various pieces of software that pupils can use to create musical compositions. Some of these pieces of software rely on what might be called 'traditional' musical skills, for example being able to play a musical keyboard. If you visit the music classroom in your school it is more than likely that you will find a number of computer workstations with musical keyboards placed in front of them. If this is the case they are almost certainly using a piece of software called a sequencer to help pupils compose music in this way. But this is not the only way that pupils can learn to make music. Other pieces of music software borrow ideas, metaphors and 'ways of working' from other curriculum areas. In the following case study, the justification for the choice of a particular piece of software for use in Key Stage 3 and 4 music lessons came from the long historical links between music and the visual arts.

Case Study 2: Mixing compositional metaphors

The relationship between music and the visual image is long established in artistic practice generally, extending back through the centuries:

> Composers and painters alike have frequently gleaned new ideas from an approximation to, or borrowings from, procedures used in the sibling art. This reciprocal relationship runs like a continuous thread through the entire [twentieth] century.
>
> (Maur 1999, p. 8)

Perhaps one of the most famous and obvious examples of a painter considering musical themes is Paul Klee, for whom music 'was the one discipline of art above all others that inspired profound insight' and showed him 'the innermost essence of nature, not a reproduction of it' (Düchting 2002, p. 88). But throughout the entire twentieth century the symbiotic artistic processes and conversations between the visual artist and the composer are apparent for all to see (and hear):

> There are no dividing walls between the arts. Music combines within itself poetry and painting and has its own architecture.
>
> (Ciurlionis 1998, p. 53)

> Colour is the key, the eye is the hammer, the soul is the piano with its many strings.
>
> (Kandinsky 1947, p. 64)

The contemporary practice of sound design, in which composers produce music and sound effects for film, television, computer games, theatre and much more besides, could be thought of as being 'the painting of sound'. It is not surprising that sound designers talk about their work with sounds by way of visual metaphors. For example, Andrew Diey talks about the brush strokes of his compositional style:

> I feel that sound design is an area in which you can either paint with very large strokes or very fine strokes. You can go as deep as you like and put as much detail in as required. Or you can just paint with broad strokes.
>
> (Andrew Diey in interview with the author, 2004)

or the relationship between the choice of sounds and particular colours:

> The overall feel and colour of the movie is washed out colours, lots of blues and dark sort of deep browns and things like that. So it automatically suggests a sort of cold feel to the actual sound itself. There's not much warmth in the colour so I have to reflect that in my choice of sound.
>
> (Andrew Diey in interview with the author, 2004)

The choice of which software I use with pupils at Key Stages 3 and 4 has been influenced by these ideas. I've chosen software that has an explicitly graphical, artistic interface. Pieces of software such as Metasynth have been useful. This allows pupils to draw in sound in an amazing way. But even with more conventional music software, I've found that there are ways of encouraging pupils to use metaphors from the visual arts as a way to get them composing. One example is to ask pupils to 'paint' sounds within the grid edit[1] function of sequencing software (Figure 5.1).

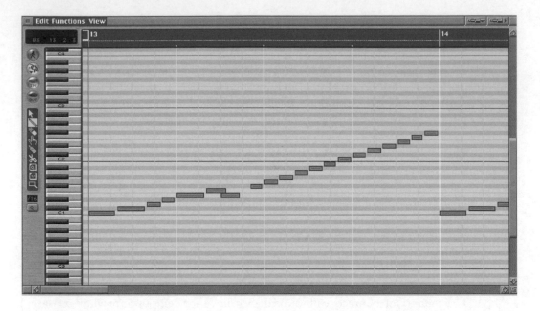

FIGURE 5.1 A typical grid editor from a music sequencer.

This case study is interesting because the teacher has drawn on a historical precedent for his pedagogical approach. This has forged his interest in developing a cross-curricular pedagogy with the visual arts through the selection of particular software tools.

Other approaches are more pragmatic. In the next case study, this ICT teacher talks about using common functions found with various pieces of software to help pupils think through a storyboard for a film.

Case Study 3: Making links with common software processes

Earlier in the year I began to reconsider my approach to teaching pupils about editing digital video. Up until this point, I think my approach would have best been described as 'traditional'. We took a standard piece of software such as Movie Maker[2] and got pupils to edit a piece of video that we provided into a short sequence.

Although this approach taught the pupils some technical skills in Movie Maker, it didn't seem to tap into their creativity. As part of the new National Curriculum we have been asked to provide opportunities for pupils to work creatively and collaboratively, and to try to forge links with other subjects. This is part of the Curriculum Opportunities statement within the National Curriculum.

I began to rethink my curriculum. I looked at some of the software processes that I was trying to get pupils to engage with through the project. One key process was that of 'cut, copy and paste'. These are common controls in many other pieces of software, e.g. word processors. This got me thinking about the video project and the possibility of including a narrative element, such as a short story.

I chatted with one of my English teaching colleagues. She talked me through some of the ways that they teach pupils to structure a large text. Part of this involved using a word processor to cut, copy and paste chunks of text into different orders. She also mentioned the way that writers use signposting-type sentences to guide the reader through a text.

This seemed like a really good approach for my digital video project. So, what's changed? Well, now pupils plan out a short digital video sequence using a word processor-based storyboard similar to that which they would use in an English lesson. They use the 'cut, copy and paste' function in the word processor to help sequence their ideas. Having done that, they shoot some video using a digital video camera and import it into the new iMacs running iMovie. As before, the editing processes are undertaken within the software, with pupils making similar choices using the cut, copy and paste functions but this time with the video (and audio) material.

The project involves them collaborating with each other more than they would have done. They also get more of a chance to be creative both in their storyboards and in the types of digital materials that they can collect and put together into their final short video story.

As these case studies have shown, using technologies that are common across all curriculum subjects and those that have specific uses in particular subjects can help you make cross-curricular links within your teaching. The accompanying titles to this book present numerous other examples of how technology can enhance this cross-curricular approach. Many go into significant detail about how particular subject cultures can be combined to great effect.

Practical Task 3

This task relies on you working with a teaching colleague from another subject area.

Each of you should choose a piece of technology that falls within the 'subject specific' type as outlined in Practical Task 1. This could be a piece of hardware or software.

Individually, think about your current use of this piece of technology. Jot down a few notes about typical uses of it that you or your pupils make within your classes

Introduce your chosen piece of technology to your colleague. Give them a very brief introduction to the technology, show them what it can do and use your notes to talk about how you or your pupils use it in your classes. Get them to do the same for their piece of technology.

Think about your colleague's piece of technology. What advice could you give about how to extend their use of that tool within their classes? Are there elements of your subject pedagogy that could be usefully applied and developed to your colleague's piece of technology? Think back through the issues we have considered in Chapters 3 and 4 for pointers if needed.

Finally, compare experiences related to the wider context within which these pieces of technology are used. This could relate to the ways that pupils are grouped within your subject when using the piece of technology, the types of tasks that pupils undertake with the piece of technology, other teaching resources that you use alongside the technology, any other instructional materials that you might use, or informal learning that the pupils may undertake in settings outside the classroom that relates to the piece of technology that you have chosen.

Curriculum collaborations and the use of ICT

But the same issues arise when teachers are seeking to collaborate with each on larger curriculum projects, involving several traditional curriculum areas. Within this setting, technology can mediate between subjects and become a key point for collaborative project work. In the following case study, pupils in a small class at a high school in south-west Manchester are creating a film from an assembly of digital materials that they have collected from their local environment. The school is for pupils who have been excluded from mainstream schooling; all pupils have statements related to their emotional, behavioural or other learning difficulties. At the point at which we pick up the story, pupils are working on their collected digital materials in a computer suite.

Case Study 4: Curriculum collaborations with ICT

I observed the pupils compiling collections of digital photographs, short video sequences, musical elements and other materials sourced from the Internet into short film segments. They did this in different ways. Some searched through collections of materials that they had assembled. Having found appropriate material for their film segment, students manipulated it in a variety of ways. For photographic material, this included using some of the basic tools in Photoshop, including cropping and panning techniques. For video materials, students used iMovie or Movie Maker to select the start and end points of particular video clips, add basic digital effects, and insert transitions between photos or video clips. The majority of students also produced narrative elements such as titles or occasional words and sentences in order to structure their film. Many of the students used the Internet to search for accompanying pieces of film footage, sound effects or music to use within their films. This produced some very interesting artistic juxtapositions that pupils found inspiring, allowing them to move their creative work forward quickly and purposefully.

As I walked around the classroom I took the opportunity to talk to several pupils. Most were happily engaged in the above activities and were concentrating hard on their work. This was impressive. All pupils within the school have emotional, behavioural or other learning difficulties (hence their referral to the school). But there was no lack of attention in this class! Several pupils commented that they had used their mobile phones to grab images, sounds and videos during the weekend prior to this class. They talked enthusiastically about how they shared these digital materials with their friends informally through sites such as YouTube. The links between this informal learning with their mobile phones were being acknowledged and built up helpfully by the teacher.

At the end of the lesson pupils were asked to talk about the work they had completed. Given the small number of pupils in the class every pupil had an opportunity to discuss what they had done and show a clip from their film. The teacher used a video camera to record these short presentations. He said that trying to get pupils to write about their work was difficult. For the purposes of assessment (these pupils were studying for a GCSE in Expressive Arts), regular video recordings of this type were included within individual pupil's e-portfolios. This way of working suited the pupils better and led to far less challenging behaviour.

In what was a successful piece of collaborative cross-curricular project work within the Expressive Arts curriculum, the use of ICT helped pupils bring together their ideas, work across a range of traditional curriculum areas and produce a number of successful short films. But there were two thoughts that struck me as I reviewed my visit.

The first of these related to the pedagogy of the teacher in the session I observed. It reminded me of another story, this time from the United States, of young people working with iMovie. Schoonmaker's (2009) account highlights the difficulty of adopting the 'right' pedagogical approach to the use of ICT. He picks up on phrases first developed by Prensky (2001) – digital native and digital immigrant – to describe a difference in mindset between those bought up with digital technologies and those who 'adopt' them but retain their 'accent' of a previous age. These thoughts are picked up at the end of his case study. Having recounted a situation in which a teaching colleague (Brad) wanted to give the students printed instructions to follow to help them learn about iMovie, he comments that:

> Digital Immigrant teachers assume that learners are the same as they have always been, and that the same methods that worked for the teachers when they were students will work for their students now. But that assumption is no longer valid. Today's learners are different. Is it that Digital Natives can't pay attention, or that

they choose not to? Often from the Natives point of view their Digital Immigrant instructors make their education not worth paying attention to compared to everything else they experience – and then they blame them for not paying attention!

In the 15 years I had been working with digital natives, I realized that I had managed to sufficiently sand down my immigrant accent. These natives wouldn't need printed instructions to refer to after the training session. They would need the time to explore and experiment. When I told Brad this, he was at first surprised, but as he watched the kids relishing the new frontier of video editing ahead of them, it made sense: "If 4th, 5th and 6th graders can get it this easily, I have some rethinking to do with my high schoolers."

At the risk of over-romanticizing the ascent of digital natives, they are in fact learners in need of teachers with timeless lessons. The question is, will teachers put the effort in to engaging with young learners in ways that fit their newly acquired and very different learning styles? If so, teachers must focus on their learning as much as their teaching.

(Schoonmaker 2009)

Within Case Study 4, much greater attention had been paid to ensuring that pupils' work with these digital technologies inspired and motivated them. The pedagogy adopted by the teacher allowed them the time and space to choose and use particular technologies within the formal classroom in a way that built on their experiences with a range of other technologies (e.g. mobile phones, YouTube, etc.) through their informal learning. This enhanced the pupils' whole educational experience.

The second thought that remained with me after my visit relates directly to our theme of cross-curricular teaching and learning. In Case Study 4 the teachers and pupils were working within an explicit, cross-curricular framework mediated by the GCSE in Expressive Arts specification. In that sense there is a clear licence for cross-curricular artistic practices that draw on at least two specific, individual art forms. By comparison, in projects that seem to be increasing in popularity, the subject dimensions of the curriculum are being collapsed in order to allow pupils to work on what are commonly called 'competency' curricula. This type of 'curriculum development' is structured around competency statements and these inform the types of activities that pupils undertake and the way that they are assessed.

My worry is that, within pieces of curriculum development of this type, the perspectives of individual subjects seem to be undervalued, not in an explicit or deliberate way, but rather through a general sense of other things being more important (perhaps by unintentional neglect). To return to the types of activities recounted in Case Study 4, the lack of subject components within a cross-curricular framework such as this could be educationally devastating. These might include:

- the artistic dimension of using these digital tools (which an art specialist could have provided) being underdeveloped;
- the skills required to construct a strong narrative throughout a film (which could have been provided by an English specialist) being weakened;

- the impact of sound and music within the film (something that a music specialist could have contributed to the project) not being considered.

Curriculum initiatives that seek to collapse the long-standing subject divisions in the secondary curriculum (whether for one day or for one term) need to consider very carefully what they are replacing them with. This is not an argument in favour of rigid subject approaches at all times and within all schools. Rather, there is a richer, cross-collaborative approach that it should be possible to initiate, develop and maintain when teachers start with their own practice and make links from that, rather than having to respond to top-down, formulaic curriculum development (whether that be something which is developed within schools or in response to wider policy initiatives).

Developing your use of ICT

Earlier in the chapter we spent some time considering how to apply Wertsch's idea of mediated action to the choice and use of a specific piece of ICT. Following that, we considered a range of examples from online learning to using digital cameras and different pieces of software to help develop our use of ICT in facilitating a cross-curricular approach to teaching and learning. This leads on to a slightly different, but very important, related question. By way of a brief detour, we will consider how you can develop your own use of ICT in your subject teaching.

Under the interesting title 'Retooling or Renaissance?', a Futurelab report has investigated how teachers learn with technology:

Change is now a constant condition in our education system, reflecting changes in the wider world. This has implications for teacher identity and role. What sort of teacher development is needed in order to keep pace with such change? We have to ask ourselves whether we want a mere 'retooling' of teacher competencies for specific purposes, or an approach that supports a renaissance in teacher development for an uncertain future. This is not about making an industrial process more efficient; rather, it is about enabling cultural change in the profession.

(Futurelab 2006, p. 39)

The discussion continues and identifies a range of features that this 'cultural change' will need to build on:

Thus, an environment for renaissance in teacher development will often include new content, which is sometimes necessary but is, alone, never sufficient for professional growth. At its heart, such an environment for CPD will necessarily offer: structured dialogue and reflection; human presence, experience and memory; and an action-researching orientation.

To such an environment, digital technologies can contribute enhanced opportunities for knowledge building, communication, distributed cognition, and engagement. . . . Thus, schools of the future will need a clear sense of the kinds of teacher professionalism and teacher learning they wish to support, in order to make wise and informed decisions about the role of digital technologies in the CPD process.

(Futurelab 2006, p. 39)

The Futurelab report argues for a change in approach to teachers' professional development. It suggests that, in respect of digital technologies, there is little research about how teachers might learn to use them. Rather, there is a pervasive assumption that they will. The report highlights that the single biggest challenge to teachers' learning about how to use digital technologies in their teaching is the time required to develop their individual skills and confidence.

So, given that the research about how teachers learn to use digital technologies is somewhat lacking, how can you seek to develop your skills with new technologies prior to implementing them in your teaching? First of all, there is no substitute for working with the pieces of technology yourself. Make sure that you spend time working through that new interactive whiteboard resource before doing so in front of Year 8 on a Wednesday afternoon. Second, you'll need to be inventive in terms of finding practical support. Videos on YouTube may be more able to solve some of the practical 'how to' questions you might have in learning to use a particular piece of software, rather than trying to get permission from your headteacher to attend an in-service training event that would take you away from your classes for a day. Third, try and find another member of staff who is slightly further ahead of you in terms of their knowledge and pedagogy with ICT. This can be a very powerful form of 'peer' professional development. As you may remember, the opening case study in Chapter 1 described how a personal friendship broadened to a form of professional development and led to significant pieces of curriculum development (Savage 2001; Savage and Challis 2001, 2002).

Finally, the report acknowledges that the processes by which teachers learn about new technologies are complicated and constricted in various ways. But:

> The possibilities for real change in the system do exist. If we can bring the technologies into situations *that resonate strongly with teachers' sense of professional and moral purposes*, we may yet see what might truly prove to be a renaissance, in which teachers would employ digital technologies for 'understanding, reflection, ingenuity and creativity', and, through these, support their own learning in new ways.

(Futurelab 2006, p. 41) [my italics]

In a similar vein to this book's theme of 'no curriculum development without teacher development', the writers of this report suggest that the best chances of technology having a positive educational impact lie with teachers aligning these powerful tools with their own sense of professional purpose. One could say that there will be no technological development without teacher development! The writers' suggestion is that, as teachers' own learning is supported through a more cohesive system, they will become more adept at creating interesting opportunities for learning with and through digital technologies for their pupils.

Reflective Task 3

The extent to which technology can 'resonate' with your sense of purpose as a teacher is clearly related to several of Wertsch's principles of mediated action, especially numbers 2, 3, 8 and 9 (see Table 5.1). The writers of the Futurelab (2006) report assert that certain purposes (e.g. understanding, reflection, ingenuity, creativity) may be more valuable than others. What do you think about this?

Consider the Key Concepts for your subject (part of the National Curriculum documentation at Key Stage 3). How do pieces of technology help promote each of the Key Concepts through skilful application and design (on your part)? Do you consider the technologies that you use to be a natural 'fit' with your wider sense of purpose as a subject specialist?

Now have a look at the Key Concepts for other subjects (http://curriculum.qcda.gov.uk/key-stages-3-and-4/subjects). As an example, creativity is a Key Concept in many subjects, including Music, English, Art and Design and Mathematics.

Compare different subjects' approaches to common Key Concepts. Are you drawn to any other subject's Key Concepts in particular? Relate this to your wider thinking about ICT through this chapter and discuss your ideas with the colleague you worked with in Practical Task 2. Are there ways that you can imagine extending your use of ICT to encompass ways of working, or thinking, contained with the Key Concepts of these other curriculum subjects?

Looking ahead

Who knows what the future of education will look like in the UK? It would be a bold writer who would predict the changes and technological developments that our future will contain. In preparing to write this book, I have spent the last year or so thinking about the themes of cross-curricularity. I have worked with colleagues who are producing the accompanying titles within this series and I have enjoyed the shared journey that we have travelled. My hope is that future developments in curriculum policy will acknowledge more explicitly the potential for cross-curricular approaches to teaching and learning. I also hope that knowledgeable and skilful subject teachers will forge forwards with these ideas and find new pedagogies that span from their subjects to others in natural, informative and pedagogically innovative ways.

However, outside the world of education, the impact of technological change moves at a faster pace. This has been a cause of frustration for some. Somekh's (2007) thesis is that twenty years of investment has rendered teachers 'powerless to direct effective change' (p. 121). She believes that ICT needs to become an integral part of teaching activity if meaningful change is to occur, but is she right to be so pessimistic? She cites NotSchool as a demonstration of how fundamental changes to teaching and learning and the 'whole institution of schooling' are both 'achievable and desirable'

(p. 119). Her argument seems to be centred on perceived contrasts between the use of ICT in the home environment and that within the school. In her concluding paragraph in the chapter, she states that:

> In the UK and the USA there are currently a number of significant initiatives aimed at radically changing aspects of schooling. These range from radical designs for new school buildings, to innovative deployment of mobile ICTs for use both at home and at school, and experimental formations of curriculum and pedagogy. They are all still considerably constrained by the technologies of national/state curricula, high-stakes testing and traditional pedagogies.
>
> (Somekh 2007, p. 119)

Educational researchers have a role to play in developing new scenarios for the use of ICT in education. But the group that Somekh fails to mention specifically is teachers themselves. This is surprising. Somekh's wider work has been to justify their place as key initiators and drivers of change through research methodologies such as action research (something that was also a key component within the Futurelab report quoted above) (Somekh 1995, 2006; Somekh and Davis 1997). You are in a powerful place to effect change in the educational system where it matters, that is, at the interchange and interplay of thoughts and ideas between you and your pupils. A thoughtful and systematic approach to the choice and use of ICT for teaching and learning is what is required along with a greater degree of communication between staff about their pedagogy and practice with technology. The ideas and principles introduced in this chapter should help you along the way. But the key foundation of this book is that you will be a reflective practitioner who makes imaginative links between theory and practice and through this activity empowers meaningful curriculum development. There is nowhere this is needed more than in the use of technological tools in education.

Earlier in the chapter we considered the research project 'Beyond Current Horizons'. We looked together at some of the key principles that informed the research, arguing that they were good foundations for our work in re-imagining the use of technology as a tool to develop cross-curricular approaches to teaching and learning. As this chapter closes, we will return to the recommendations of this piece of futures research.

'Beyond Current Horizons' is supported by a powerful set of resources. These are available online (DCSF and Futurelab 2009). A central plank in these resources is the modelling of various educational scenarios. These scenarios were developed with leading social scientists to provide insights into the different possibilities that education might face in the future. The programme clearly states that these are not predictions. Rather, 'they are stories of three different possible futures, imagining how the world could look after 2025, in order to challenge assumptions and stimulate thinking about the present' (DCSF and Futurelab 2009).

The scenarios are structured around three different, potential worlds. Each of these worlds has a different set of social values. These include increasingly individualised, increasingly collective or increasingly contested approaches towards life and education.

The final practical task will help you interrogate these and think about how your use of technology may develop over the next fifteen years.

Practical Task 4

Read through the six scenarios on the 'Beyond Current Horizons' website (DCSF and Futurelab 2009). You can also find summaries of these in Table 5.3 (taken from http://www.visionmapper.org.uk, which provides a range of other practical activities through which you can engage with the 'Beyond Current Horizons' resources). The following questions will ask you to imagine what your future role would be in these scenarios, how technology might be used and how subjects might link together in broader curriculum frameworks:

1. What would be your potential role as a subject teacher within each of these scenarios? Would that role still exist? If not, what might it be replaced by?

2. In today's terms, what technologies would support these scenarios? Are there patterns of mediated action that empower your teaching and learning (identified in Reflective Task 1) that would still be relevant within these scenarios?

3. Given that individual subjects do not appear in these scenarios, how would the knowledge, skills and understanding of your current subject area be mediated through the use of technologies identified in the previous question?

4. Reflecting on the work we have done in this chapter on how technology can help develop cross-curricular approaches to teaching and learning, what lessons can be learnt and applied within these scenarios to ensure that this approach is at least maintained (and hopefully developed further)?

Of course, futures research is a risky business. It is easy to be blasé about these things. But this research highlights, in a very responsible fashion, some of the potential issues facing education at a time of fast technological development. It also makes a range of recommendations for the intervening period (i.e. from now until 2025). The first of these has a particular relevance to the key aims of this chapter (Facer 2009, p. 7). Recommendation 1 highlights that the design of a 'curriculum for networked learning' should be a priority. This type of curriculum would:

Enable individuals to learn to work effectively within social networks for educational, social and civic purposes and to develop strategies to establish and mobilise social networks for their own purposes.

(Facer 2009, p. 7)

TABLE 5.3 Summaries of the 'Beyond Current Horizons' scenarios

SCENARIO	SUMMARY
1. Informed choice	State educational provision is more focused on early years and primary
	Students recruit mentors to help them develop lifelong and tailored learning programmes from secondary age onwards
	Curriculum and pedagogy are configured around an individual learner's history, background and experience
	Assessment is iterative and formative and produces a long-term picture of achievement, dispositions and development
	Learning never ends: age is no barrier to taking up new learning activities
	Learners produce coherent career and learning narratives that they can constantly develop and share with potential employers
2. The independent consumer	There is a diverse landscape of educational offerings, with no national curriculum
	Students choose their educational experiences from a diverse 'catalogue' of choices
	Assessment is primarily summative and for certification purposes on completion of modules
	Individuals and families are responsible for producing a coherent educational 'narrative' for learners
	Curriculum and pedagogy are not tailored to individual need, but are standardised offerings to whoever chooses to purchase them
3. Discovery	Education is all about identifying the distinctive contribution you can make to different organisations and communities
	Learning happens in a range of state, private and third-sector organisations, with learners able to move across all of these for different purposes
	Curriculum is closely tied to the needs of individual organisations; learners see knowledge as emerging from different sources and are encouraged to reflect on this
	Assessment enables learners to reflect on and communicate their skills and knowledge and match them to the diverse values and needs of different groups
	Educators are concerned with enabling learners to build reputations and networks across a range of different communities

Such a curriculum might comprise opportunities for learners to:

- learn and work within meaningful socio-technical networks not wholly within single educational institutions;

- be assessed in interaction with tools, resources and collaborators;

- develop capacities to manage information and intellectual property, build reputation and trust, develop experience of working remotely and in mediated environments;

SCENARIO	SUMMARY
4. Diagnosis	Education provision from early years onwards ties individuals into specific community, faith or employment organisations
	Education providers diagnose learners' skills, strengths and weaknesses at an early age
	Students' talents are matched to the existing and forecast skills needs of the organisations, and individualised curricula are designed to enhance this match
	Everyone has a responsibility to fulfil their economic role in exchange for their educational provision (whether privately or state funded)
	Assessment practices are bespoke to individual organisations
5. Integrated experience	Learning is a part of everyday life, a normal element of all areas of social and personal activity
	The goal of learning is to enhance participation in meaningful activities and improve contribution to collective success
	Diverse groups and individuals play roles as educators, mentors and advisors across all areas of economic, leisure, social and personal lives
	Diversity, dialogue and the capacity to understand the mutual interdependence of individuals and groups are actively fostered
	Assessment is collaborative, and focused on producing accounts of collective endeavours and meaningful achievements
6. Service and citizenship	Education is a distinct and separate part of society, playing a preparatory 'service' role to civil society and the workplace
	Education's role is to train individuals to work as effective collaborators and participants in diverse economic and social settings and to teach citizenship
	Specialised knowledge and understanding is developed in industry and other settings outside the formal education sector
	Assessment is summative, and focused on developing accounts of individual contributions to group activities, and providing indications of potential individual performance

Source: http://www.visionmapper.org.uk.

- create new learning networks;
- reflect upon how learning is connected with other areas of personal, social, and working lives and manage and negotiate these relationships;
- explore the human–machine relationships involved in socio-technical networks.

(Facer 2009, p. 7)

What are the key themes here? To my mind, the key theme in this future curriculum framework is collaboration and networking. The days of the individual teacher, teaching their individual subject in their own classroom, with the door closed to the majority of others outside, are clearly numbered. Key technological developments have already facilitated a significant shift in curriculum design and delivery. Numerous examples have been given in this chapter; I am sure that these could be matched by examples that you can cite from your own schools and colleges. The future shape and design of the formal curriculum at Key Stages 3 and 4 is uncertain and subject, as always, to political interference. But as we have considered here, the role of technology within teaching and learning is powerful. Allying technology to the promotion of a cross-curricular approach to teaching and learning makes sense in many ways, not least in the educational benefits that it brings to pupils and teachers and the way that it reflects the wider use of technology outside the world of education.

Professional Standards for QTS

This chapter will help you meet the following Q standards: Q16, Q17, Q23, Q25a

Professional Standards for Teachers

This chapter will help you meet the following core standards: C17, C27, C29a, C40, C41

6

Assessment and Evaluation within Cross-Curricular Teaching and Learning

By the end of this chapter, you will have:

- considered how assessment methodologies can be developed within a cross-curricular approach to teaching and learning;

- looked at how methods of assessment data collection, management, storage and reporting can be developed within a cross-curricular approach to teaching and learning;

- reflected on the benefits of an integrated approach to assessment and evaluation within a piece of curriculum development;

- applied an evaluation process to a piece of curriculum development based on your own teaching.

Introduction

This chapter will promote the view that processes of assessment and evaluation are essential parts of the curriculum development process. It will discuss that, although they are both distinct in their potential focus and purpose, within an educational context they become related processes that can help teachers understand the impact of curriculum development in various ways. In other words, they are two sides of the same educational coin, existing together in a symbiotic relationship. Haphazard approaches to curriculum development that bolt on old approaches to either of them, without due consideration of their fitness of purpose in relation to new models of teaching and learning, will not best serve the needs of teachers or pupils. This chapter will explore these ideas through a consideration of recent developments in educational assessment and evaluation, applying them to the framework and pedagogy of cross-curricular teaching and learning presented in the previous chapters.

In the first part of the chapter, we will turn our attention to assessment. This is an essential component of a teacher's pedagogy. As you will know, assessment processes provide important data about pupils' learning that can serve various purposes. They inform the formal outcomes of learning (i.e. qualification frameworks or external awards). But the strategies of formative assessment can also empower teachers in their day-to-day work with pupils. These types of approach have become particularly popular in recent years and have informed many pieces of educational policy and been the focus of many publications (Black, Harrison, Lee, Marshall and Wiliam 2003; Black and Wiliam 1998; Brooks 2002; Torrance and Pryor 1998). It is not this chapter's purpose to revisit these ideas. Rather, a familiarity with key terminology and practices will be assumed as we reflect on the process of assessment as it is situated within new ways of cross-curricular working at the immediate level of curriculum design and classroom interaction.

In the second part of the chapter, issues related to educational evaluation will be discussed within the context of cross-curricular teaching and learning. Educational evaluation is, unfortunately, becoming a lost art. This chapter will consider some of the key principles and purposes for evaluation, as distinct from assessment processes, and show how, through the adoption of a range of practical evaluation techniques, teachers can obtain a fuller picture of the process of curriculum development. The chapter will end with the argument that educational evaluation and assessment exist in a close relationship. They both need to be planned for as an integral part of the curriculum development process. In this sense, the boundaries of assessment and evaluation may blur and become embodied in the work of the skilful teacher. The shortcomings of recent drivers of curriculum development, such as the QCDA model of 'disciplined innovation' (QCDA 2009e), will also be briefly considered.

Reflective Task 1

As a way of summarising your existing knowledge regarding assessment, spend a few moments making a list of the various ways that you assess pupils within your subject. Having drawn together a list of assessment processes, categorise each one into one of the following three groups:

1. formative assessment (assessment for learning);

2. summative assessment (assessment of learning);

3. the formative use of summative assessment.

Reconsider each item on your list and try and decide who is doing the assessment within each assessment process. Is it you (the teacher), the individual pupil (i.e. self-assessment) or other pupils (peer assessment)? If possible, try and compare your notes within this task with a teacher from another subject. What differences or similarities in approach can you note?

The practicalities of assessment in cross-curricular teaching and learning

In adopting a cross-curricular approach to teaching and learning, teachers will need to consider a range of practicalities relating to assessment. One of the key arguments within this book has been that as you begin to consider adopting elements of a cross-curricular approach to teaching and learning it is vital that you interrogate your own subject and its associated pedagogy with greater rigour. As you begin to understand where your pedagogy, and your subject, are coming from you will be able to plan future directions with more certainty and precision. Reflective Task 1 has begun this process of analysis in respect of assessment. To what extent were your responses there balanced across the various categories? Is assessment within your subject primarily something that you do to the pupils? Or is it something that is more embedded within the various classroom activities that underpin your subject teaching? This is not a time to be judgemental. I am not suggesting that there is a perfect balance or blend of assessment processes that you need to aspire to. Rather, in coming to terms with what you currently do within your subject, I believe that you will be able to relate better to the assessment cultures of other subjects, find some common ground, develop your own pedagogy in this area in an enriching way and move forward collaboratively with other colleagues as and when required. As with all the elements of cross-curricular teaching and learning discussed within this book, addressing your assessment practices in this way will have an impact on your own teaching and also on the way that you collaborate and co-ordinate wider pieces of curriculum development with your colleagues.

Cross-curricular approaches to assessment

There are numerous debates surrounding the types and techniques of assessment. As will be clear by now, it is not the purpose of this chapter to explore these in any detail. However, it is interesting to note that recent research has reverted to asserting strong differences between traditional conceptions of summative and formative assessment.

With the wider remit of Blanchard's (2009) book being about the promotion of assessment for learning (falling clearly within the formative assessment category), it is no surprise that in his analysis approaches to summative assessment show it in a less than positive light (Table 6.1). He comments:

Assessment is traditionally summative, which means making judgements about how well pupils have learned what they should have been taught. Judgements are made by authorised examiners and teachers acting as examiners. The function of

TABLE 6.1 Differences between summative and formative assessment

(A)

SUMMATIVE ASSESSMENT HAS:	FORMATIVE ASSESSMENT HAS:
No interest in what happens next, because the activity has no history and no future	'Now what?' as a key question, as well as 'Why do it?'
A focus on performance and attainment	A focus on learning and progress
A public audience	The individual learner and those who care for and teach her/him as audience
Predictability and certainty as ideals	Tolerance of unpredictability and ambiguity
Controlled conditions	Flexible conditions
High internal validity	Low internal validity
Low external validity	High external validity

(B)

	SUMMATIVE ASSESSMENT	FORMATIVE ASSESSMENT
Learners' intrinsic interest is:	Optional, perhaps an impediment	Desirable, even necessary
Learners' active part in assessment is:	Denied and impractical	Desirable, even necessary
Criteria are:	Non-negotiable and taken from public sources	Self-made and/or taken from public sources, standards orientated/or person centred, extensive, necessarily explicit, fluid, dynamic, formative
Learners' understanding of criteria is:	Advantageous, but not required	Desirable, even necessary
Learners' goal of autonomy is:	Irrelevant	Implicit, if not explicit

Source: Blanchard (2009, pp. 143–4).

> summative assessment is to maintain standards by which examinees are qualified, and report results. . . . The summative model of assessment is linear and separates out the three elements: first there is teaching; then there is learning; finally there is assessment.
>
> (Blanchard 2009, pp. 1–2)

This seems like quite a cynical view of summative assessment. Summative assessment is undoubtedly an important element within the education process and it is seldom as simple as the model described above suggests. As an example, summative assessment can have a very helpful formative function, which is a useful addition to its traditional focus.

Figure 6.1 presents what could be described as the interplay between summative and formative assessment (often referred to as the 'formative use of summative

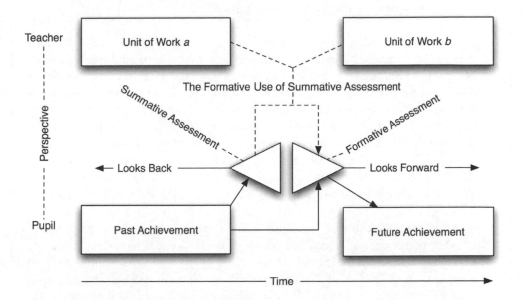

FIGURE 6.1 The formative use of summative assessment.

assessment') in which the outcomes of summative assessment are used in a formative fashion. Using assessment information in this way allows teachers to be reactive to the needs of their pupils. It involves teachers having discussions with their pupils in order to interpret what specific, summative marks and grades mean for them. So summative assessment used in a formative fashion can help take learning forward, but it needs planning for, and it requires a degree of flexibility on the part of teachers.

Within a cross-curricular approach to teaching and learning, there may be specific occasions when one or other of these assessment methodologies may be more pertinent. In this sense, teaching and learning with a cross-curricular pedagogy may not be so different from a generic subject-based pedagogy. The final, collaborative part of Reflective Task 1 could be a very useful exercise in this respect. Even if you have not been able to pin down one of your teaching colleagues and get them to complete the whole exercise, it would be worth revisiting this aspect of the task through a short discussion at some point. Having observed lessons in a range of subjects across the secondary curriculum, I am convinced that there are many subject differences in how we assess pupils. Case Study 1 presents an example from one drama teacher's pedagogy that may be unknown to teachers working in other subjects. The key point here is that there are differences in the way that individual subjects approach assessment and the techniques that they use. When considered in detail, the links between a subject's pedagogical approach and assessment processes can provide useful insights into pupils' learning from which teachers in other subjects may be able to benefit. Read what this drama teacher has to say about her pedagogy.

Case Study 1: Freeze framing and assessment

In my drama teaching I make use of a technique called 'freeze framing'. This is when the action in a particular scene is frozen at a particular point in time. Normally I will decide when this happens, although sometimes I will let pupils decide. At the particular moment when I shout 'Freeze!', every pupil involved in the scene has to stop what they are doing or saying and remain absolutely still. They stop moving, talking or anything else. This allows us to think together about the situation that the pupils are presenting through their acting. It is a technique drawn from the theatre and it allows a particular actor to talk about their perceptions in the situation they find themselves in or to give the audience further information about how they might be feeling or thinking. Some directors call this 'thought tracking'.

As a teacher, I use this technique quite a lot to help my understanding of whether pupils are really engaging with a particular scene. I would say it is a key part of my assessment for learning strategy. During the freeze frame moment I will ask questions to a particular character in the scene. Sometimes I will also ask pupils who are watching the scene with me to ask questions too. I find it a very helpful way to try to understand whether or not a particular pupil really understands the role of their character. Obviously it has limitations. In drama, pupils often feel things that they can't express in words. But when used with other assessment devices, freeze framing is a really useful assessment tool. And I'm pleased that it is an adaptation of a tool from the theatre.

In Case Study 1, a drama teacher is recounting her use of a particular tool, drawn from the world of the theatre, in the development of her approach to assessment for learning. This is a specific technique that, to my knowledge, is not used in other curriculum areas. Unless you are a drama teacher, or have investigated the performance practices of the theatre in significant detail, perhaps you have not heard about it either. However, having found out about it here, I wonder what application you could make of this within your curriculum area? What would a freeze frame technique look or sound like in a geography or science lesson? What would a teacher in these subject areas hope to find out about pupils' thoughts through such an approach? As the drama teacher mentioned in the case study, are there things in your subject that your pupils feel but might not be able to express easily in words? If so, this technique may help reveal them.

From the pupils' perspective, if this tool was being used in a number of different subjects, how would that affect their response? Would they become happier with the device and respond more positively? Or would it lose its impact as it is taken outside of the context within which it has been carefully located? These are important considerations that teachers need to explore together. To that end, your colleagues working with these types of assessment processes become important contributors to your own ongoing professional development. As a technique, freeze framing may have several benefits. But there are also limitations to it, even within drama teaching (as the teacher points out in the case study). So the tool needs to be handled carefully and with due consideration to the context from which it has been taken. However, there may be considerable benefits in enriching one subject's assessment approach by the creative borrowing of approaches of other subjects.

Practical Task 1

This task requires you to work collaboratively with at least two other colleagues working in different subject areas from your own.

Following the example in Case Study 1, choose one element of your subject pedagogy that you use to provide you with evidence about pupils' learning. Write up this subject-based assessment device in a short statement of no more than 100 words. Send your statement to the two other colleagues working with you in this exercise. When the three statements have been circulated and read, have a short discussion about the approaches and agree on a time frame within which you are going to try out the new assessment processes within your teaching.

When you have all tried out the approaches drawn from the other two subjects, reflect together about the impact that the approaches had. Consider:

1. The impact that the new approaches had on your pedagogy. Were you comfortable using them? What were the positive or limiting features of the approaches within your subject?

2. What type of assessment data did the new approaches allow you to collect? Were they any different from the data that you might collect through other processes?

3. How did pupils respond to the new approaches to assessment that you introduced? Did they spot where the new approaches had come from? Did this make a difference to their reactions?

Finally, *and most importantly*, reflect on how the assessment process that you wrote about and shared with your two colleagues was taken, adopted and adapted within their teaching. In your mind was this a successful appropriation of the assessment process? What advice would you give them should they want to continue using this technique in their teaching?

A sympathetic approach to subject identities

Subject teachers within secondary schools have a responsibility to assess their pupils, using formative and summative processes, within their own subjects. This is likely to be their main concern. However, the argument through this book has been that one's subject teaching can be helpfully developed, and perhaps even transformed, by a cross-curricular approach to teaching that transcends subject content and looks at the different ways through which one's pedagogy can develop. As Practical Task 1 has considered, this can help transform approaches to the assessment of pupils' learning within subjects. The conversations that teachers have about their pedagogy are central to this type of work, hence the strong emphasis on sharing ideas, through both written and verbal forms, in the above task.

Our discussion will move on to consider an important element of assessment that is related to subject knowledge. The conception of subjects within the secondary curriculum is very strong. As we discussed in the earlier chapters of this book, defining and interrogating the subjectivities inherent within our subjects is the first step to us making the boundaries between subjects a little more permeable. But the extent to which subject boundaries should be permeable is something on which teachers and educational researchers will hold a range of views. It seems unlikely, at least in the near future, that the secondary curriculum will be reconstituted without subjects as an organising mechanism for timetabling and, in the context of this chapter, for assessment. The potential changes needed to the qualifications framework and the political backlash would seem to make this highly unlikely. Recent events with regard to the proposed revisions for the primary curriculum are informative in this respect (DCSF 2009b).

However, within an individual teacher's subject teaching, there will be elements of different subject knowledge bases appearing across traditional subject boundaries. As an example, elements of mathematical knowledge, perhaps in the guise of functional skills (DCSF, Department for Business Innovation and Skills, the National Strategies and Learning and Skills Improvement Service 2009; QCDA 2009f), will be appearing in all other subjects across the curriculum. More informally, the case studies presented in Chapter 3 have shown how different subjects can be combined (in terms of both subject content and pedagogy). The same issues will be faced when teachers collaborate together on curriculum projects with external themes or dimensions (e.g. sustainable development; QCDA 2009d). Although I would not want to imply that it is the individual teacher's responsibility to assess each subject that they are seeking to include elements of within their teaching, the suggestion here is that there ought to be systems in place within the school that allow for the aggregation of assessment data from more than one teacher's viewpoint. In the example given above related to functional mathematical skills, teachers will be including this element within their curriculum planning following examples given in national guidance materials (DCSF, Department for Business Innovation and Skills, the National Strategies and Learning and Skills Improvement Service 2009; QCDA 2009f). Pupils will be engaging in activities that, it is hoped, will develop their mathematical skills within the subject context. What is the subject teacher to do with the assessment data gleaned from these activities? How should these findings be shared with other colleagues? This moves us into a consideration of how you might collect and manage assessment data in a cross-curricular approach to teaching and learning.

Managing the collection of assessment data

The collection of assessment data is an important first step. Across the curriculum subjects, teachers utilise a wide range of different approaches for the collection and storage of assessment data. An important consideration here is that the method of collection and storage should relate to the type of data that the teacher wants to collect. Increasingly, there is a move towards assessment data in formats other than numerical data. This might include written comments reflecting observations made of pupils working individually or collectively, photographs of pupils' work, audio recordings of their discussions or perhaps, on occasions, video evidence. As the discussion unfolds below, we will consider a number of different examples of this principle.

One of the simplest forms of 'assessment' that I can remember from my education was the weekly spelling test. Learning one's spellings was a classic homework activity that I can recall being a weekly routine of bluff and double bluff with my parents! From the teacher's perspective, the test was a double win. It provided a snapshot of a pupil's ability to spell ten or twenty words, it was easily collected and, in the ultimate time-saving form, it was marked by the pupils! Although some may doubt the value of this activity, I would maintain that the conducting of short tests like this on a weekly basis does give an indication of pupils' progress in spelling set lists of words. The spelling test as described here may have fallen out of fashion in some quarters. But through observation of the progress of my own children through primary school, I can see that the motivational dimension of this type of activity can be considerable if handled in a skilful and sensitive way by the teacher (and parent). Assessment data drawn from these types of activities can be easily stored in a mark book or electronically in a spreadsheet. It is clear by now that the collection and storage of this simple numerical data is uncomplicated.

But other situations that teachers face are much more complicated and will demand more sophisticated approaches to the collection of assessment data. In Case Study 2 we will consider the role of an English teacher at Key Stage 3 doing some work with pupils within a scheme of work that focused around Shakespeare's play *Romeo and Juliet*.

Case Study 2: Romeo and Juliet

During this term pupils have studied Shakespeare's play, *Romeo and Juliet*. Within a sequence of follow-up activities, I wanted to create some cross-curricular links using *Romeo and Juliet* as a starting point. I chose music, drama and film, specifically:

- Prokofiev's ballet score for *Romeo and Juliet* (music);
- Bernstein's *West Side Story* (drama);
- *Romeo and Juliet* (the 1996 film directed by Baz Luhrmann with Leonardo DiCaprio).

In the lesson that you came to see, I had asked the Year 9 pupils to explore each

---

of these three settings of the Romeo and Juliet story. They were working in small groups at computers watching and listening to various clips. Having spent quite a significant amount of time studying the Shakespeare text, I really wanted the pupils to have some freedom in how they analysed these three settings of the story. I was intrigued by how they might approach it.

I asked pupils to write a short piece related to their explorations. In particular, I asked them to focus on how the Shakespeare story had been interpreted in the three different genres. Specifically, I asked them to identify any similarities or differences that they could find.

I was pleasantly surprised by their work. One of the things they commented on extensively was characterisation. This is probably because I go on about it a lot! But they talked about the ways in which characterisation was portrayed in the Prokofiev score, through musical themes, the accompanying ballet (and in the West Side Story production), through gesture, and, to a lesser extent it seemed, the film (although that might be because they spent less time on that). One pupil had obviously understood it quite deeply. He commented on the way that different types of music accompanied the different characters in Bernstein's approach, with the Latin American sounds representing the Sharks, and the Jets having a different type of beat. I learnt something about it from him!

Reflective Task 2

Imagine yourself as the English teacher in this classroom. The pupils are engaged in a range of activities, exploring the three cross-curricular links that the teacher has introduced. What would your role be within this classroom? Perhaps you would circulate around the room and observe the pupils working in their groups. You might eavesdrop on a number of their conversations. The pupils are aware that you are there, observing their work, and they ask you a question or two about a particular aspect of the musical. It is outside your own specialist area of knowledge. What do you do? You cannot give a direct answer. Perhaps you are elusive and skilfully direct pupils' thinking along a new path, or point them in the direction of other resources that could help their enquiries. You observe their resulting work in process, including the errors and poor choices as well as the effective and polished responses. You observe pupils interacting with each other. You mentally note who seems to be taking the lead in a particular situation and who is quiet. You wonder why. Perhaps you are able to relate a particular pupil's work, attitude or demeanour in this lesson to previous lessons within your own subject area.

As a teacher in this scenario you are constantly making a range of judgements based on your impressions of pupils' working together, your conversations with them and your viewpoint about the quality of their work, and placing these judgements in a wider context or framework drawn from your knowledge of them and their work throughout the year. Consider the following questions:

1.   What types of assessment data can you draw from your observations in the classroom today? How can you extend the types of data collected to ensure that the data themselves reflect the nature of the activities that the pupils are undertaking?

2.   What would you do with the assessment data that you have collected?

3.   How would you distinguish between the data that are directly related to your own subject (English) and those of other subjects touched upon during the lesson?

4.   What would you do with the assessment data that fall outside your own subject area?

The English teacher in Case Study 2 gives an honest account of her first experiences of cross-curricular teaching. Building on her existing practice, she has sought to branch out into other curriculum areas through the use of a common stimulus (the Shakespeare play and its interpretation by other artists). In terms of assessment data, what is she to do with the observations about the Year 10 boy's musical learning that took place in the lesson? How could she account for this within her own assessment strategy, and how could this be shared with other colleagues?

1. Effective assessment springs from good planning

First, it is important to remember that any assessment strategies or processes within the classroom should flow from careful planning. Put simply, the initial focus for the collection of assessment data should relate to and be tied in with the stated learning objectives and associated learning outcomes for the lesson.

In this instance, the English teacher might well be right to focus on the narrow objectives related to the pupils' learning in English. This might go against the over-riding argument of this part of the chapter. But it is important to state that this is a legitimate position for any teacher to take.

However, given that the teacher has chosen to adopt an explicitly cross-curricular approach to this particular lesson within the scheme of work, we can presume that there will be learning objectives and outcomes that touch on the other subjects implicated through the lesson activities, choice of resources and associated learning outcomes. Towards this end, it will be necessary to consider a broader range of evidence that could be collected.

2. Look for broader types of generic assessment data

Second, consider the broader types of generic assessment data that can be collected. In Chapter 4 we considered the role of language and literacy in cross-curricular teaching and learning. You will remember that we began that chapter with the obvious point that language is a generic medium within which all teaching and learning takes place. This has a positive benefit for assessment. Listening to the communication that goes on between pupils, or between yourself and your pupils, will play a vital role in providing evidence for learning in subjects outside of your own specialist area.

It is essential to think through the strategies for the collection and collation of this type of data. Fragments of conversations between pupils could be noted down as you circulate around the class. Try and listen out for interesting references or verbal clues from pupils that show them working through ideas in relation to another subject area. If you have the use of portable recording technologies, these can play a useful role in recording conversations that you might have with pupils about their work at certain points in the lesson. Having a physical record of what are otherwise fleeting conversations can be very useful when reflecting on a particular lesson or sequence of learning within a lesson. Similarly, the use of visual reminders of pupils' work (e.g. by taking digital photographs or video recording) can also help you recall situations and events within lessons.

The key point here is that, when you are dealing with subject content that may be outside your own specialist area, it is important to look for generic tools, for example language, which can help you make sense of unfamiliar issues. No one is expecting teachers to know everything! But we can make useful judgements about the quality of pupil engagement with unfamiliar subject content. We can document this and, as we shall see below, report this back to colleagues who have the requisite specialist knowledge to make sense of it.

3. Maximising your time in the classroom and minimising the assessment 'burden'

Third, time with your pupils in the classroom is precious. Perhaps it does not always feel like it when you are facing particular classes for the second time within a week! But curriculum time is under an increasing amount of pressure. It is essential that we maximise the time for interacting with pupils, and that we maintain a focus on the quality of these interactions with each individual within the classroom.

Establishing a range of assessment processes is key to freeing up your time in the classroom. Processes related to self-evaluation and peer assessment are explored in great detail in many of the publications referenced throughout this chapter. They can help pupils take a greater degree of ownership of both their own, and others', work. As a vehicle for ascertaining the extent to which pupils are learning in a cross-curricular way, setting up these processes with key questions that provide the kind of data you are looking for will be vital. Remember that the division of knowledge into subject areas is an artificial construct. Within many future scenarios, pupils will need to be able to transcend these artificial boundaries, picking and choosing ideas and working practices to fit particular learning contexts. You can help them to do this through pupil-centred approaches to assessment which identify some of the common approaches to learning that underpin all subjects, as well as by highlighting, encouraging and rewarding their learning of subjects other than your own within your lessons at particular times.

4. Maintaining a balance of assessment approaches

Finally in these considerations about the collecting of assessment data for cross-curricular learning, remember that the most effective approaches to assessment maintain a balance between the collection of summative assessment data (which you can keep and reflect on at a later date) and the collection of formative assessment data (which you can use almost instantaneously to provide feedback to individuals or groups of pupils). This general point is true of teaching whether or not it is constituted as 'cross-curricular' or not. As we have seen in our earlier discussion, summative assessment, formative assessment and the formative use of summative assessment all have their place in a well-rounded approach to pedagogy. We have emphasised that fleeting, formative observations and comments may be particularly relevant for providing evidence of cross-curricular learning (particularly in areas outside your own specialist knowledge) and may provide a useful backbone for more extensive, summative statements by subject specialists at a later date.

The important thing is that all types of assessment data are collected and stored in such a way that you can begin the process of interpretation and analysis quickly and easily. It is to this aspect of storing assessment data that we will now, briefly, turn our attention.

Managing the storage and reporting of assessment data

Practical Task 2

In preparation for the following section of this chapter, briefly describe the processes by which you store assessment data. For each item, state where you store this information and whether the storage of this information is required by you or your departmental head or for a whole school assessment purpose. Your list may look something like this:

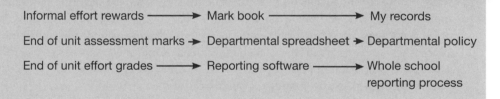

Within the secondary school context, assessment of a specific subject is probably the responsibility of the individual teacher. In larger departments this assessment process may be distributed, with different members of staff teaching the same group of pupils. But this is not common or even considered desirable by the majority of teachers who I have met in preparing for this book.

However, as you will have noticed by now, I am arguing that assessment does need to be set free from the constraints of the individual teacher and their responsibility for individual pupils' learning within their subject. As Practical Task 2 has demonstrated, your storage of assessment data takes many forms and is part of a network of accountability that is both required (by the school) and helpful to you as a teacher in many situations. But how does this argument about a more collaborative approach to assessment relate to the broader, but anecdotal, consensus amongst teachers that the status quo on assessment needs to be maintained.

I would argue that a cross-curricular approach to assessment has, in many smaller schools, been the normal, informal model for many years. In one of the schools within which I taught, it was regularly the case that individual pupils would be discussed in faculty, and even full, staff meetings. Aspects of their learning would be discussed within particular subjects and exchanges of assessment 'data' would inform these conversations. This school was small enough in terms of pupil numbers for conversations like this to take place. Similarly, the total number of staff was small and working relationships were easy to establish and maintain. Perhaps this is an argument for smaller schools in which cross-curricular links can develop informally. But what about the majority of schools that are significantly larger and in which many teachers will not even know the names of their colleagues in other curriculum areas?

Within these schools (and the smaller schools to which I refer) there will need to be a more formal approach to managing and storing assessment data in order to facilitate a truly cross-collaborative approach to teaching and learning. This will require a significant change in the culture of educational practice and assessment, which, I believe, is some way off for the majority of schools. However, I do believe that change in this direction is inevitable given the futures research for education that has recently been completed in the 'Beyond Current Horizons' project (DCSF and Futurelab 2009; Facer and Sandford 2010; for a simple analysis of this see the conclusion of Chapter 5). I also believe that in a number of schools work of this type has already begun. I will give a number of examples.

The introduction of diplomas within the secondary curriculum framework is one example in which subject specialists and others have had to work together in new ways, co-ordinating an approach to assessment that has moved beyond the notion of individual subjects. Although this has been a challenge in many schools, new ways of working have been established and, in the best practice, significant collaborative approaches to assessment have been developed. One such approach, controlled assessment, has been supported extensively by the QCA (2009) and presents an interesting possible way forwards for other areas of the curriculum.

Second, I would argue that, as a broader range of adults works alongside teachers in school settings, the need to assess pupils collaboratively is going to arise quite naturally. The role of teaching assistants is now significant in all phases of education. Whether teaching assistants are supporting individual pupils with special educational needs, or working with larger groups of pupils, they have an essential role in using assessment for learning techniques to support pupils (and teachers) that:

promotes the full participation of all pupils of all abilities and a culture in which all pupils are confident they can improve because they are aware of their successes and the progress they are making. In this environment, teaching assistants (TAs) are at the front line. Working closely with the teacher they can provide informative feedback to pupils, help discussion and sustain the pace of learning.

(DfES 2005, p. 4)

To this I would add that the positive collaborative approaches that teachers adopt to working with teaching assistants can only assist the collection, storage and analysis of assessment data to underpin subject-based and cross-curricular teaching and learning.

However, the implementation of wider changes in the storage and reporting of assessment data that supports a school-wide approach to cross-curricular teaching and learning will require strong leadership from senior management teams. As we saw in our review of the research literature in this area (in Chapters 1 and 2), without senior management support these initiatives seldom succeed. In future years it seems clear that the analytical tools and technologies that we use to manage the assessment data that we collect will become more sophisticated. They will probably allow us to track pupil learning across subjects with a greater degree of precision and meaningfulness, whilst providing more regular feedback to teachers, pupils and parents. If the curriculum continues to move in the direction of more thematic approaches, such assessment tools may highlight commonalities in styles of learning across subjects with a precision that we cannot predict today. Even if subject boundaries are defended rigorously in future curriculum frameworks, the argument here would still be that individual teachers need to provide the educational 'glue' between subjects and ensure that their subject pedagogy is enriched through broader, cross-subject pedagogical approaches. An integral part of this model is that educational assessment serves the pupils' learning first, and the subject second. To this end, pupils' learning spans the curriculum and, as such, approaches to assessment, including the collection, storage, analysis and reporting of assessment data, must do the same. To do otherwise is to fragment the curriculum on a misnomer that will reinforce individual subjects', and teachers', isolation from each other. Such a model will not withstand wider developments in technology and society and will risk school-based models of education becoming redundant.

The essential nature of educational evaluation

It is not enough that teachers' work should be studied; they need to study it themselves.

(Stenhouse 1975, p. 143)

Enquiry counts as research to the extent that it is systematic, but even more to the extent that it can claim to be conscientiously self-critical.

(Stenhouse 1985, p. 15)

The centrality of the role of the teacher in curriculum development has been a recurring theme throughout this book. In our opening chapter, we drew on Stenhouse's mantra of 'no curriculum development without teacher development'

(Stenhouse 1975, p. 142) to justify my key point that cross-curricular approaches to teaching and learning should start with the individual teacher and their pedagogy, before branching out into collaborations with others. In the above quotations, drawn from two of Stenhouse's key publications, we find him emphasising the requirement that teachers' work is worthy of study. But not only that, it is worthy of study by teachers themselves! To that end, Stenhouse equates systematic enquiry to a form of educational research, particularly when it involves teachers being self-critical of their practice.

Education is a complex activity. It involves many different elements, including people, tools and ideas. Watching education in action within a classroom or other learning environment is fascinating. Perhaps it is something that you have been able to do regularly, as part of an initial course of teacher education or subsequently through other opportunities. What would a systematic enquiry into the teaching and learning that takes place in your classroom look like? What would it involve?

Reflective Task 3

Before reading ahead any further, take a moment to pause. What are the first few things that come into your head when you hear the word 'evaluation'? What do you consider to be the differences between evaluation and assessment?

In the second part of this chapter we are going to explore educational evaluation as a means of understanding the activities that go on within our classrooms. I will argue that educational evaluation, although different from educational research, still shares many of its values. Like Stenhouse's view of educational research, evaluation should be a tool that teachers can use to investigate their own practice in a systematic and self-critical way. It can also be a tool that teams of educators could employ to investigate specific pieces of curriculum development (i.e. a broader approach to cross-curricular teaching and learning within a department or school).

Like education, evaluation involves many things and activities. It includes looking at things, asking questions, listening to others, describing events and making interpretations. It is definitely a skilful activity. Some writers relate it to an art form. As an activity, it has many benefits for those working in an educational setting. But there are some important things to consider before taking evaluation into an educational setting.

Evaluation is about making the private public

First, evaluation is about making things that are often private public. As an example, how often is your work as a teacher opened up and shared with other teachers in your school? Perhaps you are observed as part of the performance management and appraisal systems in your school, but how often is it possible for other colleagues to watch you teach? How would you feel about it if they did? And how often do you see others teach within your school? Opening up what could be seen as the private space of our classrooms to others might be one part of an evaluation methodology.

This could be uncomfortable and challenging. When thinking about using evaluation as an educational tool, it is vital to consider the conditions under which it is carried out and to ensure that it maintains respect for people and their privacy. This makes it particularly important to hold conversations before you make any final decisions about the form or shape of any evaluation you may undertake.

Evaluation is about people

Second, evaluation is not solely about educational programmes and initiatives. Although it is often used in this way to justify new ventures, it is important to reflect on the roles that people play within these. So, as you will be familiar with by now, as it has been a recurrent theme throughout this book, in evaluation, as in curriculum development, people are central. In an educational setting this would include teachers, pupils and other adults working within the school. When done well, evaluation can capture the life experiences of people within educational projects.

Evaluation extends beyond individuals

Although evaluation may start with the people within a project, it is important to recognise that it extends from them into all kinds of other contexts. Educational projects are not always what teachers or pupils inside them think or say about them. Educational projects are complicated sets of aspirations, values and experiences within which individuals' biographies, political values, contextual influences and much more besides conflict. This can cause difficulties for people on occasions. Evaluation, when done properly, is helpfully challenging but supportive.

Evaluation has a formative and summative dimension

In a similar way to our discussion about assessment in the earlier part of this chapter, evaluation has a formative and summative role to play in education. One popular application of evaluation is to look at the specific aims and objectives of a project and measure them against its outcomes or achievements. This is seldom, if ever, a straightforward judgement to make. As we have seen already in our introductory definitions of evaluation, the wider scope of an educational project requires evaluation to have a more subtle approach to measuring success or failure. A narrowly focused view on project objectives would often fail to recognise the broader efforts that the participants within that project had made. So, it is important to note that evaluation is often about keeping open educational opportunities rather that seeking to close them down prematurely. Formative approaches to evaluation emphasise this; summative evaluative comments need to be handled with care, especially if a project is still underway.

Evaluation will not find the truth

Although the notion of truth is attractive, a more pragmatic approach to evaluation acknowledges that 'truth' is always difficult to establish in a complex set of circumstances such as are found in a classroom. This is not to say that evaluation should not be truthful in its application. In fact, having an ethical approach to the collection of evaluative data and the processes by which judgements are made about that data is essential. But in terms of outcomes, there is unlikely to be one 'truth' that the evaluation process will uncover. As one experienced educational evaluator put it:

> Evaluation is always based on data. Avoid evaluations which start with a judgement about whether a project was good or bad, whether it worked or not. In good evaluations, judgements grow out of that data. . . . Evaluation usually settles for something that is persuasive.
>
> (Kushner 1992a, p. 3)

The 'educational project' of cross-curricular teaching and learning is in desperate need of educational evaluation of this type. As we have seen throughout this book, there has been little structured research in this area, and the notion of an individual teacher embodying a 'cross-curricular' pedagogy within their own teaching is almost entirely missing from educational research. Although a focus on assessment will enable teachers to examine the impact of these approaches on pupils' learning, my assertion here is that a focus on educational evaluation within the project of cross-curricular teaching and learning will enable teachers to reflect more deeply on the process of curriculum development, within which, as this book's first key principle asserts, the teacher is an integral part.

Designing an evaluation for cross-curricular teaching and learning

Having considered a number of important, operating principles for educational evaluation, we will turn our attention to how you might go about designing an evaluation for a cross-curricular teaching and learning project. Although this project might be a fictitious entity in your mind at the moment, the issues outlined below will be equally applicable whether the work is centred within your own teaching practice or it is situated as part of a wider, collaborative project with other members of staff in your department or school. In designing an evaluation, you will need to consider a range of issues including the following.

Optional practical task

The following part of the chapter discusses issues related to evaluating an educational intervention such as the development of a cross-curricular approach to teaching and learning within your subject teaching. Having reached this stage in the book (i.e. the second half of the penultimate chapter!), it might be a good opportunity to implement your ideas about cross-curricular teaching and learning within a real project. For this optional practical task, why not choose a unit of work that you are going to be teaching in the following few months. As a one-off activity, use the following advice about educational evaluation to conduct an evaluation of your own teaching during the unit of work.

Working collaboratively with another colleague in your school would make this an even more meaningful activity. You would not necessarily need to agree on cross-curricular content for the unit of work, but rather use your colleague as another source of inspiration and ideas, eyes and ears, and, when possible, get them to visit your classroom to assist in providing feedback to you about teaching during this unit of work. Perhaps you could return the favour if they were to do a similar study of their own?

Aims, objectives and activities

Most educational projects have aims and objectives. These may be set prior to the project starting. In terms of your teaching, these aims and objectives may well be drawn from your longer-term planning and relate closely to the units of work that underpin your curricula. However, in implementing a new approach, such as a cross-curricular approach within your teaching, there may be specific aims and objectives that need to be designed. Make sure that these are fit for purpose, that is, they address the questions that you, or others, are asking about the curriculum innovation. If your project is going to continue over a longer period, for example a term, then you will need to build time into your evaluation to review, and perhaps revise, your aims and objectives in light of your emerging understanding of the project. This cyclic process of revising the aims of an evaluation is similar to many processes of educational research, for example action research.

Similarly, the activities of the project are worthy of careful description. Typical activities may include various pedagogical elements that are being brought together within the project. These might cover aspects such as the application of different technological tools, a different approach to language and communication or a new approach to grouping pupils drawn from another subject pedagogy that you have identified. Either way, the activities of the project are as important as the aims and objectives. They will frame the teaching and learning that takes place and, in the Wertschian sense (Wertsch 1998), will fundamentally mediate them. As discussed above in relation to broadening approaches to assessment, communication and collaboration with colleagues in other subjects will be particularly helpful here.

Resources

Resources will include a number of different things. First, decide on the amount of time that you have to devote to the evaluation of the curriculum initiative. Although you may feel that you have limited time, trying to allow for a regular period of time during the project for reflection and note taking is worthwhile. This is better than spending a lot of time at the beginning and end of the project, with nothing or very little in-between. Although a project of this type can be done as an individual venture, perhaps the benefit of collaboration is most keenly felt here. Working with a colleague on a piece of curriculum development has many advantages, not least in sharing the workload and having that sense of a shared journey along a new educational landscape. This was certainly the case for myself as I worked with a colleague at my school (as portrayed in the first case study of Chapter 1).

Data collection

Data collection sounds very grand. In practice, it can be quite simple. Aim to collect data in your project on a regular basis. As with assessment practices, remember that data can take many shapes and forms. You may choose a particular class, or group of pupils within a class, to be the specific focus for your evaluation. If so, try to choose a representative sample of pupils that gives you the opportunity to collect a broad range of data. There is a balance here to be had between depth and breadth. It will be important that you can justify the choices you have made here within any evaluation outcomes. You might consider keeping a teaching journal for the duration of the evaluation. This could contain short comments about teaching sessions, notes about your thoughts or feelings during the evaluation process, snapshots of conversations with pupils or other things that come to your mind and might be useful later on. You will find many other published resources to assist with this aspect of evaluation, or more structured pieces of educational research (e.g. McIntosh 2010; McNiff 2005; Phillips and Carr 2010).

Originality

As with all aspects of teaching and learning, originality and creativeness can be key hallmarks of educational evaluation. These are often what will spur you on in the work and help you go that extra mile. The design of your evaluation may seem like a rather dry exercise in planning and preparation. But in the conduct of the evaluation try and build in opportunities for creativity. Be prepared to follow your hunch on occasions. I have often found that the period of time just before a lesson, or just after it when the pupils are leaving, are the times when some of the most interesting things happen. Short, snappy conversations with pupils in corridors sometimes provide the most revealing comments about what they have learnt. Formal questionnaires about classroom activities are often the least helpful in this context. So, be inventive with your evaluation design and accompanying methods and allow for (and actively seek out) the unexpected.

Establishing the wider context and sharing your design

Although the time that you have to devote to an evaluation of this type may be limited, particularly if you are working on your own, it is always worth trying to define the wider context of your proposed curriculum development. This could involve a number of different activities. First of all, have similar pieces of curriculum development been undertaken elsewhere? If you have not got time to carry out significant searches of written or electronic sources, posting a short question on a teacher website/forum (such as the *Times Educational Supplement*) may be worthwhile. Local authority advisers often have a helpful overview of work that is going on in different schools. Universities with education departments may also be a helpful point of contact.

This leads on to the second key point. Sharing your design at an early stage is key to the evaluation process. Who might you share this with? In the context of a piece of curriculum development, I urge you to share your ideas with the senior manager within your school who has a responsibility for the curriculum at the appropriate Key Stage. Although this might have an effect on the political dimension of your work (i.e. you probably do not want to upset your senior managers!), as you are working within a management system in which accountability is important, they probably have a right to know what is going on. But, more important than that, by sharing your ideas and design at this early stage you are showing yourself to be a reflective practitioner, someone who is wanting to initiate change in their teaching in a systematic and responsible way. You may also want to share your thinking about the proposed piece of curriculum development in other forums too. It is helpful to get feedback from a group of colleagues whose judgements you trust and with whom you can share ideas without fear of ridicule or rejection. Colleagues working within your own subject area in other schools may be another useful source of feedback.

Exploring the activities within an evaluation of cross-curricular teaching and learning

Your piece of curriculum development has been set up. You have identified your aims and objectives, chosen your curriculum activities, selected the classes that you are going to work with, decided on a timescale to work within and established your available resources. You have shared your ideas with your senior manager and other selected colleagues and reflected on their advice. You are ready to go. So what are you going to actually do during the evaluation itself? What are the activities that you can undertake, alongside your teaching, to help collect the data that you need to understand more fully the impact of your cross-curricular piece of curriculum development?

In this part of the chapter I want to discuss three key activities that you can undertake which are complementary to your teaching role. This is crucial. Finding the links between teaching and evaluation will help you manage your time effectively and avoid you being distracted from your key roles in the classroom. It will also make for a better evaluation and assist you in your own development as a teacher. The three activities are observing, communicating and interviewing.

Observing

As teachers we are used to observing classrooms. It is a key aspect of our work. Effective teachers make time during their lessons to take that step backwards from the complexity of classroom interactions to observe what is going on. Using observation as a key component of your evaluation methodology will enhance this generic teaching strategy.

However, familiarity with the classroom can be a barrier to effective observation.

Therefore, it will be important to find ways to challenge your own observations, particularly if you are conducting this evaluative work within your own teaching. To this end, we will briefly consider a range of issues associated with observation that will help you do this.

First, learn to live with uncertainty in your observations. As we explored above, the notion of 'truth' within an evaluation is highly contestable. What you are watching is framed by notions of objectivity and subjectivity, which you could spend a lifetime exploring. You do not have time to do that now! Rather, look for examples of activities that are 'credible and defensible rather than true' (Kushner 1992b, p. 1). Subtleties in your observations can be explored at a later date through the second and third activities discussed below. Whilst you are observing, use your instincts as a teacher to look out for interesting responses that pupils make within the lesson, unusual responses within particular activities, or that spark of creativity that a pupil may show at a given moment. Accounting for these in a simple way through your observation notes will be important, even if it is a brief comment in your teaching journal that can be returned to at a later date.

Second, use a range of technology to help you with your observations. This could include audio or video recording. The analysis of these materials can also reveal interesting material that you may miss during the busy course of a lesson. Although this technology can be a time saver and assist you in conducting the dual roles of teacher and evaluator, beware of relying too much on it. It takes a long time to review recorded materials. But the benefits can be significant if you have the time. If you want to explore and analyse your own pedagogical approach to cross-curricular teaching, why not consider video recording yourself? After you have got over the initial embarrassment of watching yourself on film (or is that just me?), this can be a very enlightening activity. If you are able to use a laptop computer with an in-built web camera directed at the position where you are standing then your pupils may not even know that you are video recording yourself. Recording yourself as a teacher is no different from recording those disciplines such as acting, dancing or athletics, in which video analysis is central to improving performance.

Finally, be focused in your observations. Your piece of curriculum development has specific aims and objectives. Try and focus on these in the early stages of your observations. But, as we discussed above, remember that these aims and objectives should not be thought of as being fixed in stone. They will develop as the piece of curriculum development unfolds and you will need to be responsive to the outworking of these throughout the curriculum activities that you have designed.

Communicating

As we discussed in Chapter 4, communication is central to teaching and learning. Communication can take many forms and you will need to be alert for these throughout your evaluation. Non-verbal forms of communication such as gesture, body language or facial expression will all be evident within your classroom. But verbal communication will probably be a major focus in all evaluations. In particular, conversations between teachers and pupils are an essential part of every classroom context. As such, they present a vital opportunity for the evaluation. How can we use the opportunities to converse with pupils to help the evaluation of cross-curricular piece of curriculum development?

First, be natural in your conversations with pupils. Build on your existing relationship with the class, or the individual pupil, and seek to nurture conversations around your key evaluation aims and objectives. But do this in a natural, not a forced, way. Do your pupils need to know that you are evaluating a particular approach within these lessons? There will be differences of opinion on this point, but if you feel that this is going to close down their responses (i.e. you think that they are going to say what they think you want to hear) then I would suggest not.

Second, take nothing for granted. Listen to the conversations that pupils are having between themselves during the various activities. These often contain really important evidence that can usefully inform your evaluation. Try and resist the urge to interrupt too soon. Maintain a critical stance and do not close down the possibilities of alternative viewpoints when you do intervene.

Third, allow conversations to touch on elements of your teaching as well as focusing on pupils' learning. This can be difficult, and even awkward, for experienced teachers. But it can prove very enlightening. So, be bold. Take a deep breath and be prepared for one or two difficult conversations. The feedback that you receive from pupils about your teaching can be extremely valuable.

Fourth, do not overdepend on the pupils' voices and forget your own. Recent educational initiatives have given a priority to 'pupil voice' that many educationalists are now finding unhelpful. For some, the emphasis on pupil voice is nothing more than adults 'copping out' and an 'abdication of their responsibilities' (Paton 2009). In the same article, Professor Hayes goes on to say:

> Everywhere I go the clearest sign of the rejection of adult authority is listening to learner, student, pupil [or] infant voice. Anybody's voice but the voice of adults. I love debating with pupils and students and getting them to research but basically they know nothing. . . . You are all professionals and you are saying that all you have to do is listen to young people. Well, you are abandoning your jobs – your role as adults – and you will make education in the future impossible.
>
> (Paton 2009)

Although such an extreme view may be seen to be unhelpful by some, perhaps a balanced view of curriculum development needs to reassert the role of the teacher as a professional. Within the sphere of educational evaluation, the teacher voice is as vital as anyone else's voice. So, do not underplay what you think and say about your own and your pupils' work.

Interviewing

The final key activity for your evaluation ought to be interviewing. Interviewing has a long history in educational research and it can prove to be a very beneficial approach within evaluations too. There are many guides on how to conduct interviews with young people either within educational research (Kvale 2007) or as part of a clinical setting (Ginsburg 1997). There are a number of important points to consider here.

First, do not get hung up on whether an interview is going to be structured, semi-structured or open-ended. All interviews are structured by the values and intentions of the interviewer. It will be more important to consider whether your interview is going to be about information retrieval or whether it will be more developmental in its nature.

Interviews that are about information retrieval make a number of assumptions. They assume that the interviewee (in our case, the pupil) knows something that the interviewer (the teacher) does not know. The task of the interview is to extract that information. The skill of the teacher in this context might be centred on putting the pupil or pupils at ease, asking them appropriate questions and facilitating the resulting conversation in a way that exposes the information that is deemed important. This is a perfectly legitimate approach to interviewing and one that, given the potential resource constraints that you may find yourself facing, may be the best use of your time.

However, there is a second way that interviews can be conducted that may be even more beneficial. The 'developmental interview' is underpinned by a different range of assumptions. As Kushner explains:

> This approach assumes that the interviewee probably does not know either and the task of the interviewer is to set up a learning situation. The interviewee is seen as someone locked up in a role and unable to take an objective role of what he or she knows, so the task of the interview is to prise the person out of the role and to ask them to look back at it and evaluate it. The interview is typified by exploration, by asking many supplementary questions to clarify and extend an idea . . . The focus is on the individual rather than the project – their life and values. The idea is to see the project in the context of the person's life.
>
> (Kushner 1992c, p. 1)

This approach to interviewing is more time-consuming. But, as Kushner points out in a later point in his exposition, it can be conducted over a longer period of time, perhaps as an interview that takes place on a number of separate occasions or stages. For teachers, this type of dialogue with a pupil could become part of a pupil's evaluative work during a particular unit of work. By asking the right sort of questions, pupils could engage with this type of focus through written responses as well as in a face-to-face interview situation. This may also be less threatening from their perspective.

This moves us on to a final point about interviewing. If you are going to include interviewing in your evaluation (and I would encourage you to), try and make the interviews a sense of occasion from the pupils' perspective. In my own evaluation work as a teacher, I would often try and find opportunities outside the formal time of a lesson to talk to pupils about their work. This might include a lunchtime 'interview', when pupils can relax, eat their lunches and you can talk about their work on a particular project. I found that this was more relaxing for me too. Group interviews are often better in this respect. Pupils can bounce their ideas off each other and, when this is going well, you can often find yourself taking a back seat in the interview process.

This is a good sign that the interview is moving beyond the information retrieval approach and really entering a developmental phase.

Making judgements about cross-curricular teaching and learning

You have reached the end of the evaluation period. You have observed pupils working through the cross-curricular activities, talked to them about their work and conducted a group interview with a selected number of pupils. In a parallel stream of activity, you have assessed their work in formative and summative ways, involving pupils in this. Your assessment data are collated and organised efficiently and you have been able to provide the appropriate data to your senior manager. You are faced with a collection of data drawn from your assessment and evaluative processes. It is time to make some judgements about your cross-curricular project.

One of the key ways of making judgements is to ask yourself questions about the data that you have collected. Perhaps this is easier when you are working collaboratively, but the kind of internal questioning that is essential to reflective practice is also a vital activity at this stage of the evaluation process. In relation to your piece of cross-curricular curriculum development, the following types of questions may be useful to consider at this moment:

- Was this the appropriate time for a piece of curriculum development for me (as a teacher), for my pupils, my department, my school? How can I be sure?

- What are the consequences of the changes I have made, for myself, my pupils and my colleagues?

- How do the changes that I have advocated relate to other changes that we are being asked to make?

- Where do the values come from that underpin this piece of curriculum development? Are they from my experiences or beliefs, or are they from somewhere else?

- Who have been the winners and losers in this piece of curriculum development?

- Has the teaching and learning been connected in this cross-curricular piece of curriculum development? How do I know?

- How would you describe your teaching approach in this project? Has it been authoritarian or democratic, formal or informal? What aspects of your pedagogy have changed or developed from my traditional, subject-based pedagogy?

- How have the pupils learnt in this project? In what ways have they learnt differently from how they might have learnt in a more traditional approach to the same topic? What have I learnt from the whole experience?

- Were my original aims, objectives and activities for the cross-curricular project appropriate? How did they change and develop over the duration of the project?

■ Whose knowledge really counts within a project like this? How did the knowledge base of my own subject specialism relate to other subjects that I was seeking to infuse within my teaching?

■ If this was a project that you did on your own, would it have worked better as a piece of collaborative curriculum development? If it was collaborative in its structure, can you conceive of it working more effectively as an independent activity? How could the collaborative dimensions of the project be translated into an individual teacher's pedagogical approach?

These questions may or may not be appropriate for the piece of curriculum development that you have undertaken. This is all part of the analytical process. Learning to ask the right questions about the work you have undertaken is part of the process of reaching a judgement about the project.

This process can continue for some time. Pragmatically, you are going to have to draw a line under the project at a particular point and move forwards. But reaching a conclusion, in your mind or as a written report of the evaluation, is an important final step. I would encourage you to write up the evaluation, however briefly, as an integral part of this process. For Stenhouse, educational research was 'systematic enquiry made public' (Stenhouse 1975, p. 142). The making public part of this definition is crucial, partly because it provides a system of accountability but, more importantly, because making your findings public will help create a dialogue of ideas about teaching and learning that will benefit yourself and others. As we have seen, a rich discourse about cross-curricular teaching and learning has been peculiarly missing from the educational debate over the last twenty years, despite many government initiatives and curriculum requirements to facilitate it. In previous chapters we have pondered over why this might be, but here is an opportunity for teachers to take ownership of their teaching and associated pedagogy and create positive changes as a result of a process of systematic enquiry.

So, as a final part of this evaluative process, submit a short report to your senior manager but also look out for opportunities to share your work with other teachers. At a recent meeting of the governing body on which I serve, we received an article, via the headteacher's termly report, from a mathematics teacher working at the school. Her evaluative study had looked at the process of implementing a more explicit assessment for learning approach within her teaching of mathematics. The report was a scholarly account of her approach, characterised by many of the attributes that we have discussed in the second part of this chapter. The pupil voice was evident within her study, but also her own professional opinions shone through, backed up with evidence drawn from various sources. Having completed the study, this teacher was asked to present her work and associated findings to the rest of the staff within the school. Her approach has been adopted and adapted to help provide a broader assessment for learning strategy within the school as a whole. Through various external links that the school has, she was invited to attend a meeting of local authority advisory staff and present her work to them. This was well received and further studies are being planned.

This type of approach empowers the individual teacher. In a political era of top-down educational initiatives, it reasserts the authority of the teacher and places them at the centre of the process of curriculum development. It does take time (and this will put some teachers off), but it is time richly rewarded for you and your pupils.

Conclusion

As symbiotic processes, assessment and evaluation are important components of a teacher's practice. Both need to be carefully nurtured and developed as part of a skilful pedagogy. As we have discussed, assessing pupil learning and evaluating one's teaching are two sides of the same coin. Done well, they can usefully inform each other. Education evaluation does take additional time but, as we have seen, this is time well spent.

Recent developments in the National Curriculum for Key Stage 3 have been accompanied by a call for 'disciplined innovation' in curriculum development (QCDA 2009e). The aim of this approach is clear:

> The new secondary curriculum offers a real opportunity to innovate and create a school curriculum that meets the needs, interests and aspirations of your learners. Over the past two years QCA has been working with schools, trying out ideas for curriculum innovation and sharing experiences. We've found that successful, effective curriculum innovation must be disciplined. It must be focused, based on evidence and closely monitored.
>
> (QCDA 2009e, p. 2)

You will note the emphasis within this quotation, and apparent within the many other QCDA documents cited in the bibliography, on the learner's needs, interests and aspirations. The seven-staged process of disciplined innovation is couched within the familiar three questions that have been used in all support materials surrounding the introduction of this latest version of the National Curriculum:

- What are you trying to achieve?
    - Identify your priorities.
    - Record your starting point.
    - Set clear goals.

- How will you organise learning?
    - Design and implement.

- How will you know when you are achieving your aims?
    - Review progress.
    - Evaluate and record the impact.
    - Maintain, change or move on.

This process has much to commend it. As the final comments in the guide from the QCDA helpfully state:

> Don't be afraid to change your approach. Curriculum innovation is a form of managed risk-taking where no one has the definitive answer. If an approach doesn't result in changes, try a different one. . . . Disciplined curriculum innovation is an ongoing process. Regularly evaluating and developing your curriculum will help ensure your changes have an impact on learners' achievements, lives and prospects.
>
> (QCDA 2009e, pp. 13–14)

However, in reading through this guidance material, I was left wondering about the role of the teacher in this process. Obviously, at a fundamental level, the teacher is the one driving this process forwards. But the material is very short on the pedagogical elements required to initiate and sustain curriculum development. Even the title reflects this view. Rather than calling it *Disciplined Curriculum Innovation: Making a difference to learners*, perhaps it could have been entitled *Disciplined Curriculum Innovation: Making a difference to teachers and learners*. Perhaps this would have been more in line with the view that curriculum development is inextricably tied to teacher development, one of the predominant themes of this book and the wider literature on curriculum development.

Professional Standards for QTS

This chapter will help you meet the following Q standards: Q6, Q7, Q11, Q12, Q13, Q26, Q27, Q28, Q29

Professional Standards for Teachers

This chapter will help you meet the following core standards: C6, C7, C11, C12, C13, C14, C35, C36

7

Metaphors for a Cross-Curricular Future

Key objectives

By the end of this chapter, you will have:

- considered a range of metaphors for cross-curricular teaching and learning and applied these to future opportunities for developing your work in this area;

- reviewed the key themes of the book and extended them in light of these metaphors;

- explored a new metaphor of curriculum development that could underpin a new, more authentic cross-curricular approach;

- identified aspects of a teaching pedagogy that would remain relevant and empowering in future educational climates.

Two metaphors for a cross-curricular disposition

Polymaths, intellectual promiscuity or intellectual polygamy?

Leon Battista Alberti was an Italian author, artist, architect, poet, priest, scientist, mathematician, inventor and sculptor. He was also, in his spare time, a skilled horseman and archer. Alberti is often cited as the archetypal 'Renaissance man', a polymath (from the Greek meaning 'having learned much'). We would use the term 'polymath' or (the less gender neutral) 'Renaissance man' to describe a person whose expertise spans numerous subject areas, or perhaps someone who is very knowledgeable. Alberti's view was that 'a man (sic) can do all things well if he will'. This ideal embodied some of the basic tenets of Renaissance humanism, which considered that human beings were the centre of the universe, limitless in their capacity for development and learning.

In today's society, the ideals of the polymath are something of an anachronism. Given that people can spend their whole life becoming experts in one field, the ideal of accumulating knowledge in multiple fields would, perhaps rightly, lead to the accusation of one being a jack of all trades and a master of none. There is undoubtedly some truth in this. But there are exceptions. Carr's (2009) exposition on the last days of the polymath makes fascinating reading. The first example of a contemporary polymath that he cites is Carl Djerassi. Djerassi had a fabulous career as a scientist, including becoming a professor of chemistry at Stanford University and inventing the contraceptive pill, before turning his hand to writing fiction. During an interview with Djerassi, Carr notes a provocative metaphor that Djerassi uses which is particularly pertinent to the theme of this book. He talks about what he considers to be the difference between intellectual promiscuity and intellectual polygamy. For Djerassi, being intellectually promiscuous is to be a 'dabbler', someone who flits between areas of knowledge in a cavalier fashion, with little regard or care for the development of a deep or sustained intellectual understanding. Rather, Djerassi aspires to intellectual polygamy. Here, he purports, there is potentially a deeper and valued commitment to each area of knowledge; intellectual understanding is developed in a systematic yet respectful way, with a sustained connection to every particular area of knowledge that one engages with, and this is maintained without favouritism.

The term 'polymath' may be anachronistic to our culture, but one cannot deny the intellectual power behind lives such as that of Djerassi. Few of us will be able to compete with the sheer breadth of such intellectual insight. For our discussion in this chapter, should an approach to cross-curricular teaching and learning be identified with intellectual promiscuity or intellectual polygamy?

This leads us on to our second metaphor, which takes a more down-to-earth tone.

The Hedgehog and the Fox

A textual fragment attributed to the Greek poet Archilochus in the seventh century BC inspired Isaiah Berlin to write his infamous essay *The Hedgehog and the Fox*. Archilochus was believed to have written the following: 'The fox knows many little things, but the hedgehog knows one big thing.' Using this as his starting point, the opening of Berlin's essay contains the following passage:

> Scholars have differed about the correct interpretation of these dark words, which may mean no more than that the fox, for all his cunning, is defeated by the hedgehog's one defence. But, taken figuratively, the words can be made to yield a sense in which they mark one of the deepest differences which divide writers and thinkers, and, it may be, human beings in general.
>
> For there exists a great chasm between those, on one side, who relate everything to a single central vision, one system, less or more coherent or articulate, in terms of which they understand, think and feel – a single, universal, organising principle in terms of which alone all that they are and say has significance – and, on the other side, those who pursue many ends, often unrelated and even contradictory,

connected, if at all, only in some de facto way, for some psychological or physiological cause, related to no moral or aesthetic principle. These last lead lives, perform acts and entertain ideas that are centrifugal rather than centripetal; their thought is scattered or diffused, moving on many levels, seizing upon the essence of a vast variety of experiences and objects for what they are in themselves, without, consciously or unconsciously, seeking to fit them into, or exclude them from, any one unchanging, all-embracing, sometimes self-contradictory and incomplete, at times fanatical, unitary inner vision. The first kind of intellectual and artistic personality belongs to the hedgehogs, the second to the foxes.

(Berlin 1953, pp. 1–2)

So, put simply, Berlin's application of Archilochus is that human beings can be categorised as being either 'hedgehogs' or 'foxes'. Hedghogs' lives are dominated by a single, central vision of reality through which they think and feel. Foxes, in contrast, live what might be called a centrifugal life, pursuing many divergent ends. Berlin goes on to give examples of each type. Famous hedgehogs that he cites include Plato, Proust and Nietzsche; famous foxes included Montaigne, Goethe and Shakespeare. The bottom line in Berlin's use of the metaphor is that there are different ways of knowing or approaching reality, namely the far-ranging generalist or the concentrated specialist.

To pursue this metaphor a little further, the power of the hedgehog in recent history and contemporary society is obvious in many senses. Bressler put it like this:

You want to know what separates those who make the biggest impact from all the others who are just as smart? They're hedgehogs. Freud and the unconscious, Darwin and natural selection, Marx and class struggle, Einstein and relativity, Adam Smith and division of labor – they were all hedgehogs. They took a complex world and simplified it.

(Bressler 2000)

Some writers believe that the original Archilochus phrase can be interpreted in different ways that reinforce the hedgehog's power more clearly. Bowman (1980), writing in the *New York Review of Books*, discusses how the word 'thing' could be interpreted as 'trick'. In his interpretation, 'the fox knows many little tricks, but the hedgehog knows one big trick' (i.e. how to curl up into a ball and survive). So, although the fox might be clever and sly, knowing many small tricks, ultimately, the hedgehog's one 'big' trick leads to its outwitting and defeating the fox.

However, I do not want to be accused of being one-sided. The fox has many positive attributes too. Reviewers of Berlin's essay often refer to his innate pluralism which, they argue, epitomises the approach that we are all better of knowing lots about different things. As an example, in an application of the hedgehog and fox metaphor to the cult of the 'expert', Kristof (2009) refers to the work of Philip Tetlock, a professor at the University of California, Berkeley. Tetlock's research tracked some 82,000 predictions by 284 experts over two decades. The experts' forecasts were tracked both on the subjects of their specialities and on subjects that they knew little about. The results were surprising. The predictions of the experts were only a little bit better than random guesses. Kristof continues:

'It made virtually no difference whether participants had doctorates, whether they were economists, political scientists, journalists or historians, whether they had policy experience or access to classified information, or whether they had logged many or few years of experience,' Mr. Tetlock wrote.

Indeed, the only consistent predictor was fame – and it was an inverse relationship. The more famous experts did worse than unknown ones. That had to do with a fault in the media. Talent bookers for television shows and reporters tended to call up experts who provided strong, coherent points of view, who saw things in blacks and whites.

Mr. Tetlock called experts such as these the 'hedgehogs'. . . . Hedgehogs tend to have a focused world view, an ideological leaning, strong convictions; foxes are more cautious, more centrist, more likely to adjust their views, more pragmatic, more prone to self-doubt, more inclined to see complexity and nuance. And it turns out that while foxes don't give great sound-bites, they are far more likely to get things right.

This was the distinction that mattered most among the forecasters, not whether they had expertise. Over all, the foxes did significantly better, both in areas they knew well and in areas they didn't.

(Kristof 2009)

That particular viewpoint puts the hedgehog well and truly in its place! But, as with all metaphors, it is best not to push them too far. As Berlin himself commented in response to the discussion in the *New York Review of Books* quoted above:

I used his isolated line as a peg on which to hang my own reflections: the metaphor of hedgehogs and foxes was not, I warned the reader, to be driven too far; it was intended, at most, as an opening to my central theme—a hypothesis about the psychological roots of Tolstoy's historical outlook. Still less did I mean to imply that foxes were superior to hedgehogs; this was (and is) not my view. I made no judgments of value.

(Berlin 1980)

However, as a second metaphor, the hedgehog and fox provide us with much to ponder upon within this concluding chapter on cross-curricular approaches to teaching and learning.

Reflective Task 1

As we have discussed, Isaiah Berlin classified intellectuals as hedgehogs or foxes. The hedgehog knows one big thing and tries to explain as much as possible within that conceptual framework, whereas the fox knows many small things and is content to improvise explanations on a case-by-case basis.

As a bit of light relief, do you think you are a hedgehog or a fox? A short quiz will help you find out: http://jsavage.org.uk/?p=528. Decide whether you agree or disagree with the twelve statements presented and follow the instructions to work out your score. Do not take it too seriously!

Reflecting on the journey so far

This book began with the identification of three key principles that, I argued, should underpin all teachers' approaches to teaching and learning. Stenhouse's famous statement that 'there is no meaningful and long-lasting curriculum development without teacher development' (Stenhouse 1975, p. 142) has underpinned our discussions throughout the book. It has been the main reason for my deliberate choice within this book to focus on the responsibility of the teacher and their key role in the development of cross-curricular approaches to teaching and learning within the classroom. Some readers may have found this approach narrow-minded. Many recent pieces of educational policy have focused on the pupil and their perceived needs and interests as a starting point for educational reform. These include recent developments in the National Curriculum for Key Stage 3.[3] I would not want to underplay the importance of considering these things as part of the teacher's role as a leader and initiator of educational change. But my argument has been that the teacher, and the development of their skilful cross-curricular pedagogy, are fundamental to the emergence of a new approach to teaching and learning. Therefore, an emphasis on teachers developing a skilful pedagogy was my third key principle.

Jumping backwards, the second key principle of the book related to the exposition of Peshkin's work (Peshkin 1988). This was developed throughout Chapter 2. His concept of subjectivity being like a garment that cannot be removed was applied in two ways: first, to the individual teacher and the way that they perceive themselves; but second, to their subject (including associated subject knowledge and its organisation) and its accompanying subject culture, and the impact of these on their sense of educational identity. As we discussed, these specific subject cultures dominate the organisation of secondary schools at the present time. These subject 'subjectivities' impact on our work in important ways. Positively, some research has argued that a strong and rigorous subject knowledge is central to the development of cross-curricular ways of working (CUREE 2009a, p. 3). It is also important for most teachers' sense of job satisfaction (Spear, Gould and Lea 2000, p. 52). More negatively, teachers can often be seen to retreat within their subject areas (both physically and metaphorically) and fail to make the kind of cross-curricular links that could enrich their own teaching and their collaborations with other colleagues. But either way, this second key principle affirms the view that, in the end, it is the teacher who will 'change the world of the school by understanding it' (Stenhouse 1975, p. 208). The amount of commitment that an individual teacher can give to the project of developing cross-curricular approaches to their teaching and learning will be the single, most influential factor in sustained curriculum development and ongoing professional development.

Drawing on these key principles, the early chapters of the book introduced a working definition for cross-curricular teaching and learning:

> *A cross-curricular approach to teaching is characterised by sensitivity towards, and a synthesis of, knowledge, skills and understandings from various subject areas. These inform an enriched pedagogy that promotes an approach to learning which embraces and explores this wider sensitivity through various methods.*

Chapter 2 identified a range of key words within this definition. These include sensitivity, synthesis, subjectivity, enriching, embracing and exploring. These words sum up, for me, the type of positive attitude and approach that teachers will need in order to develop meaningful cross-curricular approaches within their work. They are certainly attributes that the remainder of this book has explored, through issues relating to pedagogy (Chapter 3), language and literacy (Chapter 4), information and communication technologies (Chapter 5) and educational assessment and evaluation (Chapter 6).

This concluding chapter will reconsider some of these themes through a final exploration of the role of the teacher within curriculum development. It will raise questions for the future of cross-curricular teaching and learning and place these within a wider consideration of the possible future for cross-curricular education over the next fifteen years. It will structure these considerations under three main headings:

1.   a renaissance of curriculum development;
2.   the pull towards centrifugal teaching;
3.   the future possibilities for cross-curricular teaching and learning.

A renaissance of curriculum development

Ross's (2000) work on curriculum development is a helpful way to begin this process of summing up our discussion about cross-curricular teaching and learning. For our purposes, I will draw on two of his models for curriculum analysis and apply them to our ongoing discussion.

First, Ross (2000) provides us with a metaphorical view of the curriculum. Within his model (Table 7.1) there are four metaphors: the 'baroque' curriculum, the 'natural landscaped' curriculum, the 'dig for victory' curriculum and the 'cottage' curriculum.

Alongside these curriculum metaphors, Ross (2000) provides a helpful historical model of curriculum development from the mid-1980s onwards (Table 7.2). Again, in a similar way to one's consideration of Ross's metaphorical curriculum model

TABLE 7.1 Ross's curriculum metaphors

CURRICULUM METAPHOR	DEFINITION
Baroque	'The curriculum of clearly demarcated subjects, classified by both content knowledge and by the discourse forms appropriate and specific to each discipline' (Ross 2000, p. 3)
Natural landscaped	'Subjects are portrayed as artificial, dividing forms of knowledge with contrived distinctions or process, knowledge and procedure. . . . The apparent freedom of the learner is conditioned by the constant surveillance of the teacher' (Ross 2000, p. 4)
Dig for victory	'The idea that curriculum must be in some way useful and, in particular, that the learning that takes place in schools must in some way prepare children for their future roles in work and in society (Ross 2000, p. 5)
Cottage	'A preservation of cultural forms achieved through time honoured processes, resistant to challenge or criticism . . . the result of competing claims to truth, or bargaining and negotiation' (Ross 2000, p. 7)

TABLE 7.2 Ross's curriculum types

CURRICULUM TYPE	
The imposed curriculum	This curriculum type is about political power and ideology. It is about maintaining the status quo and imposed from central, organisatory bodies (this could be governmental or regulatory in origin). Ross described this as 'a curriculum that eschews relevance and the present, concentrating on the heritage and the canon based on temporal disengagement; a curriculum suspicious of the popular and immediate, made up of echoes of past voices, the voices of a cultural and political elite; a curriculum that ignores the past of women and the working class and the colonised – a curriculum of the dead' (Ross 2000, pp. 81–2)
The social transformative curriculum	Within this model, individuals get the opportunity to escape from the limitations of the social or class group in which they were born through exposure to a broader environment of learning and knowledge. Ross draws on Dewey here [especially Dewey's view of knowledge being something that is actively constructed by the learner (Dewey 1916, p. 20)], the teacher's role being that of provoking this type of enquiry from the pupil
Content-driven curriculum	This is an academic, subject-based and content-driven curriculum model. Although the actual forms of content and delivery within this curriculum model (and across the particular subjects within it) will vary, the outcomes of this model would be construed as being 'academic' (Ross 2000, pp. 81–2)

TABLE 7.2 (continued)

CURRICULUM TYPE	
The objectives-driven curriculum	This is characterised as being a utilitarian or vocational curriculum model. It might be referred to as being an 'applied' curriculum and, historically, would be for pupils who would not be studying under the 'academic' content-driven curriculum model (Ross 2000, pp. 81–2)
The process-driven curriculum	This is a progressive and developmental curriculum model. It could also be labelled the 'child-centred' curriculum. It is characterised by an approach that places the student at the centre of the curriculum, empowering their choices and allowing them plenty of opportunity to discover things for themselves (Ross 2000, pp. 81–2)

presented above, these categories are not fixed and there will be elements of each in any given situation.

Ross's paper was published in 2000, before the most recent set of curriculum initiatives at Key Stages 3 and 4. The following reflective task will help you apply his thinking to recent developments.

Reflective Task 2

Reflect on the most recent series of curriculum reforms. These will include the revision of the National Curriculum at Key Stages 3 and 4 in 2007, the introduction of diplomas in the 14–19 curriculum from 2007 onwards, and the plethora of competency-based, learning-to-learn or 'opening minds' type curriculum innovations that have become increasingly popular in recent years.

Using Ross's models, for each piece of curriculum reform try and ascertain the blend of curriculum metaphor and curriculum type that it contains. Each piece may, and probably will, contain more than one.

Finally, to what extent do Ross's metaphors and types allow for the possibility of a cross-curricular model of curriculum development?

Kirk's warning that 'courses and subjects that fail to reinvent themselves in the face of new circumstances are liable to decline or disappear' (Kirk, Macdonald and Tinning 1997, p. 273) is worth repeating at this point. By extension, we could hypothesise that curricula that fail to reinvent themselves in light of new circumstances are equally likely to decline and, in the worst (or should that be the 'best'?) case, disappear. The metaphors for curriculum that Ross has developed seem, in the majority of cases, to emphasise the delineation of subjects along lines that are, by now, familiar to all teachers. This is certainly the case for the 'Baroque' and 'landscaped' metaphors. The 'dig for victory' curriculum metaphor is functional in its design and has grown in prominence throughout the last ten years in all phases of secondary education. The 'cottage' curriculum metaphor provides a broader historical perspective but, again, seems unable to escape the shackles that preserve its dominating cultural forms established by an elite. Similarly, within the curriculum types that Ross identifies there are echoes of many recent initiatives. Perhaps Ross's social transformative and process-driven curriculum types present the best opportunity for cross-curricular approaches to teaching and learning.

But in surveying Ross's curriculum metaphors and types I was struck by the lack of reference to cross-curricularity. There seems to be an opportunity to develop a new curriculum model that acknowledges more explicitly the cross-curricular frameworks and pedagogies that we have been discussing throughout this book. A playful approach to the metaphors that were introduced during the opening of this chapter might find a useful alternative.

Taking a cue from Ross's use of the term 'Baroque', and from the metaphor of the polymath introduced above, perhaps a 'Renaissance' metaphor for the curriculum is worth developing. The Renaissance period of history was characterised by many things, but one of the key elements was a renewed emphasis on learning. Interestingly, this focused on a rediscovery of subjects within the classical antiquities. But Renaissance scholars have identified two themes that are pertinent to the possible formation of a 'Renaissance' curriculum model (Cassirer 2000; Kristeller 1990): first, universal orderliness and, second, universal interdependence.

Universal orderliness was premised on the concept that every existing thing in the universe had its place in a divinely planned hierarchical order. It divided objects according to the proportion of 'spirit' or 'matter' that they contained, with those objects that contained more 'spirit' being higher up the order. So, for example, the lower levels contained inanimate objects (such as water, air and fire); and moving up the order we reach vegetative classes (trees, flowers) and then animals, humans and angels. There was also a hierarchical structure within each of these large groups (e.g. gold had more 'spirit' than lead). There were also overlaps between the tops and bottoms of particular levels.

Universal interdependence held the belief that different segments of this great chain of universal orderliness reflected each other in particular ways in what were known as 'correspondences'. This is put most powerfully by Faivre, who wrote:

> We find again here the ancient idea of microcosm and macrocosm or, if preferred, the principle of universal interdependence. These correspondences, considered more or less veiled at first sight, are, therefore, intended to be read and deciphered. The entire universe is a huge theater of mirrors, an ensemble of hieroglyphs to be decoded. Everything is a sign; everything conceals and exudes mystery; every object hides a secret.

> (Faivre 1994, p. 10)

As an example, Renaissance thinkers viewed a human being as being a microcosm of the world as a whole. As the world comprised four elements (earth, water, air and fire), so the human body was composed of four 'humours' (sanguine, choleric, phlegmatic and melancholy). This had implications for medical science, philosophy and psychology within the period. These types of correspondences were made everywhere, on many levels throughout the chain of universal orderliness. As a literary example, in Shakespeare's *King Lear*, the mental anguish that the King experiences, including his loss of reason, is paralleled with a reversal in the natural order of things. This leads King Lear to equate his mental disorders to the natural disorders (i.e. the storm) that surround him:

> Thou think'st 'tis much that this contentious storm
> Invades us to the skin; so 'tis to thee.
> But where the greater malady is fixed,
> The lesser is scarce felt. Thou'dst shun a bear,
> But if thy flight lay toward the raging sea,
> Thou'dst meet the bear i'th' mouth. When the mind's free,
> The body's delicate. The tempest in my mind
> Doth from my senses take all feeling else
> Save what beats there – filial ingratitude.
>
> (Act III, Scene IV)

Applying any metaphor is often simultaneously helpful and problematic. This is certainly the case with the twin concepts of universal orderliness and universal interdependence in the construction of a provisional Renaissance curriculum model. Existing curriculum models could be conceived as presenting an orderly model of subjects, arranged in a hierarchical structure of sorts by perceived academic value (hence we have core or foundation subjects; optional or compulsory subjects at particular ages), akin to Ross's Baroque curriculum model. For each subject culture within this model there will be categorisations or levels of knowledge, skills and understanding, some of which are valued more highly than others.

The notions of universal interdependence and correspondences become the metaphors for cross-curricularity within the Renaissance curriculum model. The challenge here is to find correspondences that relate to and enforce the natural orderliness found within the particular subject cultures. Although there will not be exact parallels (and this is where the metaphor begins to fall down), working across and between the subject cultures in a way that promotes orderliness in knowledge, thinking and understanding may help to facilitate or stimulate cross-curricular learning. To do the contrary will lead to 'disorder' in thinking and educational 'anguish'.

In a final extension to this development of a Renaissance curriculum metaphor, perhaps it is helpful to explore in a little more detail one further art form from the Renaissance period that has survived to this day. Renaissance music is often characterised as being polyphonic (literally, many sounds) as opposed to monophonic (literally, one sound), as is found in Medieval plainchant. As the Renaissance period merged into the Baroque (around 1600), polyphonic musical textures transformed to become homophonic (i.e. having the same sound), which resulted in a melodic line being supported by a chordal accompaniment, that is, the melodic line became of primary importance, with the bass line and chordal parts supporting it. In contrast, in the Renaissance period the art of writing polyphonic music centred on the composer's ability to write for many voices as if they were one. Composers tried to do this by:

- sharing common melodic materials between the voices;
- allowing different voices to take the lead at different times;
- ensuring that the voices were equally important and that one voice did not dominate the music at any given point;
- handling dissonance (i.e. what could be perceived as 'clashes' in the sound of the music at a particular point) in a specific way, making sure that any of these tensions in the music were both prepared and resolved for the listener.

Renaissance polyphonic music expressed the metaphors or universal orderliness and interdependence within a perfect musical form. The result of this approach was the most beautiful religious music, characterised by its many interweaving parts sounding as one that can be heard, daily, in cathedrals and other large churches.

For our Renaissance curriculum model, this type of subject polyphony would be something to aspire to. It would permeate through our Renaissance curriculum model by allowing key knowledge, skills and understanding which are initiated by individual subjects (voices) to be shared across subjects (between voices) in a way that allows them to exist alongside each other with an equal sense of value. It could allow particular subjects to take the lead at particular times, but always within a combined, overall sense of balance, purpose and direction. It could highlight a specific theme for a certain period, sharing it amongst subjects and allowing each to present it with its own particular subject tone or resonance. It could handle potential clashes of knowledge or learning by carefully preparing learners for the potential dissonance, allowing them to enjoy the creative tension that the dissonance allows before resolving it for them in a sensitively managed and appropriate way.

Ultimately, a Renaissance curriculum is one of many potential metaphors that could encourage a sympathetic approach to cross-curricular teaching and learning. But curriculum models are fine in theory. It is time to turn our attention briefly to the second, key part of these concluding thoughts. What style of teaching would facilitate such a model?

The pull towards centrifugal teaching

Centripetal forces move or direct something towards the centre. In physiology, nerve impulses are sent centripetally to the central nervous system; in botany, the florets nearer the edge of a flower open first and they open centripetally as they move towards the centre. A centripetal approach to life characterises the perspective and attitude of hedgehogs (see Berlin 1953, pp. 1–2, quoted above) who, despite their many strengths, are unable to see life in any other way apart from through their particular mindset or disposition.

In contrast, centrifugal forces move away from the centre. Centrifugal comes from an amalgamation of two Latin words, *centrum* meaning 'centre', and *fugere* meaning 'to flee'. For Berlin (1953), foxes characterise a centrifugal approach to life. Their thought patterns are, in his words, 'scattered or diffused'. They move on multiple levels, drawing on a vast range of experiences and objects without trying to fit them together within one all-embracing rationale. They are happy to live with the incomplete, the contradictory and, unlike hedgehogs, thrive on the multiple meanings that life throws at them.

As equally tentatively as I suggested a Renaissance curriculum model, I would like to put forward the concept of centrifugal teaching, which, over the coming years, may provide the best way to develop cross-curricular teaching and learning. What elements define this approach?

Centrifugal teachers are, by instinct, outward looking. They have many interests and they are happy moving between multiple areas of knowledge, pulling together diverse patterns and ideas from different subject areas without worrying too much about a final framework for their co-existence or ultimate meaning. They are willing to pursue metaphors and explore the tensions within them, without closing down patterns of thought too early. For the centrifugal teacher, contradictions between subjects and self-contradictions in their work are creative forces that spur them onwards and outwards to further discoveries. For these teachers, the spiralling, centripetal forces associated with traditional subject cultures and associated pedagogies are an anathema. These suck their creative forces dry and lead them to educational and professional implosions. But centrifugal teachers can often be misunderstood. Their ability to live with uncertainty can be threatening to those who value certainty and see it as a pre-requisite for action. Their pragmatism is seen by some as a lack of ability to establish what is right or wrong within curriculum development; their cautiousness is dismissed as hesitancy, and their self-doubt and provisionality as woolly-headed thinking.

Perhaps you feel that this is a bit strong? Maybe it is. But perhaps there does need to be a significant shift towards a more centrifugal teaching approach if we are to shake the current approaches to curriculum development and pedagogy to their core and develop new curriculum models with cross-curricular pedagogies at their heart. It is easy to meddle around the edges of our subject pedagogies, to do what we have always done and re-package them according to the current educational climate and philosophy.

However, this is not what is required to initiate and sustain a cross-curricular approach to teaching and learning that is sensitive and sympathetic to traditional subject cultures, whilst at the same time enriching, exploring and embracing new pedagogical avenues and directions. As we will consider below, a failure to respond to wider changes in society will result in traditional models of teaching and learning losing currency and value amongst young people.

To return to the metaphors that opened this chapter, teaching seems dominated by hedgehogs. We need more foxes. We need more teachers to think and act centrifugally rather than centripetally. Whilst it is unrealistic and unhelpful to use the term 'educational polymaths', we do need teachers who are able to handle knowledge and understanding from diverse areas with a significant degree of authenticity. Intellectual promiscuity of the type decried by Djerassi (Carr 2009) is not the answer. Nor is intellectual polygamy despite the apparent democratic value it might bestow upon its particular subjects. As we have seen, powerful subject discourses are a real and defining force within our identities and subject cultures, which imbue us with a particular tone or, in Prensky's term, accent which it is impossible to lose (Prensky 2001, pp. 2–3). To return briefly to our discussion of Renaissance polyphonic music, if all the voices in an ensemble sounded the same the result would be bland; a key component of its beauty would be lost. A centrifugal disposition as a teacher will, in part at least, lead to the development of a successful cross-curricular pedagogy. It will also underpin a disposition and ability to collaborate meaningfully with other teachers within a Renaissance curriculum model based on equality of discourse, expression and interaction.

The future possibilities for cross-curricular teaching and learning

So, given the focus on curriculum and pedagogy discussed above, what is the future for cross-curricular teaching and learning?

This depends on how teachers respond to the challenges within books like this. Formal, top-down policy initiatives for greater degrees of cross-curricular activities within schools seem to fail. History has taught us that. This book has argued that a cross-curricular practice and pedagogy needs to be reborn and re-situated within the pedagogy of individual teachers. Within the contemporary secondary context, the notion of the subject specialist, and the accompanying subject cultures, are firmly established in curricular and assessment frameworks. There will need to be a major shift in pedagogical thinking and practice for this type of cross-curricular practice to emerge. It seems likely that this kind of shift will only take place in the medium to long term. In the shorter term, I am optimistic that teachers will rise to the challenge and, providing the key principles that we have explored together within this book are adhered to, there is a strong possibility that an authentic cross-curricular approach to teaching and learning will emerge. One of the keys for our work over the next few years will be to find appropriate platforms for the sharing of successful approaches to cross-curricular teaching and learning. Lawrence Stenhouse had another famous aphorism, 'research is systematic enquiry *made public*' [my italics] (Stenhouse 1983). Teachers need to be empowered to share their stories in a more systematic way.

However, this is only one component of an anticipated educational future. As we saw in Chapter 5 when we examined the use of technology as a tool to develop cross-curricular teaching and learning, the wide array of thinking behind futures educational research such as 'Beyond Current Horizons' (DCSF and Futurelab 2009) has identified a broad range of future concerns that will need to be addressed. For an alternative look at the future of education see the interactive timeline Education Futures, a resource put together by a team of American researchers (Education Futures 2009). The challenges of globalisation, environmental concerns, issues associated with well-being and health, technological development and much more besides will all impact on the shape and format of educational practice in years to come. It seems that the concept and organisation of the school as we know it today will change radically in the medium to long term.

How should one prepare for these changes? In my opinion, the concepts of individual subjects have a limited currency in education. In the short term they will remain as an organising principle. But an analysis of recent changes in the curriculum show these being replaced by more generic curriculum themes and approaches on a regular basis. Within these changes, subject knowledge still plays an important part and teachers are able to react and re-organise their approaches with minimal impact on their pedagogy and practice. But I do not think that this will be the case for too much longer. More significant changes to curriculum design and implementation will emerge that stretch the traditional organising principles of subjects and subject cultures to breaking point. Subjects in the curriculum, at least in the way that we have them today, may cease to exist. Subject specialists will need to re-think the ways in which subject knowledge contributes to these new curriculum and pedagogical frameworks. I suspect that some teachers will be able to do this and others will not. Educational practice in twenty years from now will be very different from what it is today.

Of course, all of this might not happen. But how would you feel if it did? I cannot help but feel a sense of loss. Changes like this would worry me in several ways. But this response shows a natural inclination to reflect inwards, centripetally, to what I value and know, to curl up like a hedgehog and withstand the assault of the fox. A new breed of teachers, those that think centrifugally, will grasp the inherent challenges of the above scenarios. They will naturally think in a cross-curricular way and be able to bridge the gaps between what we refer to as 'subjects' today. Their pedagogical approach will undoubtedly be different in ways that we have yet to perceive. But I hope that ideas in this book have paved the way for a significant review of what we currently do and how we might respond to the new challenges ahead.

Professional Standards for QTS

This chapter will help you meet the following Q standards: Q6, Q7a, Q8, Q10, Q11, Q14

Professional Standards for Teachers

This chapter will help you meet the following core standards: C6, C7, C8, C15, C16, C30, C40, C41

Links to Other Books in this Series

I hope you have enjoyed reading this title. This book is one of a series of books published by Routledge investigating cross-curricular approaches to teaching and learning. The other titles take a detailed look at the possibilities of developing a cross-curricular approach within each of seven, different disciplinary areas. Each takes a predominantly practical approach to issues that have been raised here. As such, we urge you to explore these ideas further through these accompanying titles:

- Cross-Curricular Teaching and Learning in the Secondary School . . . The Arts
- Cross-Curricular Teaching and Learning in the Secondary School . . . English
- Cross-Curricular Teaching and Learning in the Secondary School . . . Foreign Languages
- Cross-Curricular Teaching and Learning in the Secondary School . . . Humanities
- Cross-Curricular Teaching and Learning in the Secondary School . . . Using ICT
- Cross-Curricular Teaching and Learning in the Secondary School . . . Mathematics
- Cross-Curricular Teaching and Learning in the Secondary School . . . Science.

Notes

1. The 'grid edit' function of music sequencing software allows the user to enter notes to be played by 'colouring in' elements of a grid. A piano-style keyboard is displayed on the left-hand side of the screen (with the lower notes at the bottom left-hand corner of the screen and the highest sounding notes at the top left-hand corner). Users enter notes within the grid and can determine their pitch (by how high or low the notes are on the screen), their duration (by how long the coloured rectangle is) and their relative volume (by the density of the colour or by adjusting the appropriate point of the graph that runs along the bottom of the screen).

2. Movie Maker is a piece of free software designed for creating a digital video. It comes as part of Windows Vista or XP (see http://www.microsoft.com/windowsxp/using/moviemaker/default.mspx for further details). The equivalent piece of software from Apple is called iMovie (see http://www.apple.com/ilife/imovie/ for further details).

3. As an example of this, consider the change of words within each of the Key Process statements within the National Curriculum documentation. Previous versions of the National Curriculum contained the phrase, 'Pupils should be taught how to . . .'; the current National Curriculum phrases the same sentence as, 'Pupils should be able to . . .'. Although I would not want to build my justification for this point solely on this change of words, I think it does signal a significant shift in the perceived roles of teachers and pupils.

Bibliography

Alexander, R. J. (2004) 'Still No Pedagogy? Principle, pragmatism and compliance in primary education'. *Cambridge Journal of Education* 34:1, 7–34.

Alexander, R. J. (2007) *Education for All: The quality imperative and the problem of pedagogy*. New Delhi, Department for International Development.

Alexander, R. J. (2008) *Essays on Pedagogy*. London, Routledge.

Alexander, J., Walsh, P., Jarman, R. and McClune, B. (2008) 'From Rhetoric to Reality: Advancing literacy by cross-curricular means'. *The Curriculum Journal* 19:3, 23–35.

Altrichter, H., Posch, P. and Somekh, B. (1993) *Teachers Investigate Their Work*. London, Routledge.

Anderson, L. W. and Krathwohl, D. R. (2001) *A Taxonomy for Learning, Teaching, and Assessing: A revision of Bloom's taxonomy of educational objectives*. New York and London, Longman.

Anderson, T. (2002). *Getting the Mix Right: An updated and theoretical rationale for interaction*. ITFORUM, Paper no. 63. Available from http://it.coe.uga.edu/itforum/paper63/paper63. htm [last accessed 3 December 2009].

Anderson, T. and Elloumi, F. (2004) *Theory and Practice of Online Learning*. Athabasca, Canada, Athabasca University. Available from http://cde.athabascau.ca/online_book/ [last accessed 15 October 2009].

Anderson, T., Rourke, L., Archer, W. and Garrison, R. (2001) 'Assessing Teaching Presence in Computer Conferencing Transcripts'. *Journal of the Asynchronous Learning Network* 5:2, 1–17.

Bakhtin, M. M. (1981) *The Dialogic Imagination: Four essays by M. M. Bakhtin*. Emerson, C. and Holmquist, M. (eds) (trans. McGee, V. W.). Austin, University of Texas Press.

Bakhtin, M. M. (1986) *Speech Genres and Other Late Essays*. Emerson, C. and Holmquist, M. (eds) (trans. McGee, V. W.). Austin, University of Texas Press.

Ball, S. J. (1990) *Politics and Policy Making in Educational Settings: Explorations in policy sociology*. London, Routledge.

Beck, J. (1996) 'Citizenship Education: Problems and possibilities'. *Curriculum Studies* 4:3, 349–66.

Bell, W. (1997) *Foundations of Futures Studies*. London, Transaction Publishers.

Bennett, C. (2009) 'So Many Weird Lessons, Yet So Little Time for Proper Teaching'. Available from http://www.guardian.co.uk/commentisfree/2009/nov/29/education-domestic-violence [last accessed 5 January 2010].

Berk, R. (1996) 'Student Ratings of Ten Strategies for using Humor in College Teaching. *Journal on Excellence in College Teaching* 7:3, 71–92.

Berk, R. (1998) *Professors are from Mars, Students are from Snickers*. Madison, WI, Mendota Press.

Berlin, I. (1953) *The Hedgehog and the Fox: An essay on Tolstoy's view of history*. London, Weidenfeld & Nicolson.

Berlin, I. (1980) 'The Hedgehog and the Fox Continued'. *New York Review of Books* 27:15 (9

October 1980). Available from http://www.nybooks.com/articles/7279 [last accessed 8 January 2010].

Bernstein, B. (1999) 'Official knowledge and pedagogic identities', in Christie, F. (ed.) *Pedagogy and the Shaping of Consciousness*. London, Cassell.

Bernstein, B. (2000) *Pedagogy, Symbolic Control and Identity: Theory, research and critique* (revised edn). London, Lanham, Rowman & Littlefield.

Biesta, G. J. J. (2007) 'Education and the Democratic Person: Towards a political understanding of democratic education'. *Teachers College Record* 109:3, 740–69.

Black, P. and Wiliam, D. (1998) *Inside the Black Box: Raising standards through classroom assessment.* London, School of Education, King's College.

Black, P., Harrison, C., Lee, C., Marshall, B. and Wiliam, D. (2003) *Assessment for Learning: Putting it into practice.* Maidenhead, Open University Press/McGraw-Hill Education.

Blanchard, J. (2009) *Teaching, Learning and Assessment.* Buckingham, Open University Press.

Bloom, B. S. (1956) *Taxonomy of Educational Objectives, Handbook I: The cognitive domain.* New York, David McKay.

Board of Education (1921) *The Teaching of English in England* (Newbolt Report). London, HMSO.

Bowers, C. (1993). *Critical Essays on Education, Modernity, and the Recovery of the Ecological Imperative.* New York, Teachers' College Press.

Bowers, J. and Archer, P. (2005) 'Not Hyper, Not Meta, Not Cyber but Infra-Instruments'. Proceedings of the 2005 International Conference on New Interfaces for Music Expression, Canada, Vancouver, BC.

Bowman, J. S. (1980) 'The Hedgehog and the Fox'. *New York Review of Books* 27:14 (25 September 1980). Available from http://www.nybooks.com/articles/7297 [last accessed 8 January 2010].

Boyle, B. and Bragg, J. (2008) 'Making Primary Connections: The cross-curriculum story'. *The Curriculum Journal*, 19:1, 5–21.

Brehony, K. J. (2005) 'Primary Schooling under New Labour'. *Oxford Review of Education* 31:1, 29–46.

Bressler, M. (2000) 'In conversation with Jim Collins'. Available from http://www.kheper.net/topics/typology/Fox_and_Hedgehog.html [last accessed 8 January 2010].

Brooks, V. (2002) *Assessment in Secondary Schools: The new teacher's guide to monitoring, assessment, recording, reporting and accountability.* Buckingham, Open University Press.

Bruner, J. (1996) *The Culture of Education.* Cambridge, MA, Harvard University Press.

Buck, M. and Inman, S. (1993) 'Making Values Central: The role of the cross curricular themes'. *Careers Education and Guidance*, February, 10–14.

Campbell, A. and Kerry, T. (2004) 'Constructing a New KS3 Curriculum at Brooke Weston CTC: A review and commentary'. *Educational Studies* 30:4, 391–408.

Carr, E. (2009) 'The Last Days of the Polymath'. *Intelligent Life*, Autumn. Available from http://www.moreintelligentlife.com/content/edward-carr/last-days-polymath [last accessed 8 January 2010].

Cassirer, E. (2000) *The Individual and the Cosmos in Renaissance Philosophy*. New York, Dover Publications.

Central Advisory Council for Education (1959) *15 to 18, vol. 1* (Crowther Report). London, HMSO.

CfBT (2008a) 'Planning to Lead or Contribute to Cross-Curricular Opportunities: RE, citizenship and history'. Available from http://www.newsecondarycurriculum.org [last accessed 23 November 2009].

CfBT (2008b) 'Strange Fruit: A cross-curricular approach to the blues at Key Stage 3'. Available from http://www.newsecondarycurriculum.org [last accessed 23 November 2009].

CIDREE (2005) *Cross-curricular Themes in Secondary Education: Report of a CIDREE collaborative project.* Sint-Katelijne-Waver, Belgium, CIDREE. Available from http://www.cidree.be/uploads/documentenbank/4854365076a88c8ba93cbebe04fd9196.pdf [last accessed 20 July 2009].

Ciurlionis, M. K. (1998) 'M. K. Ciurlionis' (exhibition catalogue). Cologne, Wallraf-Richartz-Museum.

Claxton, G., Pollard, A. and Sutherland, R. (2003) 'Fishing in the fog: Conceptualising learning at the confluence of cultures', in Sutherland, R., Claxton, G. and Pollard, A. (eds) *Learning and Teaching: Where world views meet*. London, Trentham Books.

Conle, C. (2000) 'Narrative Inquiry: Research tool and medium for professional development'. *European Journal of Teacher Education* 23:1, 49–63.

Cooper, B. (1983) 'On Explaining Change in School Subjects'. *British Journal of Sociology of Education*, 4:3, 207–22.

Crawford, K. (2000) 'The Political Construction of the "Whole Curriculum"'. *British Educational Research Journal* 26:5, 615–30.

CUREE (2009a) *Map of Research Reviews (QCA Building the Evidence Base Project): September 2007–March 2011*. Coventry, CUREE. Available from http://www.curee-paccts.com/our-projects/qca-building-evidence-base [last accessed 24 July 2009].

CUREE (2009b) *Review of Individual Studies from Systematic Research Reviews: February 2008–August 2008*. Coventry, CUREE. Available from http://www.curee-paccts.com/our-projects/qca-building-evidence-base [last accessed 24 July 2009].

Dannels, D. P. and Housley Gaffney, A. L. (2009) 'Communication across the Curriculum and in the Disciplines: A call for scholarly cross-curricular advocacy'. *Communication Education* 58:1, 124–53.

DCSF (2009a) 'Learning Outside the Classroom'. Available from http://www.dcsf.gov.uk/everychildmatters/ete/schools/learningoutsidetheclassroom/learningotc/ and http://www.lotc.org.uk/ [last accessed 14 January 2010].

DCSF (2009b) 'Independent Review of the Primary Curriculum'. Available from http://www.dcsf.gov.uk/primarycurriculumreview/index.shtml [last accessed 15 December 2009].

DCSF and Futurelab (2009) 'Beyond Current Horizons'. Available from http://www.beyondcurrenthorizons.org.uk/ [last accessed 24 July 2009].

DCSF and QCDA (2007) *The National Curriculum: Statutory requirements for Key Stages 3 and 4*. London, DCSF and QCDA.

DCSF, Department for Business Innovation and Skills, the National Strategies and Learning and Skills Improvement Service (2009) 'Functional Skills Support Programme'. Available from http://www.fssupport.org/ [last accessed 15 December 2009].

de Bono Thinking Systems (2009) 'Six Thinking Hats'. Available from http://www.debonothinkingsystems.com/tools/6hats.htm [last accessed 14 January 2010].

Deleuze, G. and Guattari, F. (1988) *A Thousand Plateaus*. London, Athlone.

Dewey, J. (1916) *Democracy and Education*. New York, Macmillan.

DfES (2005) *Key Stage 3 National Strategy: Working together: teaching assistants and assessment for learning*. London, DfES. Available from http://nationalstrategies.standards.dcsf.gov.uk/node/86723 [last accessed 15 December 2009].

DfES (2007) *Teaching, Speaking and Listening* (Secondary National Strategy CD-ROM). London, DfES.

Dorion, K. (2009) 'Science Through Drama: A multiple case exploration of the characteristics of drama activities used in secondary science lessons'. *International Journal of Science Education* iFirst Article, 1–24.

Düchting, H. (2002) *Paul Klee: Painting music*. London, Munich and New York, Prestel.

Dufour, B. (ed.) (1990) *The New Social Curriculum: A guide to cross-curricular themes*. Cambridge, CUP.

Education Futures (2009) 'The Education Futures Timeline of Education: 1647–2045'. Available from http://www.educationfutures.com/resources/timeline/ [last accessed 12 January 2010].

Edwards, D. and Mercer, N. (1987) *Common Knowledge: The development of understanding in the classroom*. London, Methuen.

Eikenberry, K. (2009) 'The Kevin Eikenberry Group'. Available from http://kevineikenberry. com/ [last accessed 5 January 2010].

Eisner, E. (1987) 'Celebration of Thinking'. *Educational Horizons* 66:1, 1–4.

Eisner, E. (2005) *Reimagining Schools: The selected works of Elliot. W. Eisner*. London, Routledge.

Eraut, M. (2001) 'Non-formal learning, implicit learning and tacit knowledge in professional work', in Coffield, F. (ed.) *The Necessity of Informal Learning*. Bristol, Policy Press.

Estyn (2002) *Standards and Quality in Personal and Social Education in Primary and Secondary Schools in Wales*. Cardiff, Estyn.

Facer, K. (2009) 'Educational, Social and Technological Futures: A report from the Beyond Current Horizons Programme' . London, DCSF and Futurelab.

Facer, K. and Sandford, R. (2010) 'The Next 25 Years? Future scenarios and future directions for education and technology'. *Journal of Computer Assisted Learning* 26, 74–93.

Faivre, A. (1994) *Access to Western Esotericism*. Albany, State University of New York Press.

Futurelab (2006) 'Teachers Learning with Digital Technologies: A review of research and projects'. Bristol, Futurelab. Available from http://www.futurelab.org.uk/resources [last accessed 20 October 2009].

Galison, P. (1997) *Image and Logic: The material culture of micro-physics*. Chicago, University of Chicago Press.

Garner, R. (2005) 'Humor, Analogy, and Metaphor: H.A.M. it up in teaching'. *Radical Pedagogy* 6:2. Available from http://radicalpedagogy.icaap.org/content/issue6_2/garner.html [last accessed 14 January 2010].

Ginsburg, H. P. (1997) *Entering the Child's Mind: The clinical interview in psychological research and practice*. Cambridge, CUP.

Glynn, S. and Takahashi, T. (1998) 'Learning from Analogy-Enhanced Science Texts'. *Journal of Research in Science Teaching* 35, 1129–49.

Goodson, I. F. (1991) 'History, context and qualitative methods', in Goodson, I. F. and Walker, R. (eds) *Biography, Identity and Sociology*. Basingstoke, Falmer Press.

Goodson, I. F. and Mangen, J. F. (1995) 'Subject Cultures and the Introduction of Classroom Computers'. *British Educational Research Journal* 21:5, 613–29.

Goodson, I. F. and Mangen, J. M. (1998). 'Subject cultures and the introduction of classroom computers', in Goodson, I. F. (ed.) *Subject Knowledge: Readings for the study of school subjects*. London, Falmer Press.

Gorden, D. (1978) *Therapeutic Metaphors*. Cupertino, CA, Meta.

Gove, M. (2008) 'Michael Gove Attacks Proposed Changes to Primary Curriculum'. Available from http://conservativehome.blogs.com/torydiary/2008/12/michael-gove--1.html [last accessed 29 November 2009].

Grainger, T., Barnes, J. and Scoffham, S. (2004) 'A Creative Cocktail: Creative teaching in initial teacher education'. *Journal of Education for Teaching* 30:3, 243–53.

Hargreaves, D. (2003) 'Teachers Must Become Networking Wizards'. *The Independent*, 26 June.

Hargreaves, D. H. (1991) 'Coherence and Manageability: Reflections on the National Curriculum and cross-curricular provision'. *The Curriculum Journal* 2:1, 33–41.

Harris, R. and Ratcliffe, M. (2005) 'Socio-scientific Issues and the Quality of Exploratory Talk: What can be learned from schools involved in a "collapsed day" project'. *The Curriculum Journal* 16:4, 439–53.

Harris, V. (2008) 'A Cross-Curricular Approach to "Learning to Learn" Languages: Government policy and school practice'. *The Curriculum Journal* 19:4, 255–68.

Heppell, S. (2010) 'Playful Learning's the Answer. What is the question?' Available from http://agent4change.net/index.php?option=com_content&view=article&id=492:playful-learnings-the-answer-whats-the-question&catid=98:innovation&Itemid=478 [last accessed 6 January 2010].

Higham, J. and Yeomans, D. (2009) 'Working Together? Partnership approaches to 14–19 education in England'. *British Educational Research Journal* iFirst Article, 1–23.

Hill, D. (1988) *Humor in the Classroom: A handbook for teachers*. Springfield, IL, Charles C. Thomas.

Hoffman, R. (1983) 'Recent Research on Metaphor'. *Semiotic Inquiry* 3, 35–62.

Inspectie van het Onderwijs (2001) *Onderwijsverslag 2000*. Utrecht, Inspectie van het Onderwijs.

Jephcote, M. and Davies, B. (2007) 'School Subjects, Subject Communities and Curriculum Change: The social construction of economics in the school curriculum'. *Cambridge Journal of Education* 37:2, 207–27.

Jerram, L. (2009) 'Play Me, I'm Yours'. Available from http://www.lukejerram.com/projects/play_me_im_yours/ [last accessed 12 December 2009].

Jewitt, C. (2008) 'Multimodal discourses across the curriculum', in Hornberger, N. H. (ed.) (2008) *Encyclopaedia of Language and Education* (2nd edition). New York, Springer.

John, P. (2005) 'The Sacred and the Profane: Subject sub-culture, pedagogical practice and teachers' perceptions of the classroom uses of ICT'. *Educational Review* 57:4, 469–88.

Johnson, G. C. (2002) 'Taking Up a Post-Personal Position in Reflective Practice: One teacher's account'. *Reflective Practice* 3:1, 21–38.

Kandinsky, W. (1947) *Über das Geistige in der Kunst*. New York, Wittenborn.

Kerr, D. (1999) *Re-examining Citizenship Education: The case of England*. Slough, NFER.

Kerr, D. (2000) 'Citizenship Education: Some lessons from other countries'. *Topic* 24, 1–9.

Kirk, D., Macdonald, D. and Tinning, R. (1997) 'The Social Construction of Pedagogic Discourse in Physical Teacher Education in Australia'. *The Curriculum Journal* 8:2, 271–98.

Kristeller, P. O. (1990) *Renaissance Thought and the Arts*. New Jersey, Princeton University Press.

Kristof, N. D. (2009) 'Learning How to Think'. *The New York Times*, 26 March. Available from http://www.nytimes.com/2009/03/26/opinion/26Kristof.html?_r=1 [last accessed 8 January 2010].

Kroeker, K. (2004), 'Technology Meets Music: An interview with composer-singer Paul Korda'. *Tech News World*. Available from http://www.technewsworld.com/story/32952.html [last accessed 23 March 2009].

Kushner, S. (1992a) *The Arts, Education and Evaluation: An introductory pack with practical exercies*. 'Section 1: Introduction'. Norwich, Centre for Applied Research in Education, University of East Anglia.

Kushner, S. (1992b) *The Arts, Education and Evaluation: An introductory pack with practical exercies*. 'Section 5: Making observations'. Norwich, Centre for Applied Research in Education, University of East Anglia.

Kushner, S. (1992c) *The Arts, Education and Evaluation: An introductory pack with practical exercies*. 'Section 6: Interviewing'. Norwich, Centre for Applied Research in Education, University of East Anglia.

Kushner, S. (1993) 'One in a million? The individual at the centre of quality control', in Elliott, J. (ed.) *Reconstructing Teacher Education: Teacher development* London, Falmer Press.

Kushner, S. (2000) *Personalising Evaluation*. London, Sage.

Kvale, S. (2007) *Doing Interviews*. London, Sage.

Lakoff, G. and Johnson, M. (1981) *Metaphors We Live By*. Chicago, Chicago University Press.

Latour B. (1993) *We Have Never Been Modern*. Hemel Hempstead, Harvester Wheatsheaf.

Leat, D., Lofthouse, R. and Taverner, S. (2006) 'The Road Taken: Professional pathways in innovative curriculum development'. *Teachers and Teaching: Theory and Practice* 12:6, 657–74.

McIntosh, P. (2010) *Action Research and Reflective Practice*. London, Routledge.

McNiff, J. (2005) *Action Research for Teachers*. London, Routledge.

Maes, B., De Coninck, C., Sleurs, W. and Van Woensel, C. (2001) European Conference of Experts on Cross-Curricular Themes in Secondary Education. Pre-conference document. Questionnaire Analysis. Brussels, 11–12 October.

Marland, M. (1977) *Language Across the Curriculum*. London, Heinemann.

Maur, K. (1999) *The Sound of Painting: Music in modern art*. London and New York, Prestel.

May, S. (2007) 'Sustaining Effective Literacy Practices Over Time in Secondary Schools: School organisational and change issues'. *Language and Education* 21:5, 387–405.

Mercer, N. (2000) *Words and Minds: How we use language to think together.* London, Routledge.

Morrison, K. (1994) *Implementing Cross-Curricular Themes.* London, David Fulton Publishers.

National Curriculum Council (NCC) (1989) *Circular No.6.* York, NCC.

North American Simulation and Gaming Association (NASAGA) (2009) 'Creating Metaphors and Analogies to Use in Training and Other Learning Events'. Available from http://www.nasaga.org [last accessed 15 December 2009].

O'Brien, J. and MacBeath, J. (1999) 'Co-ordinating Staff Development: The training and development of staff development co-ordinators'. *Journal of In-service Education* 25, 69–83.

Ofsted (2001a) *Ofsted Subject Reports (1999–2000): Secondary personal, social and health education (PSHE).* London, Ofsted.

Ofsted (2001b) *Inspection Report 122153.* London, Ofsted.

Ofsted (2008) *Curriculum Innovation in Schools.* London, Ofsted.

On Track and Field (2009) Available from http://www.ontrackandfield.com/main/catalog/2009/polevaulthistory.html [last accessed 29 November 2009].

Owen, M. (2006), 'The Myth of the Digital Native'. Available from http://www.futurelab.org.uk/viewpoint/art26.htm [last accessed 6 April 2009].

Parker, J. (2004) 'The Synthesis of Subject and Pedagogy for Effective Learning and Teaching in Primary Science Education'. *British Educational Research Journal* 30:6, 819–39.

Parker, J. and Heywood, D. (2000) 'Exploring the Relationship between Subject Knowledge and Pedagogic Content Knowledge in Primary Teachers' Learning about Forces'. *International Journal of Science Education* 22:1, 89–111.

Partnership for Schools (2010) 'Library'. Available from http://www.partnershipsforschools.org.uk/library/library.jsp [last accessed 5 January 2010].

Paton, G. (2009) 'Adults 'Abdicating Responsibility' for Children'. Available from http://www.telegraph.co.uk/education/6598138/Adults-abdicating-responsibility-for-children.html [last accessed 10 December 2009].

Peshkin, A. (1988) 'In Search of Subjectivity – One's Own'. *Educational Researcher* 17:7, 17–22.

Peshkin, A. (1991) *The Color of Strangers, the Color of Friends: The play of ethnicity in school and community.* Chicago, University of Chicago Press.

Phillips, D. K. and Carr, K. (2010) *Becoming a Teacher through Action Research.* London, Routledge.

Polanyi, M. (1967) *The Tacit Dimension.* New York, Anchor Books.

Pollio, H. and Humphreys, W. (1996) 'What Award-Wining Lecturers Say About Their Teaching: It's all about connection'. *College Teaching* 44, 101–6.

Pope, A. (1711) *An Essay on Criticism.* Available from http://poetry.eserver.org/essay-on-criticism.html [last accessed 5 January 2010].

Popkewitz, T. (1998) *Struggling for the Soul: The politics of schooling and the construction of the teacher.* New York, Teachers College Press.

Prensky, M. (2001) 'Digital Natives, Digital Immigrants'. *On the Horizon* 9:5. Lincoln, NCB University Press.

Pumfrey, P. (1993) 'Cross-curricular elements and the National Curriculum', in Verma, G. and Pumfrey, P. (eds) (1993) *Cross-Curricular Contexts: Themes and dimensions in secondary schools.* London, Falmer Press.

QCA (2000) *Language for Learning at Key Stage 3.* London, QCA.

QCA (2001) *Language at Work in Lessons.* London, QCA.

QCA (2007) *The National Curriculum: Statutory requirements for Key Stages 3 and 4.* London, QCA.

QCA (2008a) *The New Secondary Curriculum: What has changed and why.* London, QCA.

QCA (2008b) *Disciplined Curriculum Innovation: Making a difference to learners.* London, QCA.

QCA (2009) *Controlled Assessment in Diploma Principal Learning: A consortium guide.* London, QCA.

QCDA (2009a) 'A Big Picture of the Curriculum'. Available from http://www.qcda.gov.uk/5856.aspx [last accessed 3 November 2009].

QCDA (2009b) *Cross-Curriculum Dimensions: A planning guide for schools.* London, QCDA.

QCDA (2009c) 'Support for the New Secondary Curriculum'. Available from http://www.newsecondarycurriculum.org [last accessed 3 November 2009].

QCDA (2009d) *Sustainable Development in Action: A curriculum planning guide for schools*. London, QCDA.

QCDA (2009e) *Disciplined Curriculum Innovation: Making a difference to learners*. London, QCDA. Available from http://www.qcda.gov.uk/22095.aspx [last accessed 10 December 2009].

QCDA (2009f) 'Functional Skills'. Available from http://www.qcda.gov.uk/6062.aspx [last accessed 15 December 2009].

Reid, A. and Scott, W. (2005) 'Cross-Curricularity in the National Curriculum: Reflections on metaphor and pedagogy in citizenship education through school geography'. *Pedagogy, Culture and Society* 13:2, 181–204.

Rico, G. L. (1983) *Writing the Natural Way*. Los Angeles, J. P. Tarcher.

Rosenbaum, M. (2009) 'An Illustrated History of Pole Vault'. Available from http://trackandfield.about.com/od/polevault/ss/illuspolevault_2.htm [last accessed 30 November 2009].

Ross, A. (2000) *Curriculum: Construction and Critique*. London, Falmer Press.

RSA (2009) 'The Manchester Curriculum'. Available from http://www.thersa.org/fellowship/journal/archive/spring-2009/news/manchester-curriculum [last accessed 12 September 2009].

Ruddock, J. (ed.) (1995) *An Education that Empowers: A collection of lectures in memory of Lawrence Stenhouse*. Clevedon, Avon, Multilingual Matters.

Salavuo, M. (2008) 'Are University Students Digital Natives?' Available from http://weblog.siba.fi/msalavuo/2008/09/12/are-university-students-digital-natives/ [last accessed 20 March 2009].

Saunders, L., Hewitt, D. and MacDonald, A. (1995) *Education for Life. The cross-curricular themes in primary and secondary education*. Slough, NFER.

Savage, J. (1999) 'Approaches to Composition with Music Technology'. Available from http://www.music-journal.com/english/htm/musunt/approach/appr1.htm [last accessed 3 November 2009].

Savage, J. (2001) 'Sound Reflections: The influence of acoustic ecology on classroom composition'. *Soundscape,* 2:2, 36–9.

Savage, J. (2007a) 'Reflecting through Peshkin's I's'. *International Journal of Music Education* 25:3, 193–204.

Savage, J. (2007b) 'Reconstructing Music Education through ICT'. *Research in Education* 78, 65–77.

Savage, J. and Challis, M. (2001) 'Dunwich Revisited: Collaborative composition and performance with new technologies'. *British Journal of Music Education* 18:2, 139–49.

Savage, J. and Challis, M. (2002) 'A Digital Arts Curriculum? Practical ways forward'. *Music Education Research* 4:1, 7–24.

Savage, J. and Fautley, M. (2007a) *Assessment for Learning and Teaching in Secondary Schools*. Exeter, Learning Matters.

Savage, J. and Fautley, M. (2007b) *Creativity in Secondary Education*. Exeter, Learning Matters.

Schaff, A. (1973) 'Language and Cognition', in Cohen, R. S. (ed.) *Linguistics: From Herder to the theory of the 'linguistic field'*. New York, McGraw-Hill.

Schon, D. (1983) *The Reflective Practitioner: How professionals think in action*. New York, Basic Books.

Schon, D. (1987) *Educating the Reflective Practitioner: Toward a new design for teaching and learning in the professions*. San Francisco, Jossey-Bass.

Schoonmaker, M. (2009) 'Thinking like a Digital Native'. Available from http://www.school-video-news.com/index.php?option=com_content&view=article&id=597:thinking-like-a-digital-native&catid=24:concepts&Itemid=39 [last accessed 7 January 2010].

Scott, P., Mortimer, E. and Aguiar, O. (2006) 'The Tension Between Authoritative and Dialogic

Discourse: A fundamental characteristic of meaning making interactions in high school science lessons'. *Science Education* 90, 605–31.

Selwyn, N. (1999) 'Differences in Educational Computer Use: The influence of subject cultures'. *The Curriculum Journal* 10:1, 29–48.

Selwyn, N., Dawes, L. and Mercer, N. (2001) 'Promoting Mr. "Chips": The construction of the teacher–computer relationship in educational advertising'. *Teaching and Teacher Education* 17:4, 3–14.

Sergeant, H. (2009) 'Too Many Initiatives, Not Enough Teaching'. Available from http://www.guardian.co.uk/education/mortarboard/2009/nov/27/too-many-iniatives-not-enough-teaching [last accessed 30 November 2009].

Silbeck, M. (1983) 'Lawrence Stenhouse: Research methodology'. *British Educational Research Journal* 9:1, 11–20.

Somekh, B. (1995) 'The Contribution of Action Research to Development in Social Endeavours: A position paper on action research methodology'. *British Educational Research Journal,* 21:3, 339–55.

Somekh, B. (2006) *Action Research: A methodology for change and development.* Maidenhead, OUP.

Somekh, B. (2007) *Pedagogy and Learning with ICT.* London, Routledge.

Somekh, B. and Davis, N. (eds) (1997) *Using Information Technology Effectively in Teaching and Learning: Studies in pre-service and in-service teacher education.* London, Routledge.

Somers, M. (2001) *Implementatie van gezondheidsbevordering in het basisonderwijs en de eerste graad van het secundair onderwijs.* Studie in opdracht van de Vlaamse Onderwijsraad. Brussel: Vlaamse Onderwijsraad.

Spear, M., Gould, K. and Lee, B. (2000) *Who Would be a Teacher? A review of factors motivating and demotivating prospective and practising teachers.* Slough, NFER.

Stein, P. (2007) *Multimodal Pedagogies in Diverse Classrooms: Representation, rights and resources.* London, Routledge.

Stenhouse, L. (1975) *An Introduction to Curriculum Research and Development.* London, Heinemann Educational.

Stenhouse, L. (1980a) 'Product or process? A reply to Brian Crittenden', reprinted in Ruddock, J. and Hopkins, D. (eds) (1985) *Research as a Basis for Teaching.* London, Heinemann Educational.

Stenhouse, L. (1980b) *Curriculum Research and Development in Action.* London, Heinemann Educational.

Stenhouse, L. (1983) 'Research is Systematic Enquiry Made Public'. *British Educational Research Journal* 9:1, 11–20.

Stenhouse, L. (1985) *Research as a Basis for Teaching.* London, Heinemann Educational Books.

Sutherland, R. and John, P. (2005) 'Affordance, Opportunity and the Pedagogical Implications of ICT'. *Educational Review* 57:4, 405–13.

TDA (2007) *Professional Standards for Teachers.* London, TDA. Available from http://www.tda.gov.uk/teachers/professionalstandards/downloads.aspx [last accessed 20 July 2009].

TDA and Lifelong Learning UK (2008) *A Guide to Support the Professional Development of Diploma Teachers.* London, TDA/LLUK.

Terry, R. and Churches, R. (2009) *The NLP Toolkit: For teachers, trainers and school leaders.* Carmarthen, Crown House Publishing.

Tetlock, P. E. (2005) *Expert Political Judgment: How good is it? How can we know?* New Jersey, Princeton University Press.

Théberge, P. (1997), *Any Sound you can Imagine: Making music/consuming technology.* London, Wesleyan University Press.

Torrance, H. and Pryor, J. (1998) *Investigating Formative Assessment.* Buckingham, Open University Press.

Triggs, P. and John, P. D. (2004) 'From Transaction to Transformation: ICT, professional development and the formation of communities of practice'. *Journal of Computer Assisted Learning* 20:6, 426–40.

Turner-Bisset, R. (2001) *Expert Teaching*. London, David Fulton.

University of Bristol (2010a) 'InterActive Education Project: Subject cultures'. Available from http://www.interactiveeducation.ac.uk/sub_cult.htm [last accessed 8 January 2010].

University of Bristol (2010b) 'InterActive Education Project: Learning'. Available from http://www.interactiveeducation.ac.uk/learning.htm [last accessed 8 January 2010].

Van Looy, L. (ed.) (2002) *Zelfstandig en coöperatief leren. Kroniek van een Vlaams experiment*. Brussels, VUBpress.

Van Manen, M. (1977) 'Linking Ways of Knowing with Ways of Being Practical'. *Curriculum Inquiry* 6:3, 205–28.

Verma, G. and Pumfrey, P. (eds) (1993) *Cross Curricular Contexts: Themes and dimensions in secondary schools*. London, Falmer Press.

Walker, A. (2002) 'Assessment and evaluation of cross-curricular themes', in Colpaert, K. (ed.) *Cross-Curricular Themes*. Conference Proceedings, Brussels, 11–12 October, 53–7.

Waters, M. (2006) 'Seizing Success: Leading a dynamic school system'. Presentation at the National College of School Leadership Annual Conference, Nottingham, UK.

Waters, S. (1994) *Living Without Boundaries*. Bath, Bath College of Higher Education Press.

Watson, D. M. (2001) 'Pedagogy Before Technology: Re-thinking the relationship between ICT and teaching'. *Education and Information Technologies*, 6:4, 251–66.

Watson, J. S. and Wilcox, S. (2000) 'Reading for Understanding: Methods of reflecting on practice'. *Reflective Practice* 1:1, 57–67.

Wertsch J. (1991) *Voices of the Mind*. Cambridge, HUP.

Wertsch, J. (1998) *Mind as Action*. Oxford, OUP.

Wertsch, J. (2003) 'Dimensions of culture-clash', in Sutherland, R., Claxton, G. and Pollard, A. (eds.) *Learning and Teaching: Where world views meet*. London, Trentham Books.

Whetton, C. (2009) 'A Brief History of a Testing Time: National curriculum assessment in England 1989–2008'. *Educational Research* 51:2, 137–59.

White, J. (2004) *Rethinking the School Curriculum: Values, aims and purposes*. London, Routledge/Falmer.

Whitty, G., Rowe, G. and Aggleton, P. (1994) 'Discourse in Cross-Curricular Contexts: Limits to empowerment'. *International Studies in Sociology of Education* 4:1, 25–42.

Woolgar S. (ed.) (2002) *Virtual Society? Technology, cyber-bole, reality*. Oxford, Oxford University Press.

Index

aims of assessment and evaluation 157, 159–60, 161

Alberti, Leon Battista 167–8

Alexander, J., Walsh, P., Jarman, R. and McLune, B. 77, 78–9, 79–80

Alexander, Robin 44–6, 46–7, 47–8, 56–7, 58–9, 63; definition of pedagogy 45–6

alternative viewpoints, allowing for possibilities of 161

Altrichter, H., Posch, P. and Somekh, B. 68

ambiguity of language 82

analysis: cross-case analysis, development of 56–7; intrinsic I's, analysis in personal context 28; of language and literacy 102, 103; longitudinal curriculum data, ten-year analysis of 12; of mediated action through ICT 121, 122; reflective analysis 21

Anderson, L.W. and Krathwohl, D.R. 65, 101, 102

Anderson, T. 120

Anderson, T. and Elloumi, F. 119–20

Anderson, T., Rourke, L., Archer, W. and Garrison, R. 120

anthropomorphic analogies 51

application: in language and literacy 102, 103; of metaphors to cross-curricular teaching and learning 90–4

Archilochus 168–70

artistic responses to common stimulus 56

artistically appeasing I 26–7, 30–1

assessment: balance of assessment approaches 151; 'burden' of, maximisation of classroom time and minimisation of 150; data in cross-curricular situation, collection of 148–9; data storage processes 151; formative assessment 142–3, 145–6, 151, 163; freeze framing and 144–5; methodologies 141–3, 145–6, 151, 163; principles and purposes 39–40; process of, cross-subject comparisons 145; summarising existing knowledge on 140–1

assessment and evaluation: aims, objectives and activities 157; alternative viewpoints, allowing for possibilities of 161; assessment 'burden', maximisation of classroom time and minimisation

of 150; assessment methodologies 141–3, 145–6, 151, 163; balance of assessment approaches 151; collection and collation of generic data 150; collection of assessment data, management of 147–9; communication 160–1; conception of subjects, strength of 146; conversations with pupils, naturalness in 161; coordination of assessment approaches 152–3; cross-curricular approaches to assessment 141–5; crossing subject boundaries 146; data, management of storage and reporting of 151–3; data collection 158; design sharing 158–9; designing an evaluation 156–63; developmental interviews 162; disciplined innovation, seven-staged process of 140, 165–6; essential nature of educational evaluation 140, 153–6; establishment of wider context 158–9; evaluation extends beyond individuals 155; exploration of activities within cross-curricular evaluation 159; fitness for purpose 139–40; formative assessment 142–3, 145–6, 151, 163; formative evaluation 155; generic assessment data 149–50; interviewing 161–3; judgements about cross-curricular teaching and learning 163–5; key objectives 139; leadership, requirement for 153; listening 161; making the private public, evaluation as 154–5; maximisation of classroom time and minimisation of assessment 'burden' 150; non-verbal communication 160–1; observation 159–60; occasion, sense in interviews of 162–3; originality 158; people, evaluation and 155; planning, effective assessment and 149; practicalities 140, 141–51; 'pupil voice' 161; questions for judging cross-curricular activities 163–4; reporting judgements of cross-curricular activities 164–5; resources 157–8; structures of interviews 161–2; subject identities, sympathetic approach to 145–6; summative assessment 141–3, 145–6, 151, 163; summative evaluation 155; symbiotic relationship 139–40, 165; teacher's role 166; teaching practice, openness to criticism of 161; technologies in observation, use of range